Why Christians Will Suffer "Great Tribulation"

The Sequel to
The End Times Passover

by

Joe Ortiz

Bloomington, IN Milton Keynes, UK

authorHOUSE®

AuthorHouse™
1663 Liberty Drive, Suite 200
Bloomington, IN 47403
www.authorhouse.com
Phone: 1-800-839-8640

AuthorHouse™ UK Ltd.
500 Avebury Boulevard
Central Milton Keynes, MK9 2BE
www.authorhouse.co.uk
Phone: 08001974150

First published by AuthorHouse 2/1/2007

ISBN: 978-1-4259-8486-1 (sc)

Library of Congress Control Number: 2006911255

Printed in the United States of America
Bloomington, Indiana

This book is printed on acid-free paper.

Dedication

This book is dedicated to my precious wife Martha. Thank you for your love, affection, companionship and genuine concern for my physical, emotional and spiritual well-being. Thank you for showing me how to laugh again, and to live life at its fullest.

"The End Times Passover," the book by Joe Ortiz, is not just another prophecy book out of thousands. But I dare not tell you the conclusion because I don't want to spoil your journey. Whatever you do, don't pass over Joe's well-thought-out and scriptural work," Dave MacPherson, March 8, 2002.

Dave MacPherson is the author of
The Rapture Plot, The Incredible Cover Up,
The Great Rapture Hoax,
Unbelievable Pre-Trib Origin and
Late Great Pre-Trib Rapture.]

"The reader will find *The End Times Passover* to be a scholarly sound and profound work that will straighten out a lot confusion surrounding biblical issues related to end times prophecy. It will cause many teachers and students of the Bible to rethink much of what they have accepted as 'fact' concerning the end times. Joe Ortiz has done a magnificent job of researching and writing this important book. This is the book I wish I would have written, and I'm sure there are a few others who will wish they had written it as well," Bill Somers, May 28, 2004.

Bill Somers is the host of the
End Time Prophetic Vision web site.
http://www.etpv.org]

Photo credit

The Martyrdom of the Apostle Stephen

(Painting by Juan De Juanes, 1523-1579,

housed at the Prado Museum, Spain)

The author chose this marvelous painting by *Juan De Juanes* for the front cover of both books because it illustrates so convincingly how and why many of God's disciples will experience great tribulation before the return of Christ.

Contents

Introduction

This author believes he provided more than enough scriptural evidence in his first book, *The End Times Passover*, to prove that there will be no Pre-Tribulation Rapture. Not only will there be no Pre-Tribulation Rapture, there will be no Mid-tribulation, nor any Post-tribulation Rapture, if the question has to do with Christians being taken to heaven while all hell breaks loose on earth before Jesus Christ returns. For that matter, the author believes the word Rapture should be entirely taken out of the Christian Church's lexicon!

Yes! We believe that Jesus Christ is going to 'snatch (harpazo)' His *called out ones* on His downward flight to earth, and there will be a meeting held with Him in the air; however, the *church* will not be taken directly to Heaven, but will be involved in the greatest meeting (in the air) that has ever been held in the history of mankind.

Some may still doubt the material we provided in our first book was sufficient to prove this point, and their hopes still lie in being rescued up to heaven before the Lord returns to rule and reign on earth forever. Whether they believe this reality or not, many of the disciples of Jesus Christ (who will be alive during that great return) will be persecuted, tortured, possibly beheaded, and may even experience such a horrific torture unto death they could ever imagine. This may not sound like *Good News* to the traditional Christian; but, then again, throughout history, millions of Christians and believers in the Messiah have suffered greatly for not only their belief in Him, but for standing tall in their gospel broadcasting efforts.

As we mentioned in our first book, records exist of the myriad of Christians who chose death rather than renouncing Christ, including Foxe's Book of Martyrs. Most recently other great books have also chronicled stories of the dastardly torture and deaths experienced by believers throughout the world. Works such as *By Their Blood* by James and Marti Hefley and *Their Blood Cries Out* by Paul Marshall with Lela Gilbert, provide us with stories of the most ghastly kind regarding people who have literally been slaughtered in the cause of Jesus Christ.

Most American Christians, especially (if they were to read these great books), would be stunned by the revelation of the many who willingly gave up their lives in quest of spreading the gospel and standing up for Jesus. Most Americans would shudder in complete horror to learn that thousand upon thousands have died for Christ not just in 'olden' days, but who are currently dying for Christ in remote villages and (some in big) cities daily! Some Americans are familiar with reports of Christians being persecuted throughout the world, like The Voice of Martyrs; but, for the most part, your average American Christian has no idea. Many, unfortunately, are blissfully living day to day in the hopes that Jesus Christ will any moment step out of His abode in heaven and secretly whisk them away to heaven to be with Him while all hell breaks loose on earth during a time they call, *The Great Tribulation!*

The reader may think that incidents like these could never happen to Christians because they have been saved by grace and are not destined for wrath. True! The disciples of Christ are not destined for wrath, and they quote 1 Thessalonians 5:9 as biblical proof: *For God hath not appointed us to wrath, but to obtain salvation by our Lord Jesus Christ.*

This is profound truth! However, as we have stated before, wrath and tribulation are two different experiences. The wrath of God is intended for non-believers; however, throughout the bible, it clearly states that tribulation (or persecution) is the fate of all true believers. The great apostle Paul clearly warned us of this fact when he stated in Acts 14:22, *Confirming the souls of the disciples, and exhorting them to continue in the faith, and that <u>we must through much tribulation enter into the kingdom of God.</u>*

But why should that be so?

After reading this book, this question will be exhaustively answered with scripture to prove Christians will be persecuted before the return of Christ just as they have experienced persecution throughout history. But more importantly, the purpose God has for each and every single Christian, will be unveiled in a dramatic but yet fulfilling manner, for the glory of God, as we examine why Christians will suffer "Great Tribulation!"

Chapter One
JESUS? WHY TRIBULATION?

Yes! Jesus Christ our Lord and our God, currently residing in heaven, definitely has an earth-bound journey. His *called out ones* are hoping and praying that He will come soon. Yes! A myriad of uninformed or deceived *called out ones* today are praying they will be caught up to heaven at any moment, primarily to escape the woes predicted throughout the Bible. Unfortunately (for those whose 'Blessed Hope' lies solely in a secret escape to heaven), the reality is that the *Christian Church* will have to remain on earth awaiting His arrival. Not realizing that to spend an eternity, as co-inheritors of the Kingdom of God, and all that it entails, this *is* our *true* Blessed Hope. Scripture upon scripture clearly state, *that we must through much tribulation enter into the kingdom of God*, (Acts 14:22, KJV). There will be no secret escape to heaven before *The Second Advent*. Therefore, and unfortunately, many *called out ones* will not be prepared to experience great tribulation and the many horrific persecutions from anti-Christian forces prophesied in Revelation 11:7: 13:1, 4, 11, 12, 15, 17, and 18. Many *called out ones* will fall victim to his terror. Why? What's the purpose? Jesus? Why tribulation?

1

In the author's first book, he believes he provided sufficient scripture to prove that God's *called out ones,* the *ecclesia* of Jesus Christ, will remain on earth until He returns at His Second Advent. But why do we have to remain on earth until He returns? What's the purpose? If a secret escape to heaven before His return appears unlikely, then what purpose is served by having believers remain on earth during this great time of sorrow and persecution? Some Christians are probably saying, "Why did I accept Jesus Christ as my Lord and Savior only to have to experience pain and tribulation? What good does it do for a non-Christian to accept Jesus Christ as Lord and Savior if they have to go through tribulation?"

Good questions. The author himself was relieved when he came to the Lord on January 5, 1975 and was told that Christians would escape the so-called Great Tribulation and all the horrors described in Revelation. For him, one of the most thrilling aspects of becoming a Christian was the so-called secret escape to heaven. The verse in 1 Thessalonians 5:9, where we are told that, *God did not appoint us to suffer wrath but to receive salvation through our Lord Jesus Christ,* has been a great comfort to him all these years. Also, the verse in Romans (8:1) that says, "*There is now no condemnation for those who are in Christ Jesus,*" gives him great comfort and assurance concerning his relationship with the Lord and his eternal future with Him. But now it appears that believers (if still alive before *The Second Advent*) will not only be on earth, but face the strongest possibility of being horribly persecuted, much more so if they stand up and testify to the Lordship of Jesus Christ! What is served for believers to endure such a fearsome trial? Did the Lord say believers had to experience tribulation in order to qualify for salvation? Is there scripture that specifically states that Christians must go through tribulation? Let's examine first if Jesus himself said we would go through and experience great tribulation.

In the Beatitudes (Matthew 5:1-12), we find the first exhortation to God's chosen people concerning sorrow and persecution:

2

And seeing the multitudes, he went up into a mountain: and when he was set, his disciples came unto him: 2 and he opened his mouth, and taught them, saying, 3 blessed are the poor in spirit: for theirs is the kingdom of heaven. 4 Blessed are they that mourn: for they shall be comforted. 5 Blessed are the meek: for they shall inherit the earth. 6 Blessed are they which do hunger and thirst after righteousness: for they shall be filled. 7 Blessed are the merciful: for they shall obtain mercy. 8 Blessed are the pure in heart: for they shall see God. 9 Blessed are the peacemakers: for they shall be called the children of God. 10 **Blessed are they which are persecuted for righteousness' sake: for theirs is the kingdom of heaven**. 11 **Blessed are ye, when men shall revile you, and persecute you, and shall say all manner of evil against you falsely, for my sake.** 12 Rejoice, and be exceeding glad: for great is your reward in heaven: for so persecuted they the prophets which were before you, Matthew 5:1-12, KJV). [Bold and underline is by the author, solely for emphasis]

The Beatitudes are well known in the Christian community and have brought much comfort to many people throughout the years, especially for the promises that are provided in verse 12. However, later on, in Matthew 10:17-18, Jesus is talking about a future time when His disciples will be punished by various entities for testifying for the Lord:

But beware of men: for they will deliver you up to the councils, **and they will scourge you in their synagogues**; 18 **and ye shall be brought before governors and kings for my sake**, for a testimony against them and the Gentiles, (Matthew 10:17-18, KJV). [Bold and underline is by the author, solely for emphasis]

Then, in verses 21 and 22, possibly one of the most dreaded things that could happen to any one person is the betrayal by brothers, parents and even our very own children, maybe even resulting in our death! What kind of horrific society will we be living in during that period? Even now, the divisiveness that is being felt in today's society compares little to the familial treachery that lies in store for the believer during this great time of horror. Everyone who does not believe as we do (in Jesus Christ as Lord and Savior) will hate us as never before. We live in a period of time today that sees Christianity as being an oppressing philosophy to a humanistic society. What greater trauma and persecutions lay in the future? It's not necessary to cite examples, one only has to pick up the newspaper, hear on radio and see on television the stories of Christians throughout the world being persecuted for their belief in Jesus Christ. Even in the United States, we see many of the religious liberties that were once the main threads of the tradition fabric of this country, unraveling before our very eyes due to legal and pseudo-moral challenges by secular entities. While Americans are not experiencing physical persecutions for their religious beliefs like many in various Third World and Communist controlled countries, the rapid decline of respect for religious liberty could very well turn into acts of physical persecution toward those who remain adamant in their belief of Jesus Christ. As we have seen in the past few decades, those things that were once called good are now being called bad, and vice verse. But, through this persecution, Jesus' exhortation to God's *called out ones* is to choose between Him and a non-believing society (which can include family members), even if it means being killed!

> He that loveth father or mother more than me is not worthy of me: and he that loveth son or daughter more than me is not worthy of me. 38 **And he that taketh not his cross, and followeth after me, is not worthy of**

me. 39 He that findeth his life shall lose it: and he that loseth his life for my sake shall find it, (Matthew 10:37-39, KJV). [Bold and underline is by the author, solely for emphasis]

Many Christians today see the aforementioned verse (38) and apply it solely to normal problems being experienced in their homes, communities and businesses. A friend of the author, in response to his concern about his employer's harsh treatment toward him, jokingly said, "My boss is a real taskmaster, but I just pick up my cross daily." I smiled back at him and told him to count his blessings because a time is coming when the *cross* he next picks up might very well be the instrument that will be used for his virtual execution. The author doesn't believe this verse was meant to be taken solely as a metaphor describing the normal hardships we face daily. But, rather, we need also to receive it as a message that our physical bodies could very well be subjected to much torture and even death at the hands of anti-Christian forces. The cross is not to be viewed solely as a symbol of weight, as if carrying a heavy domestic or financial burden; but it is meant to symbolize exactly what it is, an instrument of death, the same meaning it had for Jesus.

In Matthew 11:29, Jesus specifically asks His disciples to join Him in His sufferings, these being an even better way of living than the way those destined for destruction live out their lives:

> Take my yoke upon you and learn from me; for I am gentle and humble in heart, and you will find rest for your souls, (Matthew 11:29, NIV).

In Matthew 16:24-26, Jesus is challenging the sincerity of believers who claim to be willing to leave everything to follow him:

> Then Jesus said to his disciples, "If anyone would come after me, he must deny himself and take up his cross and

follow me. 15 **<u>For whoever wants to save his life will lose it, but whoever loses his life for me will find it</u>**. 26 What good will it is for a man if he gains the whole world, yet forfeits his soul? Or what can a man give in exchange for his soul, (Matthew 16:24-26, NIV)? [Bold and underline is by the author, solely for emphasis]

Once again, He tells us that the price for following Him can, and often does, include death. He specifically tells us that if we try to save our own life through our own means (worldly power, money, societal status, etc.), we will lose it; but, if we are willing to lose our life for Him, we will find it!

In Matthew 20:20-23, the disciples (in their egotistical and frail humanness) were primarily concerned about gaining a high place in the coming kingdom. Jesus told them that their positional status therein would be determined by the Father; however, the important message to them was not what would be their role in the Kingdom of God, but the fact that they too would experience death:

Then came to him the mother of Zebedee's children with her sons, worshipping him, and desiring a certain thing of him. 21 And he said unto her, what wilt thou? She saith unto him, Grant that these my two sons may sit, the one on thy right hand, and the other on the left, in thy kingdom. 22 But Jesus answered and said, Ye know not what ye ask. **<u>Are ye able to drink of the cup that I shall drink of, and to be baptized with the baptism that I am baptized with</u>**? They say unto him, We are able. 23 And he saith unto them, **<u>Ye shall drink indeed of my cup, and be baptized with the baptism that I am baptized with</u>**: but to sit on my right hand, and on my left, is not mine to give, but it shall be given to them for whom it is prepared of my Father,

(Matthew 20:20-23, KJV). [The "drinking' (PINO in the Greek) of His cup here literally means to "share in the sufferings of Christ," the same message we find in Mark 10:38, 39. Underline and bold is by the author, solely for emphasis]

Unfortunately, it appears that many in Christendom are working very hard to also gain preeminence in the kingdom through ministerial activities that currently bring them much temporal fame, money and status. While the author doesn't necessarily question their true motives, his spirit tells him that many more Christians who labor (and have labored in preaching the Gospel of Jesus Christ) in the remote jungles, mountains and deserts of the world (even unto death) will be receiving greater honor in God's kingdom, more so than some of today's much publicized *Christian Church* leaders. The author believes that when we see Him face-to-face, and rewards are given, many of today's famous evangelists and "prophecy experts" will be taking a back seat to those unknown soldiers who, by their death, have added others to the kingdom without receiving the acclaim and fame so many seek in modern day Christianity.

In Matthew 23, Jesus, in His address to the teachers of the law and the Pharisees, chided them for their hypocrisy and warned them of their impending condemnation. In verse 34, He reiterates the fact that He is sending them prophets, wise men and teachers and that they will kill and crucify some of them, while flogging and pursuing others from town to town:

> "You snakes! You brood of vipers! How will you escape being condemned to hell? 34 **Therefore I am sending you prophets and wise men and teachers. Some of them you will kill and crucify; others you will flog in your synagogues and pursue from town to town.** 35 And so upon you will come all the righteous blood that

> has been shed on earth, from the blood of righteous
> Abel to the blood of Zechariah son of Berakiah, whom
> you murdered between the temple and the alter 36 I tell
> you the truth, all this will come upon this generation,
> (Matthew 23:33-36, NIV). [Underline and bold is by the
> author, solely for emphasis]

This very same message is also seen in Luke 11:49-51. Many readers and critics of this particular message will say that these prophecies by Jesus were fulfilled during the times of the early apostles and have nothing to do with our modern day *Christian Church*! How terribly sad for them to believe that somehow all in today's Christian community have acquired some spiritual (or physical) immunity from the events to come, solely by their experiencing a religious (so-called *born again*) moment of euphoria and adopting (with questioning) a belief in a secret escape to heaven myth. But, as we shall see further in this book, this will not be the case.

Many scholars and theorists have disputed Chapter 24, the famed Mount of Olives discourse, as to its timing, and it is not our intention to present any further arguments pro or con. However, if the scriptures we have presented so far negate a secret escape to heaven, then this entire chapter speaks boldly to the imminent tribulation the *Christian Church* can expect:

> Jesus left the temple and was walking away when his
> disciples came up to Him to call his attention to its
> buildings 2 "Do you see all these things?" He asked.
> "I tell you the truth, not one stone here will be left on
> another; every one will be thrown down." 3 As Jesus
> was sitting on the Mount of Olives, the disciples came
> to him privately. "Tell us," they said, "when will this
> happen, and what will be the sign of your coming and
> of the end of the Age?" 4 Jesus answered: "Watch out

that no one deceives you. 5 For many will come in my name, claiming, 'I am the Christ,' and will deceive many. 6 You will hear of wars and rumors of wars, but see to it that you are not alarmed. Such things must happen, but the end is still to come. 7 Nation will rise against nation, and kingdom against kingdom. There will be famines and earthquakes in various places.8 **All these are the beginning of birth pains**, (Matthew 24: 1-8, NIV). [Bold and underline is by the author, solely for emphasis]

This group of verses deals specifically with Jesus' exhortation concerning two events separated by thousands of years, including the destruction of the temple in Jerusalem (which was fulfilled in 70 AD), and then the signs of His coming at of the end of the age. He proceeds to cite the conditions immediately before His return, stating that many "deceivers" will come proclaiming that the Christ has come, that there will be wars and rumors of wars, that nations will rise against nations, kingdoms against kingdoms and there will be increased famines and earthquakes in various places. All these things are likened to the labor pains a woman experiences before giving birth to her child. Then, in the following verses, Jesus reiterates the same persecutions that he cited in Matthew 10:17-18; however, here He also states that during that time, many will turn away from the faith:

Then you will be handed over to be persecuted and put to death, and you will be hated by all nations because of me. 10 At that time **many will turn away from the faith and will betray and hate each other.** 11 and many false prophets will appear and deceive many people. 12 Because of the increase of wickedness, the love of many will grow cold, (Matthew 24:9-12, NIV). [Underline and bold is by the author, solely for emphasis]

Could it be that what is called the Great Apostasy, spoken in context with the immediate increased tribulation period that precedes the anticipated meeting of the Lord in the air, will be so horrific that grounded Christians will turn away from their faith in Jesus Christ? Could the impending horrors at the hand of the man of lawlessness cause such terror and pain that believing Christians will crumble under the beast system and turn away from Christ?

Speaking of a woman experiencing labor pains, in verses 19 through 21, the Lord commences to describe how it will be during that time, which includes the dreadfulness of this period, so dreadful that the joy women experience during pregnancy, and the blessed experience of nursing a beloved child, will become a living nightmare. Also, many theorists interpret the "flight" to mean that people shouldn't be on airplanes during this period; however, the word "flight" in the Greek is *phuge* from *pheugo* which means *to flee*. This is mentioned in connection with praying that your fleeing be not in the winter or the Sabbath, which indicates that the beginning of this horror could commence on a Sabbath Day or during a winter period. Verse 22 goes on to say that those days are going to be so horrible, that if they had not been shortened, no one would be able to survive:

> How dreadful it will be in those days for pregnant women and nursing mothers! 20 Pray that your flight will not take place in winter or on the Sabbath. 21 For then there will be great distress, unequaled from the beginning of the world until now – and never to be equaled again. 22 if those days had not been cut short, no one would survive, but for the sake of the elect those days will be shortened. 23 At that time if anyone says to you, 'Look, here is the Christ!' or, 'There he is!' do not believe it. 24 For false Christs and false prophets will

appear and perform great signs and miracles to deceive even the elect – if that were possible. 25 See, I have told you ahead of time, (Matthew 24:19-25, NIV).

Jesus is telling His disciples that one of the biggest horrors of that period will be great signs and miracles by false prophets and false Christs who will attempt to deceive the chosen ones of God. Many of these signs and miracles will be especially designed to fool even Christians into believing that Jesus has returned; however, the spirit-filled believers will be able to see through the ruse, barely!

These are the things that Jesus said would be experienced by His disciples then, and, Matthew 24, specifically talks about the things His disciples will experience in the future. Then, the horror of all horrors, universal chaos, including the sun being darkened, the moon's brightness shut, stars falling and a completely devastating realignment of the planets, to the point of total annihilation. Such tremendous horror that it will even make the most horrendous science fiction movie ever made look like animated cartoons kids watch on television. The minds of those who produce Armageddon-themed science fiction motion pictures are incapable of imagining how truly horrible it will be during this end times period.

The books of Mark (Chapter 13:1-25) and Luke (21:7-36, 17:20-37) speak about this period of time also, but not with the descriptive imagery found in Matthew 24. However, in Mark 8:34-38 and Luke 9:23-24 and 14:26-27, we find a repeat of picking up and carrying our cross, choosing Christ over family and friends, trusting in nothing or no one but Christ, unto death, for the saving of our souls. In Mark 10:39, we see a repeat of Jesus telling us that we also will "drink" the cup (of suffering), and we will also be "baptized" in the same manner He was to be "baptized," indicating that the disciples will also suffer as He did, (Luke 12:50). In Mark 13:9-13, we also see a repeat of the disciples being handed over to authorities to be flogged and tried.

Verse 12 describes again the betrayal by family members resulting in our death. This is graphically described in Luke 12:52-53. The interesting thing about all of these persecutions (so far), is the fact that Jesus Himself sends us (believers) out among the world, allowing us to become exposed to these tribulations:

> Go! I am sending you out like lambs among wolves, (Luke 10:3, NIV).

Not only does Jesus say He sends disciples out among the wolves, Jesus specifically states that His command for us is to "love each other" as He has loved us, by our willingness to lay down our lives for our friends:

> My command is this: Love each other as I have loved you. 13 Greater love has no one than this that one lay down his life for his friends, (John 15:12-13, NIV).

Here Christ is asking the *called out ones* to make that supreme sacrifice. To be His disciple requires a commitment unheard of these days. In this "Me" oriented society of today, a person would be considered a masochist to adopt such behavior. "Only lunatics, suicidal psychopaths or the mentally deranged would ever consider such a course," so say today's psychologists. "Only super-crazed macho, kamikaze-oriented fools ponder such absurdities," so says the rational man. But this is exactly what Christ asks of those who want to be His disciples. Is there another way to live our lives as Christians? Is Christianity that important that we (believers) must be willing to die in order to enter the kingdom of God? Jesus said, "*If the world hates you, keep in mind that it hated me first*, (John 15:18, NIV)." He also said,

> If they persecuted me, they will persecute you also, (vs. 20). He said, "They will treat you this way because of my name, for they do not know the One who sent me, (vs. 21)." In John 16:1, Jesus states: "All this I have told

you so that you will not go astray." He goes on to say, "They will put you out of the synagogue; in fact**, a time is coming when anyone who kills you will think he is offering a service to God.** They will do such things because they have not known the Father or me. I have told you this; so that when the time comes you will remember that I warned you. I did not tell you this at first because I was with you, (John 16:2-5, NIV). [Bold and underline by the author solely for emphasis]

Can you imagine that? Verse 2 states that those who kill us will actually believe that they are offering a service to God!

In answer to the many who still might believe in a secret pre-tribulation escape to heaven, Jesus, while praying to the Father in John 17:15, prays to God for Him *not* to take us out of the world; but, rather that He protects us from the evil one! What does this protection involve, if not an End Times Passover? How will God do this? We will answer this question in a later chapter that specifically deals with our experiencing "The End Times Passover." However, as we have read from the four gospels, Jesus Christ specifically answered our questions concerning what the living *called out ones* on earth will experience during this period of time! But, Jesus, why tribulation? Why should the Christian have to remain on earth during this horrendous time? Why must this be?

As we continue this topic in the next few chapters, the answers to this question will be unveiled through specific examples and corroborating scriptures. As we have done so far, examples and scriptures will be provided to prove that great tribulation (not a secret Rapture to heaven) is in store for God's *called out ones* before *The Second Advent*. However, many of you may become unsettled by the truths contained in God's words about the purpose of tribulation. In the next few chapters we will be examining the tribulations Paul experienced,

13

and the messages about tribulations spoken directly to the church, which will scripturally prove that it will remain to experience these tribulations and the reasons why. As we close this chapter, the author provides a brief clue to this answer:

The author has always been intrigued by war movies, not relishing them in some macho-seeking excitement, but intrigued especially by those movies that depicted a courageous soldier falling on a live hand grenade, thereby saving the lives of his buddies close by. Was this an act of courage? Was this foolishness? Did this soldier have a suicidal death wish, or was he demonstrating a true sacrificial love for the friends he was protecting? Like Jesus said, *"Greater love has no one than this, that one lay down his life for his friends,* (John 15:13, NIV)." What did this soldier know or feel at that exact moment the grenade exploded? Mankind has been searching for answers to the death experience from the very beginning, even to the point of killing people in hopes they could resuscitate their victims to ask them what it was like. What experiential knowledge has the Bible withheld from us about the death experience that mere mortals fail to comprehend? What is it about death that causes us so much fear? We will discuss this further in a later chapter. For now, the central issue is tribulation. If we can accept that great tribulation is definitely in store for the *called out ones,* more so as the Day of the Lord draws closer, we ask again: "Is tribulation truly necessary? If so, what is its purpose?" Unfortunately, not many people (even Christians) want to know, nor are they ready for the answer:

> And we rejoice in the hope of the glory of God. 3 Not only so, but we also rejoice in our sufferings, **because we know that suffering produces perseverance**; 4 **perseverance, character; and character, hope**. 5 And hope does not disappoint us, because God has poured out his love into our hearts by the Holy Spirit, whom he has given us, (Romans 5:2-5, NIV). [Underline and bold is by the author, solely for emphasis]

Chapter 2
PAUL'S TRIBULATIONS!

In the four gospels, we briefly touched on what Jesus had to say about the impending persecutions and tribulation that Christians can expect before His return. What do the Book of Acts and the Epistles say about tribulation? They have much to say about this subject matter and, in the Book of Acts, we get a first hand commentary about the tribulations that lay before God's *ecclesia*, directly from a *called out one* who experienced more than his share of persecution for Christ, the apostle Paul.

In Acts, we don't see any persecution of Christians until we come to Chapter 7. This is one of the author's all time special chapters in the Bible because, here, the entire recapitulation of Israel's history, including the promises God made to her, is so eloquently recited by the brave disciple Stephen. The end of this chapter, where we see Stephen being stoned to death because the Sanhedrin became furious when they heard the truth, has to be a tremendous source of inspiration (and a cause of deep introspection) for all Christians.

The author can see in Chapter 7 of Acts a vivid picture of the manner in which many dedicated-to-the-end believers will be conducting themselves in the face of all forms of persecutions and adversity. More importantly, he can also see how Stephen's spirit-filled discourse was directly responsible for many non-believers coming to faith in Jesus Christ as a result of that incident. Actually, the author believes that Stephen's last prayer was directly responsible for the eventual conversion of Saul, one of the antagonists among the hostile crowd that stoned him to death. The author believes that God always answers prayer, and that only God Himself knows how He will answer it; but He always makes all things work to the good according to His purpose, (Romans 8:28). Saul, one of the major instigators of the stoning siege of Stephen, went on to become Paul, possibly the greatest apostle that ever lived. Who is to say that the prayer or testimony of Jesus and His Gospel on the lips of a dying person has not been responsible for many non-believers turning to Christ? But the most beautiful part of Chapter 7 is where we see Stephen, in his last dying breath, praying to the Lord to receive his spirit. As he fell to his knees, we see in verse 60 how beautifully similar were the last words to escape from his mouth to Jesus' last words on the cross: *Lord, do not hold this sin against them*, (Luke 23:34).

In Chapter 9, we see where it speaks about the conversion of Paul, who is primarily responsible for writing the majority of the epistles to the *ecclesia*. Paul had much to say about the conduct of the God's *called out ones*, as he defined and articulated in great detail the purpose of Christ's mission, and how the disciples should respond to the Gospel of Jesus Christ. He had much to say about the prophecies and the impending trials and persecutions the *ecclesia* would experience, he being one of its chief victims. Let's review the verses that allude to Paul's great trials, persecutions and tribulation.

In Acts 9:15 and 16, the Lord speaks to Ananias about Paul's mission, which was to include much suffering for upholding the name of Jesus:

> But the Lord said unto him, Go thy way: for he is a chosen vessel unto me, to bear my name before the Gentiles, and kings, and the children of Israel: 16 **For I will shew him how great things he must suffer for my name's sake**, (Acts 9:15-16, KJV). [Underline and bold is by the author, solely for emphasis]

In Acts 9:18-31, we begin to see the metamorphosis that Saul went through, preaching in synagogues with such great effectiveness, that plots were devised to silence him (vs. 22, 23); but the apostles (still leery and doubtful about Paul's purpose and commitment to the Gospel), nevertheless, sheltered him. We don't see too much of Saul until Chapter 13:9, at which time Saul becomes Paul, after he receives power from on high from the Holy Spirit. Paul and Barnabas proceed to preach the Gospel throughout the land and persecution is stirred up against them (vs. 50) as they moved on to other cities. After preaching the Good News throughout Lystra, Paul experienced a stoning (vs. 19) that would provoke him to make the most profound statement about tribulation that he ever made: *that we must through much tribulation enter into the kingdom of God*, (Acts 14:22, KJV).

The word *tribulation* in Acts 14:22 is the Greek (in the plural) noun *thlipsis* (many afflictions), the same word used in the phrase *great tribulation* in Revelation 7:14, which theorists claim is describing a seven-year time framed season. However, solely by virtue of the adjective *great* preceding the word *tribulation*, many theorists have somehow added new meaning to these two words, a phrase which is mentioned only once in the entire Bible. They somehow have concluded a unique meaning for these two words (*great tribulation*) to engender them as a specific (seven year) period of time, and have now given these two words a proper noun (*The Great Tribulation*) status; this by inference, of course! It's as if placing the word "great" before "tribulation" somehow identifies these two words as a special event or a specific (seven year) period of time, a conclusion they base solely on an unproven theory they call "Daniel's Seventieth Week."

However, if examined closely, the word *great* in this verse is the Greek word *megas*, the same Greek word used to define the intensity of the strong angel's voice in Revelation 5:2, who is hereby making a most profound proclamation in a *loud* (*megas*) voice: *"who is worthy to open the book!"* It's also used for the word *loud* in Revelation 5:12 to describe, "In a *loud* voice they sang." The word *megas* means (according to Vine) *"of external form, size, measure."* However, no specific identification is made in the Bible of this great tribulation as being a special season or event unto itself; but, rather, it is merely stating that the *degree* of tribulation that will ensue immediately before Christ returns will be greatly and mightily intensified. The reader should be made aware that many Bible versions (except for the King James) use the article (the) before *great tribulation,* in Revelation 7:14, as if it supposedly means the phrase is giving identity to a proper noun describing a special event or day, such as The Feast of Tabernacles, The Sabbath Day or The Passover. The author believes that no article was intended or is required before these two words (*great tribulation*) because it is not speaking about a specific three and a half to seven year period of tribulation preceding the return of Jesus Christ; although, intensified tribulation as has never been witnessed before *will* definitely occur immediately before He returns. Nevertheless, to label the intensity of tribulation in a proper noun sense, calling it *The Great Tribulation* (and infer a specific event not specifically stated in scripture) is as ludicrous as calling the *caught* phase of the Lord's return *The Rapture.* The word *great* is not capitalized in this passage (vs. 14), any more than is the Greek adjective *harpazo* (caught) in 1 Thessalonians. 4:17. When the Bible mentions the Sabbath Day, the Feast of Tabernacles and the Passover, each are identified as specific days or events. Read this verse again, in the King James Version, where the article is not seen before the words *great tribulation:*

> And I said unto him, Sir, thou knowest. And he said to
> me, these are they which came out of **<u>great tribulation</u>**,
> and have washed their robes, and made them white
> in the blood of the Lamb, (Revelation 7:14, KJV).
> [Bold, underline and italics by the author, solely for
> emphasis]

Revelation 7:14 is not talking solely about the martyred *called out
ones* who come out of the so-called period theorists call *The Great
Tribulation*; this verse is describing all the members of the *ecclesia*
that have suffered for their belief in Messiah, a myriad who have
experienced great tribulation for God throughout history, (See all of
Hebrews 11)! Are we to believe that only those martyred three and
a half to seven years before the Lord returns are the only ones that
have washed their robes in the blood of the Lamb? Are we to believe
that the millions of *called out ones* who have labored and suffered for
God throughout history will be afforded less honor and glory than
those who are martyred during the perilous times preceding *The
Second Advent*?

No Bible scholar has proven beyond a shadow of a doubt that the
Book of Revelation contains a chronological beginning or ending
of any specific seven-year period of time, neither has anyone
proven conclusively that the so-called "Daniel's Seventieth Week"
theory (Daniel 9:24-27) is describing a specific seven-year period of
tribulation. We have hundreds of theories, but no definitive doctrine
has been presented that would pass canonization, as has the death and
resurrection of Jesus Christ. Theorists have attempted to configure
various days, weeks and years mentioned in the Book of Daniel
to determine a specific timeline for the return of Christ. But they
have never been able to justify or validate their theories. No specific
timeline has been factually established. Much conjecture, inference
and theory has been proffered, but no scriptural substantiation that
has passed exegetical muster exists today.

How can theorists propose any specific time frame conclusions as biblical fact (or even try to build a doctrinal foundation for the Daniel's Seventy Weeks theory) when there exists varying numerical times mention in the Book of Daniel. For example, in Daniel 8:13-14, when Daniel heard from a holy one about how long it would take to see the vision to be fulfilled, the answer was 2,300 evenings and mornings:

> Then I heard a holy one speaking, and another holy one said to him, "How long will it take for the vision to be fulfilled—the vision concerning the daily sacrifice, the rebellion that causes desolation, and the surrender of the sanctuary and of the host that will be trampled underfoot?" 14 He said to me, "It will take 2,300 evenings and mornings; then the sanctuary will be reconsecrated, (Daniel 8:13-14, NIV).

Then, in Daniel 12:11-13, speaking about the same issues he addresses in Daniel 8:13-14, two different numbers of days (1290 and 1,335) are mentioned:

> And from the time that the daily sacrifice shall be taken away, and the abomination that maketh desolate set up, there shall be a thousand two hundred and ninety days. 12 Blessed is he that waiteth, and cometh to the thousand three hundred and five and thirty days. 13 But go thou thy way till the end be: for thou shalt rest, and stand in thy lot at the end of the days, (Daniel 12:13-14, NIV). [Underline is by the author, solely for emphasis]

From which sets of numbers above do they build their dispensational time frames concerning a proposed and specific seven years of tribulation? Too many theorists have in vain tried to develop their own Apocalypse time-setting configurations by including various mathematical formulae and combinations of weeks for years, including the sixty-two sevens and seven more weeks (of seven years), with a major Gentile fulfillment Church gap in between (Luke 21:24) another seventh week to occur immediately before *The Second Advent* - and these other three different numbers (2,300, 1290 and 1,335) of days – solely (and in attempts) to validate a special seven year-long period they call *The Great Tribulation* that supposedly precedes The Lord's Parousia. This is dangerous theorizing of which we have been warned not to promote or concern ourselves with, (Acts 1:7-8).

If the author digressed a little, it is only to clarify some points the Lord has quickened in his heart concerning these unsubstantiated theories, which are primarily based solely on the conjecture and inferences made by many theorists who consistently disregard the Lord's admonitions concerning times and epochs: *It is not for you to know the times or dates the Father has set by His own authority,* (Acts 1:7-8, NIV). The Lord's exhortation for the evangelical community is, *You will be my witnesses in Jerusalem, and in all Judea and Samaria, and to the ends of the earth,* (verse 8). It is therefore incumbent on all disciples to direct all efforts to that great commission and move away from times and epochs that can (and have) become stumbling blocks for many. The Bible specifically states that Christians must go through many hardships (tribulations) to enter the Kingdom of God. Let us all join together for the purpose of strengthening and edifying the *ecclesia* in preparation for that horrific onslaught that will precede the Lord's return. Let us not be found titillating our brethren with soothing myths for the purpose of earthly glory, nor attempting to allay fearful hearts and souls from what could very well be the plan almighty God has in store for His *called out ones*. Let us follow through on the Lord's exhortation to preach the Good News of God's salvation and God's grace, let us take heed of Paul's message in 2 Timothy 4:2-5:

Preach the word; be instant in season, out of season; reprove, rebuke, exhort with all long suffering and doctrine. 3 **For the time will come when they will not endure sound doctrine; but after their own lusts shall they heap to themselves teachers, having itching ears; 4 And they shall turn away their ears from the truth, and shall be turned unto fables.** 5 But watch thou in all things, **endure afflictions**, do the work of an evangelist, make full proof of thy ministry, (2 Timothy 4:2-5, KJV). [Underline and bold is by the author, solely for emphasis]

As we continue examining Paul's tribulations, in Acts 15:26 it is said that apostles and elders of the whole church decided to send some men to Antioch to help Paul and Barnabas, *men who have risked their lives for the name of our Lord Jesus Christ.* Later in Chapter 16, we see where Paul and Silas were thrown in prison for supposedly causing uproar in regards to Roman law. They were stripped and flogged (vs. 23) publicly and without a trial (vs. 37), even though Paul and Silas were Roman citizens. Paul is eventually released and travels hither and yon, preaching the Gospel of Jesus Christ under great peril.

While in Ephesus, Paul once again reaffirms the perils that face him, but in Chapter 20: 23, 24, he declares his need to persevere:

Save that the Holy Ghost witnesseth in every city, saying that **bonds and afflictions abide me.** 24 But none of these things move me, **neither count I my life dear unto myself,** so that I might finish my course with joy, and the ministry, which I have received of the Lord Jesus, to testify the gospel of the grace of God, (Acts 20:23, 24, KJV) [Bold and underline is by the author, solely for emphasis]

22

Paul, knowing that he would soon be leaving them to continue his evangelistic mission, warns the Ephesians to also be on guard from those who distort the truth, an act that in and of itself should be viewed as a form of suffering:

> Take heed therefore unto yourselves, and to all the flock, over the which the Holy Ghost hath made you overseers, to feed the church of God, which he hath purchased with his own blood. 29 For I know this that after my departing **shall grievous wolves enter in among you, not sparing the flock**. 30 **Also of your own selves shall men arise, speaking perverse things, to draw away disciples after them.**31 Therefore watch, and remember, that by the space of three years **I ceased not to warn every one night and day with tears**, (Acts 20:28-31, KJV). [Underline and bold is by the author, solely for emphasis]

The words, *draw away disciples after them*, is an issue that deserves an entire book. The author personally has witnessed and experienced this sad phenomenon in the various congregations he has attended or been involved with. He has witnessed many instances where the pastor of a church has been literally sabotaged by upstart and ersatz leaders in their respective congregations, posturing themselves as being more biblically informed or more charismatic than the leadership God placed in their midst. True, many of those leaders probably faltered in their respective mission for one reason or another. But leaders of an assembly can come together in prayer and biblical wisdom to make such determinations.

The author's biggest concerns regarding today's churches, however, is that too many congregations place too much emphasis on fund raising, using electronic wizardry and secular promotion tactics to increase their coffers and respective ministries, rather than praying for the wisdom of God to open their journey doors to accomplish His will. Unfortunately, the *electronic church* has pried away parishioners from their local congregations with a myriad of secular-style activities such as programs involving Wall Street-oriented methods to increase wealth, secular-oriented game shows, health and muscle-building programs, cartoon shows, soap operas, Christian-oriented rock concerts, grandiose musicals and other theatrical productions that must have the Lord both crying and laughing at the same time. While these activities are not necessarily sinful in and of themselves, the preoccupation to entertain and comfort the Christian has taken a back seat to sound biblical exhortation. The moneychangers in the temple are alive and doing very well in today's *Christian Church*!

Even many of today's sermons, by well-intended preachers, are more geared to helping their parishioners solve their everyday problems of marital relationships, parenting and self-esteem issues. While the Bible provides much wisdom for church leaders to use in dealing with their respective flocks on these matters, modern day Christian leaders spend more time on soothing and comforting their parishioners, rather than preparing them for the imminent return of Jesus Christ (not to secretly catch them up to heaven, but) to judge the world!

Where are the truly committed *called out ones* that once gathered together for prayer and study, seeking to help the poor and needy, conducting neighborhood and home visitations of the infirm, orphans and elderly, bringing with them both tangible and spiritual sustenance? Where are the Jeremiahs, Ezekiel's and Isaiah's of centuries past? Where are the prophets of yesteryear, those who prophesied the impending judgment that is in store for those who ignore God's warning to repent; those, who, sadly, are resting too comfortably in their hope for a secret escape to heaven? They are probably at home, switching their radio and television channels back and forth to the popular evangelist of the hour, not realizing that the perils that precede the Day of the Lord are closer than ever before!

Unlike today's church, Paul was determined to preach the word regardless of the perils that he knew awaited him in Jerusalem. In Acts, Chapter 21, after hearing that the Jews were plotting to hand him over to the Gentiles, Paul responded thusly:

> Then Paul answered, "What mean ye to weep and to break mine heart? **for I am ready not to be bound only, but also to die at Jerusalem for the name of the Lord Jesus.**" 14 And when he would not be persuaded, we ceased, saying, "The will of the Lord be done, (Acts 21:13, 14, KJV)" – [Bold and underline is by the author, solely for emphasis]

It has been said by several Pre-Tribulation expositors that anyone who believes the *Christian Church* will remain on earth during increased times of persecution before the Lord returns, supposedly view themselves as "super macho" Christians. If those of us who have seen the light concerning the *End* (no Pre-Tribulation secret escape to heaven) *Times* reality, should we be insulted for wanting to emulate Christ, or even Paul? If this also were the Lord's will, as it states above that it is, do we really have any choice in the matter? Machismo has nothing to do with realizing the impending persecutions the *Christian Church* will experience before the Lord's return.

Nevertheless, Paul was once again arrested:

> When the seven days were nearly over, some Jews from the Province of Asia saw Paul at the temple. They stirred up the whole crowd and seized him, 28 shouting, "Men of Israel, help us. This is the man who teaches all men everywhere against our people and our and this place." 29 (They had previously seen Trophimus the Ephesian in the city with Paul and assumed that Paul had brought him into the temple area.) 30 The whole

city was aroused, and the people came running from all directions. **Seizing Paul, they dragged him from the temple**, and immediately the gates were shut. 31 While **they were trying to kill him**, news reached the commander of the Roman troops that the whole city of Jerusalem was in an uproar. 32 He at once took some officers and soldiers and ran down to the crowd. When the rioters saw the commander and his soldiers, **they stopped beating Paul**, (Acts 21:27-32, NIV). [Underline and bold is by the author, solely for emphasis]

Later on, we see the Jews conspiring to kill him (Acts 23:12-21); however, Paul was assisted by the commander of the Roman troops to get a fair hearing from the governor after many legal battles concerning the jurisdiction of where (and by whom) Paul would be tried. He was finally afforded the *opportunity* (Gr. *topos*, condition, license, room, opportunity) to present his case before King Agrippa. After Paul presented his case to Agrippa, and almost persuaded him to become a Christian (Acts 26:28), he was finally released. This aspect of Paul's persecution is a perfect example of why *called out ones* will remain on earth and experience great tribulation immediately before the Lord's return. The author believes that the possible Christianization of kings and rulers (and many other people, as well) during this period will come about as a result of the spirit-filled testimonies coming from the *called out ones* during that period of increased tribulation. [More on this aspect later]

The remainder of Acts is filled with stories concerning the tribulations that Paul and the apostles endured as the *ecclesia* was flourishing by virtue of the newly gained power from the Holy Spirit on the Day of Pentecost, and by the preaching of the Word of God. They experienced storms, shipwrecks, death plots, snake attacks and other tribulations too numerous to mention.

As the Book of Acts comes to a close, regardless of the persecutions he experienced, Paul is last seen in his own rented house greeting all who come to see him and, *Boldly, and without hindrance, he preached the Kingdom of God and taught about the Lord Jesus Christ,* (Acts 28:31, NIV). It appears that during this time of peace, Paul took some time out and wrote the letters to the Romans, Corinthians, Ephesians and all other churches, letters that have become so precious to those who call themselves New Testament believers.

The author in this chapter focused primarily on Paul's experiences in the Book of Acts, dwelling more so on his personal tribulations rather than the subject matter and the wisdom contained in the words he preached. It was (and is) important to this work that we read the accounts of Paul's trials and tribulations, because what follows next, is going to be a book-by-book description of not only the tribulations Paul endured, but also those he says the *Christian Church* will experience in the times of great and mighty persecutions. And Paul should know best, he lived (and died) through them!

Chapter 3
MESSAGES OF TRIBULATION
TO THE CHURCHES

Paul's history of experiencing persecution obviously gave him deeper spiritual insights into the plan God has in store for those who "pick up the cross and follow Him." The Book of Romans, like the four synoptic Gospels and the Book of Acts, speaks very clearly about the expected trials that the *Christian Church* will endure until *The Second Advent* of the Lord Jesus Christ.

Whereas Paul's message is primarily directed to the Roman community, and contains in the first four chapters the consequences of wrath for the unbeliever, Paul also tells the *called out ones* the purpose behind suffering great tribulation:

> And not only so, but we glory in tribulations also: **knowing that tribulation worketh patience;** 4 **And patience, experience; and experience, hope**: 5 And hope maketh not ashamed; because the love of God is shed abroad in our hearts by the Holy Ghost which is given unto us, (Romans 5:2-5, KJV). [Underline is by the author, solely for emphasis]

The Greek word for *experience* is *dokime*, which (according to W. E. Vine) means (a) "the process of proving;" it is rendered "experiment" in 2 Cor. 9:13, AV, RV, "the proving (of you);" in 2 Cor. 8:2, AV, "trial," RV, "proof;" (b) "the effect of proving, approval, approvedness," RV, "probation," Rom. 5:4 (twice), for AV, "experience;" AV and RV, "proof" in 2 Cor. 2:9; 13:3; Phil. 2:22. See EXPERIENCE, PROOF. Cp. dokimos, "approved," dokimazo, "to prove, approve;" see APPROVE. (W. E. Vine, *An Expository Dictionary of Biblical Words*, Thomas Nelson Publishers, page 392)

In these verses, Paul points out a few of the reasons why *Christian Church* must suffer great tribulation; however, this particular aspect will be discussed in greater detail in a future chapter. In Romans 6, though, Paul once again reminds the *Christian Church* that suffering is to be associated with its union to Christ, because through His death, our resurrection is also guaranteed. Our being united with Christ therefore makes us heirs to all that He inherits, which also includes sharing the same sufferings he endured:

> And if children, then heirs; heirs of God, and joint-heirs with Christ; **if so be that we suffer with him, that we may be also glorified together**, (Romans 8:17, KJV). [Underline and bold is by the author, solely for emphasis]

The fact that Paul tells us that we will never be separated from Christ, regardless of the persecutions to come, also confirms that these persecutions are part of God's overall plan:

> Who shall separate us from the love of Christ? Shall tribulation, or distress, or persecution, or famine, or nakedness, or peril, or sword? 36 As it is written, **For thy sake we are killed all the day long; we are accounted as sheep for the slaughter.** 37 Nay, in all these things we are more than conquerors through him

that loved us. 38 For I am persuaded, that neither death, nor life, nor angels, nor principalities, nor powers, nor things present, nor things to come, 39 nor height, nor depth, nor any other creature, shall be able to separate us from the love of God, which is in Christ Jesus our Lord, (Romans 8:35-39, KJV). [Underline and bold is by the author, solely for emphasis]

It is obvious from these verses (especially vs. 36) that, as followers of Christ, facing death as sheep before the slaughter is an expected reality. This is just a small part of the anticipated persecutions that await the *called out ones*, now and in future times. Once again, Paul reminds the *ecclesia* that not only will there be persecution at the hands of unbelievers, he plainly states that the brethren will not need to arm and defend themselves from these persecutions; but, rather, they need to be prepared to volunteer their bodies for the Lord's service:

I beseech you therefore, brethren, by the mercies of God, **that ye present your bodies a living sacrifice,** holy, acceptable unto God, which is your reasonable service, (Romans 12:1, KJV). [Underline and bold is by the author, solely for emphasis]

Paul goes on to say that no matter what types of persecution lay ahead for the *called out ones*, they must be prepared to go all the way with their commitment to Christ, regardless of the cost:

For whether we live, we live unto the Lord; **and whether we die, we die unto the Lord:** whether we live therefore, or die, we are the Lord's, (Romans 14:8, KJV). [Bold and underline is by the author, solely for emphasis]

As Paul concludes his letter to the Romans, he gives the *Christian Church* a hint that part of the persecutions will include doctrinal divisiveness among the Christian community. While some may not view differences in doctrine as a form of persecution, to be denied the truth about what God truly is saying through His word, is to deny a fellow servant – especially new converts - all the tools of the faith needed to endure the impending tribulations to come:

> Now I beseech you, brethren, **mark them which cause divisions and offences contrary to the doctrine which ye have learned**; and avoid them.18 for they that are such serve not our Lord Jesus Christ, **but their own belly; and by good words and fair speeches deceive the hearts of the simple**, (Romans 16:17-18, KJV). [Underline and bold is by the author, solely for emphasis]

This divisiveness (for many) will unfortunately be more sorrowful than death itself. Earlier, it was noted that many of the Christian's very own relatives will turn on them (Matthew 10:21); but, even these betrayals compare little to the treachery that will come upon many Christians at the hands of their fellow church members who are supposedly *the true relatives of God*, (Luke 8:21). We will deal with this aspect in greater detail in the chapter regarding the Apostasy.

In Paul's letters to the Corinthians, we see him reiterating the fate of Christians who "pick up their cross" for the word of Jesus:

> For I think that God hath set forth us the apostles last, as it were appointed to death: for we are made a spectacle unto the world, and to angels, and to men, (1 Corinthians 4:9, KJV).

Here we see a picture of the accepted realities befalling an apostle during the times of Paul, Barnabas, et al. Theorists would state that the persecution and tribulations mentioned so far pertained solely to those ordained apostles during that era. It is true that to become an apostle one had to meet the apostolic criteria set forth in Acts 1:21-26 (specifically chosen by Christ, who knows a man's true heart). However, the Lord has still been choosing apostles since he first chose the original twelve, and continues to do so daily. Paul specifically states that all who are members of the body of Christ, which includes individuals with many different areas of ministry and church responsibility (1 Corinthians. 12:12-30), whether they are apostles or not, will suffer together: *If one part suffers, every part suffers with it*, (1 Corinthians 12:26, NIV).

In 2 Corinthians, the apostle Paul continues to convey his message concerning sufferings and persecutions, albeit he assures the Christian that the Lord's comfort will be in abundance during those times of great affliction:

> For just as the sufferings of Christ flow over into our lives, so also through Christ our comfort overflows, (2 Corinthians 1:5, NIV).

Paul goes on to say that the expected distresses of life, and even the possibility of death, have a specific purpose:

> If we are distressed, it is for your comfort and salvation; if we are comforted, it is for your comfort, which produces in you patient endurance of the same sufferings we suffer. 7 And our hope for you is firm, because we know that as you share in our sufferings, so also you share in our comfort. 8 We do not want you to be uninformed, brothers, about the hardships we suffered in the province of Asia. We were under great pressure, far beyond our ability to endure, so that we despaired even of life. 9 Indeed, in our hearts **we felt the sentence of death**. **But this happened that we**

might not rely on ourselves but on God, who raises the dead, (2 Corinthians 1:6-9, NIV). [Bold and underline is by the author, solely for emphasis]

In these verses, we see Paul emphasizing (from his past experiences) that the sufferings are purposely allowed by God to bring us to the point where we depend on nothing else but Him for deliverance. Paul gives the Christian a perfect example of why God allows this persecution in his "jars of clay" analogy:

But we have this treasure in jars of clay to show that this all surpassing power is from God and not from us. 8 We are **hard pressed** on every side, but not crushed; **perplexed**, but not in despair; 9 **persecuted**, but not abandoned; **struck down**, but not destroyed. 10 We always carry around in our body the death of Jesus, so that the life of Jesus may also be revealed in our body. 11 **For we who are alive are always being given over to death for Jesus' sake, so that His life may be revealed in our mortal body**, (2 Corinthians 4: 7-11, NIV). [Bold is by the author, solely for emphasis]

Once again, Paul is providing the Christian not only with words of comfort for those who fear death, but a beautiful example of how these persecutions (including death) will reveal Christ in us. It will also cause more and more people to participate, at all costs, and give more generously in support of those ministries that are doing the will of God, thereby gaining Him more glory. Paul cites a specific example in 2 Corinthians 8:1-4 of how this type of suffering by the churches in Macedonia produced great results:

And now, brothers, we want you to know about the grace that God has given the Macedonian churches. 2 **Out of the most severe trial, their overflowing joy and**

their extreme poverty welled up in rich generosity. 3 For I testify that they gave as much as they were able, and even beyond their ability. Entirely on their own, 4 **they urgently pleaded with us for the privilege of sharing in this service to the saints,** (2 Corinthians 8:1-4, NIV). [Bold and underline is by the author, solely for emphasis]

In Chapter 11 of 2 Corinthians, Paul proceeds to boast about the sufferings he has endured for preaching the gospel. In this, he is telling Christians that not only will they suffer for the sake of Jesus, but that they ought to take pride in this, to the point of even becoming fanatical about the expected sufferings:

To my shame I admit that we were too weak for that! **What anyone else dares to boast about – I am speaking as a fool – I also dare to boast about.** 22 Are they Hebrew? So am I. Are they Israelites? So am I. 23 Are they servants of Christ? (I am out of my mind to talk like this.) I am more. **I have worked much harder, been in prison more frequently, been flogged more severely, and been exposed to death again and again.** 25 three times I was shipwrecked, I spent a night and a day in the open sea, 26 I have been constantly on the move. I have been in danger from rivers, in danger from bandits, in danger from my own countrymen, in danger from Gentiles; in danger in the city, in danger in the country, in danger at sea; **and in danger from false brothers.** 27 I have labored and toiled and have often gone without sleep; I have known hunger and thirst and have often gone without food; I have been cold and naked, (2 Corinthians 11:21-27, NIV). [Bold and underline is by the author, solely for emphasis]

The psychology community would consider it sheer folly these days to express Paul's sentiments about suffering for Christ, because it knows not, nor can it understand the things that Christians (through the power of the Holy Spirit) realize and accept about trials and tribulations. Practitioners of (especially modern-day) psychology don't realize that as the Christian surrenders all claims to worldly (and emotional) strength, then (and only then) can the power of God begin its work. Paul knew this well and so beautifully states this in 2 Corinthians 12:7-10:

> To keep me from **becoming conceited** because of these surpassingly great revelations, there was given me a thorn in my flesh, a messenger of Satan, to torment me. 8 Three times I pleaded with the Lord to take it away from me. 9 But he said to me, "My grace is sufficient for you, **for my power is made perfect in weakness**." Therefore I will boast all the more gladly about my weaknesses, in insults, in hardships, in persecutions, in difficulties. For when I am weak, then I am strong, (2 Corinthians 12:7-10, NIV). [Bold and underline is by the author, solely for emphasis]

Many theorists have attempted to identify specifically what was that "thorn" in the flesh that plagued Paul; however, it appears that what is a "thorn" to one person can be something entirely different to another. Only the individual Christian and the Lord truly know what specific maladaptive traits or inherent weaknesses might exist within each of us that rob us from being able to walk a guilt-free lifestyle.

However, in these verses we may see a deeper insight into the thorn issue, which can very well allude to the dangerous issue of pride. This is revealed in the Biblical fact that Paul was the only human being who was caught up to the third heaven and heard inexpressible words that were virtually unspeakable that no man is permitted to tell another human being. Who truly knows what Paul heard? Whatever it was, he is the only person in recorded history to be caught up (he didn't know if in the spirit or in the body) and returned to earth. Such an experience could cause anyone to become conceited and to boast and exalt themselves above others. It appears, therefore, that the buffeting from Satan could well have been a diabolical effort to make Paul boastfully reveal the words he heard, things that God probably did not want anyone to know yet. Nevertheless, this heavenly knowledge could very well make anyone believe himself to be extra special.

This aspect is also an important reminder that needs to be brought into greater focus to the *ecclesia* and many of its leaders. Many evangelists, bible scholars, commentators and even novice students of God's word have been given deep insights to God's overall redemption plan and message to mankind. Many modern day prophets have indeed been responsible for turning many to Christ, and they have even received many accolades and gained great fame in the church and even in the secular arena. Many, however, have also been victim to great attacks from Satan, because the closer one gets to God the more they will be persecuted. Therefore, it is crucial to remember that these messages of wisdom come from God and not from the messenger's intellect. Too many great men and woman of God have been mightily used by Him to deliver His messages and thereafter find them basking and languishing in their temporal fame and glory, to the point of becoming ineffective in the long haul of their ministerial journey. The Bible gives us many examples of those whom God gave great strength and wisdom to fulfill His purpose, such as Samson and Solomon, only to see them falter at the end of their careers.

Therefore, the message from Paul is a great reminder that although many receive great wisdom from God, this wisdom must be handled carefully and judiciously, always remembering that it is God who is to receive the glory, rather than the messenger. In these verses, Paul delights in his persecutions, focusing more on these than any glory for himself. Paul recognized that no good thing comes from him, and whatever idiosyncratic millstones (such as arrogance, ego, haughtiness, conceit) he may have carried in his heart and mind, he exalted in these persecutions in the realization that his true strength came from submission to God's will and grace, rather than through any perceived strength or intellect of his own. These afflictions are allowed by God as a reminder that the Lord's "grace is sufficient" because in (our) weakness His "power is made perfect."

It is interesting to note that Paul, in his epistle to the church at Galatia, dwelled not much on persecution, per se. However, he warned that the maintenance of the gospel requires the Christian be imminently aware of those who will distort the word of God through vain preaching:

> I am astonished that you are so quickly deserting the one who called you by the grace of Christ and are turning to a different gospel – 7 which is really no gospel at all. **Evidently some people are throwing you into confusion and are trying to pervert the * gospel of Christ.** 8 But even if we or an angel from heaven should preach a gospel other than the one we preached to you, let him be eternally condemned! 9 As we have already said, so now I say again: If anybody is preaching to you a *gospel other than what you accepted, let him be eternally condemned, (Galatians 1:6-9, NIV). [Underline and bold is by the author, solely for emphasis]

*And what is the Gospel? The Gospel is that by Jesus' propitiatory sacrifice at Calvary, God provided all mankind the opportunity to share in the grace and inheritance promised to His chosen people. This Gospel was made plain and evident directly to the person He promised it to, Abraham: *The Scripture foresaw that God would* *justify the Gentiles by faith, and announced the gospel <u>in advance</u> to Abraham: "<u>All nations will be blessed through you,</u>* (Galatians 3:8, Genesis 12:3; Acts 3:25, Acts 4:3-16; Romans 4:16, NIV). [Underline is by the author]

The spirit-filled Christian knows too well that in these latter days there will be an increase of false teachers and so-called prophets, twisting and distorting the true Gospel to suit their needs, which thereby will be denying the glory to God. As the author of 1 John so eloquently states, *even now many antichrists have come,* (1 John 1:18, 19). The amazing thing about this prophetic utterance is that in today's world, a myriad of sects and so-called religious groups are found to be preaching not only a humanistic gospel, but, also, many are openly advocating satanically induced theologies. If the Gospel or doctrines they preach are not the true Gospel of God, then obviously they are satanically inspired! The unfortunate reality of this increasing phenomenon is that many of these proponents originated from your basic orthodox groups that originally professed a belief in the true Gospel. It is one thing to suffer for professing the Christian faith (in its truest sense), but the worst persecution that Christians are becoming exposed to and seduced by (and acquiesce to) is a doctrine that distorts the gospel. Too many well intended evangelists preach a gospel that glorifies persons, groups or dogma, rather than one that clearly proclaims that *all nations will be blessed through you* (Abraham), by virtue of the atoning works on Calvary by Jesus Christ! This Gospel (*that God would justify the Gentiles by faith*) was an announcement and a promise of glad tidings beforehand, prior to the crucifixion and before the Lord's resurrection.

In the Book of Ephesians, most of Paul's message concerns the spiritual blessings found in Christ, being made alive and one in Christ, Paul's administration of God's grace, our need to live as children of the light, being imitators of God (that of loving one another as Christ loved and gave Himself for the *ecclesia*), the proper relationship between wives and husbands, children and parents and, most importantly, putting on the armor of God to combat "against the devil's schemes." This particular group of scriptures (Ephesians 6:10-18) will receive greater attention in a later chapter.

In Philippians, Paul continues to boast about him being *chained for Christ* (Philippians 1:12-14), and its positive results. After much boasting and rejoicing about his tribulations, Paul reminds the Christian that to believe in Christ includes the sharing in His suffering:

> For it has been granted to you on behalf of Christ **not only to believe on him, but also to suffer for him**, (Philippians1:29, NIV). [Bold and underline is by the author, solely for emphasis]

In Chapter 2, Paul is found exhorting Christians that their attitude should be exactly as Christ's, one of total submission to the will of God:

> Who, being in very nature God, did not consider equality with God something to be grasped, 7 but made himself nothing, taking the very nature of a servant, being made in human likeness. 8 **And being found in appearance as a man, he humbled himself and became obedient to death – even death on a cross**, (Philippians 2:6-8, NIV). [Bold and underline is by the author, solely for emphasis]

Probably the most puzzling, but yet ignored, verse in the Bible is verse 12:

> Therefore, my dear friends, as you have always obeyed – not only in my presence, but now much more in my absence – **continue to work out your salvation** with fear and trembling, (Philippians 2:12, NIV). [Bold is by the author, solely for emphasis]

The Greek word for *work* is the verb *kategazomai*, which literally means "to achieve, effect by toil and to be free from strife and vain glory." This "work out your own salvation" obviously does not refer to the obtaining of salvation by works. But, rather, as a Christian, it is our responsibility to exercise our faith by doing the works that God requires, as seen in James, Chapter 2, which is a condition for believers chosen by God: *You see that a person is justified by what he does and not by faith alone*, (vs. 24), for *As the body without spirit is dead, so faith without deeds is dead*, (James 2:26, NIV).

There has been, and still exists today, a large group within the Christian community that believes in the doctrine of "once saved, always saved;" however, it appears from scripture that many of today's professing Christians will "rebel" and "fall away" during times of persecution (See Luke 8:11-14). [More on the "Apostasy" will be discussed in a later chapter]

Further, in Ephesians, Paul makes a statement that goes contrary to contemporary human thought (and more so within the Psychology community) concerning his desire to not only share in the same sufferings that Christ experienced, but also to look death squarely in the face, knowing full well that he will be resurrected when Christ returns:

> I want to know Christ and the power of his resurrection
> and the fellowship of sharing in his sufferings, becoming
> like him in his death, 11 and so, somehow, to attain to the
> resurrection from the dead, (Philippians 3:10, 11, NIV).

In the book of Colossians, Paul's message includes the Christian's need for constant thanksgiving and prayer, the supremacy of Christ, more about Paul's labor for the *ecclesia*, warnings about hollow and deceptive philosophy, rules for holy living, rules for Christian households and other instructions. The author mentions here that Paul's exhortation concerning a wife's responsibility toward her husband and vice verse might not be considered within the realm of persecution; however, much of the social ills confronting modern society can be directly linked to the breakdown of the family structure. This subject alone is worth writing about in great detail; however, let us suffice by stating that as the family unit goes, so goes the basic foundation for the successful Christian community. The old adage that "The family that prays together, stays together" still holds true today, and will be needed much more so as the times of great distress approaches:

> Wives, submit to your husbands, as is fitting in the Lord. 19 Husbands, love your wives and do not be harsh with them. 20 Children, obey your parents in everything, for this pleases the Lord. 21 Fathers, do not embitter your children, or they will become discouraged, (Colossians 3:18-21, NIV).

Chapter 4

THE TIME OF TRIALS WILL INCREASE!

As we venture further through the epistles for scripture regarding the tribulations that *called out ones* can expect before the return of the Lord, we see the apostle Paul offering encouragement to the *ecclesia* at Thessalonica, concerning the fate of those who die in Christ and those who remain waiting for the Lord's return. His message, however, continues to remind the *ecclesia* that persecutions are not only on the increase, but *called out ones* are destined to experience them until the Lord returns. Paul is telling the Thessalonians that even during those trials, a time when even He, Timothy and Silas needed as much help as possible, they nevertheless sent one of their most able disciples to strengthen and encourage the Thessalonians, who also were enduring hardship:

> So when we could stand it no longer, we thought it best to be left by ourselves in Athens. 2 We sent Timothy, who is our brother and God's fellow worker in spreading the gospel of Christ, to strengthen and encourage you in your faith, 3 so that no one would be unsettled by these trials. **You know quite well that we were destined**

for them. 4 **In fact, when we were with you, we kept telling you that we would be persecuted**. And it turned out that way, as you well know. 5 For this reason, when I could stand it no longer, I sent to find out about your faith. I was afraid that in some way the tempter might have tempted you and our efforts might have been useless, (1 Thessalonians 3:1-5, NIV). [Underline and bold is by the author, solely for emphasis]

In 2 Thessalonians, we not only see Paul boasting about his trials, but we see him boasting about their faithfulness amid the persecutions that they themselves (the Thessalonians) are experiencing:

Therefore, among God's churches we boast about your perseverance and faith in all the **persecutions and trials** you are enduring, (2 Thessalonians 1:4, NIV). [Underline and bold is by the author, solely for emphasis]

In 2 Thessalonians 2:1-12, we see the famous exhortation from Paul concerning their redemption, which specifically states that it will not come about until first the *apostasy* (believers falling away from their faith in God) and *the man of lawlessness* is revealed, in accordance with Satan's authority. That period of intensified tribulation will include some of the most horrific persecutions imaginable at the hands of the satanically inspired Beast (or antichrist).

Throughout the book of 1 Timothy, we see Paul touching on several issues, which includes warnings to the *ecclesia* to be aware of more persecutions (which will include false teachers), and the Lord's grace to Paul and instructions on worship, overseers and deacons. In the book of 1 Timothy 4:1-3, we see specific warnings to God's *called out ones* that, in the later times, some believers will abandon the faith and follow deceiving spirits:

The Spirit clearly says that in later times some will abandon the faith and follow deceiving spirits and things taught by demons. 2 Such teachings come through hypocritical liars, whose consciences have been seared as with a hot iron. 3 They forbid people to marry and order them to abstain from certain foods, which God created, to be received with thanksgiving by those who believe and who know the truth, (1 Timothy 4:1-3, NIV). [Underline and bold is by the author, solely for emphasis]

In 2 Timothy, Paul continues to exhort the *called out ones* to be faithful and bold in ministering to others, and not to be ashamed about testifying about the Lord Jesus, which will include suffering:

So do not be ashamed to testify about our Lord, or ashamed of me his prisoner. **But join with me in suffering for the gospel**, by the power of God, 9 who has saved us and called us to a holy life – not because of anything we have done but because of his own purpose and grace. This grace was given us in Christ Jesus before the beginning of time, (2 Timothy 1:8, 9, NIV). [Underline and bold is by the author, solely for emphasis]

In Chapter 2, Paul's exhortation implies hardship is inevitable, as is expected from one who is a soldier of Christ Jesus:

Endure hardship with us like a good soldier of Christ Jesus. 4 No one serving as a soldier gets involved in civilian affairs – he wants to please his commanding officer, (2 Timothy 2:3, 4, NIV). [Bold and underline is by the author, solely for emphasis]

In 2 Timothy, Chapter 3, verses 10 through 12, we see Paul sharing about his way of life, where he makes one of the most profound statements ever concerning the true Christian life:

> You, however, know all about my teaching, my way of life, my purpose, faith, patience, love, endurance, 11 **persecutions, sufferings**--what kinds of things happened to me in Antioch, Iconium and Lystra, the persecutions I endured. Yet the Lord rescued me from all of them. 12 **In fact, everyone who wants to live a godly life in Christ Jesus will be persecuted**, (2 Timothy 3:10-12, NIV). [Bold and underline is by the author, solely for emphasis]

Once again, we go back to the beginning of our discussion of tribulation in Chapter 16, where we asked the proverbial question: "Why did I accept Jesus Christ as my Lord and Savior if I have to experience pain and persecution? What good does it do for a non-Christian to accept Christ if they have to go through tribulation?" Based on 2 Timothy 3:12, wanting to live a godly life *will* result in persecution. For many in the *Christian Church* (or society in general) this doesn't make any sense at all. If you try to live a godly life, you will be persecuted. If you live an ungodly life, you may enjoy the momentary pleasures of sin, but you will eventually pay the price. Some would say it's kind of like being caught between a rock and a hard place.

However, those *called out ones* of Christ know the true answer. Being a Christian is not about gaining worldly power, riches, fame and all the other creature comforts that the ungodly live for. Many evangelists spend much time preaching prosperity messages that a prayer formula exists within God's word that riches can be gained by righteous living, and many such cases can be documented that those of faith did achieve great wealth. However, as we turn the corner on history and enter the end times, the word of God requires the *ecclesia* to prepare itself for the imminent return of Christ, where great tribulations are definitely in store for *called out ones* in the near future. Creature comforts will matter little during those horrific times. While millions will continue to pursue (and depend on) worldly possessions and pleasure, their actions will indirectly affect the *ecclesia*. Therefore, the *called out ones* need be ready and willing to lay aside everything (material possessions, jobs, friends, and even family) and pick up their crosses and follow Him. Paul tells us what it's going to be like in those days, which will include a spiritual malaise which (to a great degree) already exists at this precise moment:

> But mark this: **There will be terrible times in the last days**. 2 People will be lovers of themselves, lovers of money, boastful, proud, abusive, disobedient to their parents, ungrateful, unholy, 3 without love, unforgiving, slanderous, without self-control, brutal, not lovers of the good, 4 treacherous, rash, conceited, **lovers of pleasure rather than lovers of God** – 5 **having a form of godliness but denying its power.** Have nothing to do with them. 6 They are the kind who worm their way into homes and gain control over weak-willed women, who are loaded down with sins and are swayed by all kinds of evil desires, 7 always learning but never able to acknowledge the truth. 8 Just as Jannes and Jambres opposed Moses, so also these men oppose the truth – men of depraved minds, who, as far as the faith is concerned, are rejected. 9 **But they will not get very far because, as in the case of those men, their folly will be clear to everyone,** (2 Timothy 3:1-9, NIV). [Underline and bold is by the author, solely for emphasis]

Although Paul here is talking about the Godlessness that will be prevalent in the last days, Christians can be assured that by virtue of this type of behavior by their unbelieving (and some believing) friends, neighbors and family members, the truly committed *called out ones* will be affected (and persecuted) by its spillover into their lives. If just one of our unbelieving loved ones manifests these behavior traits (lovers of money, boastful, proud, abusive, disobedient, etc.), you can be assured that much sorrow will be experienced by the *ecclesia* as a result of these activities, regardless of its non-participatory stance. Sorrowfully, many, who today proclaim they are Christian, once they see the financial pressures and other horrors begin to mount, will fall away and seek worldly solutions to their problems, denying God's help and wisdom, and they will even turn against their fellow Christian brothers and sisters. As verse 5 clearly states, they will be *having a form of godliness but denying its power.* We see these things happening increasingly so on a daily basis. Many professing Christians (and some churches and charitable Christian organizations, as well) are falling apart under financial and political pressures and scandals they never experienced before. Many profess the name of God and Christ, yet have no faith in God to provide for them and their respective missions. Many of these faithless and frustrated leaders have lost sight of their mission and waste much time and energy bickering over titles, territorial authority and petty financial issues. Many even deride and curse their brethren Christian workers who seek to live by faith and trust in God to provide the resources to accomplish their respective tasks. Human hearts are turning colder and colder toward each other, as we speak:

> At that time **many will turn away from the faith and will betray and hate each other,** 11 and many false prophets will appear and deceive many people.12 **Because of the increase of wickedness, the love of most will grow cold**, (Matthew 24:10-12, NIV). [Bold and underline is by the author, solely for emphasis]

Unfortunately, even as the dedicated and committed Christian holds firm, to either rebuke or provide Godly instruction to these rebellious factions, they will be met with force, insults, hostility, legal maneuvers, physical abuse and other increased forms of retaliation, which will result in great persecutions, some resulting in death. This is why Paul exhorts the *called out ones* to preach the *true* word of God (as challenging and frightening as it may seem for many, including fellow Christians) while it can still be received:

> Preach the Word; be prepared in season and out of season, correct, rebuke and encourage – with great patience and careful instruction. 3 **For the time will come when men will not put up with sound doctrine. Instead, to suit their own desires, they will gather around them a great number of teachers to say what their itching ears want to hear.** 4 **They will turn their ears away from the truth and turn aside to myths**. 5 But you, keep your head in all situations, **endure hardship**, do the work of an evangelist, discharge all the duties of your ministry, (2 Timothy 4:2-5, NIV). [Bold and underline by the author, solely for emphasis]

As he begins to close his second letter to Timothy, Paul knows that his death is soon at hand; although weary, tired, exhausted, in much pain from years of beatings, floggings, and many other sorrows. Knowing and expecting to be executed soon by his persecutors, he is at peace, knowing the mission Christ gave him of evangelizing the gospel has been completed. He knows his reward will be given to him on that glorious day (not any sooner than) when Christ appears; but, yet he continues to exhort his fellow servants in the Lord about the rewards they will also receive, on that great day, as He promised:

> **For I am already being poured out like a drink offering**, and the time has come for my departure. 7 I have fought the good fight, I have finished the race, **I have kept the faith.** 8 Now there is in store for me the

crown of righteousness, which the Lord, the righteous Judge, will **award to me on that day** – and not only to me, but also to all who have longed for **his appearing**, (2 Timothy 4:6-8, NIV). [The Greek word for *poured* is *spendo*, which literally means and is used of one whose blood is poured out in a violent death for the cause of God. Bold and underline is by the author, solely for emphasis]

In Titus, the apostle Paul is seen exhorting the Christian concerning the criteria for appointing elders, the negative aspects about Cretans, the teaching of sound doctrine to women and young men; about slaves being subject to their masters and the famous passage (Titus 2:13, NIV) about the blessed Hope, which is "*The glorious appearing of our God and Savior, Jesus Christ.*" Paul also reminds the Christian about being subjected to rulers and authorities, avoiding foolish controversies about the Law and the warnings that should be given to divisive people. However, no mention is made of any specific suffering or tribulation in the Book of Titus. The same is true of the Book of Philemon, where Paul communicates about prayer and thanksgiving and his request that his disciple Onesimus be cared for.

In the Book of Hebrews, a litany of scriptures address the "new covenant" that was fulfilled by Jesus' death on the cross, and how all who believe (including Jew and Gentile alike) have been made one in Christ. However, a group of scriptures that weighs tremendously on the whole concept of this book is found in Hebrews 2:14 and 15, and it should be read at this point:

Since the children have flesh and blood, he too shared in their humanity so that by his death he might destroy him who holds the power of death – that is, the devil – 15 **and free those who all their lives were held in slavery by their fear of death**, (Hebrews 2:14, 15, NIV).

[We will be discussing these two verses at great length in a future chapter, but since we are citing scriptures that make reference to persecutions, sufferings and tribulation, the author felt it would be profitable for *called out ones* to read these now. Underline and bold by author, solely for emphasis]

As we move forward concerning the expected tribulations that *called out ones* will experience, we now examine the Book of Hebrews. The author of Hebrews first mentions the subject of persecution in Chapter 11:24 as he discusses the tribulations that Old Testament *called out ones* experienced due to their faith, in particular, Moses the Law Giver:

By faith Moses, when he had grown up, refused to be known as the son of Pharaoh's daughter. 25 **He chose to be mistreated along with the people of God rather than to enjoy the pleasures of sin for a short time.** 26 He regarded disgrace for the sake of Christ as of greater value than the treasures of Egypt, because he was looking ahead to his reward, (Hebrews 11:24-26, NIV). [Underline and bold is by the author, solely for emphasis]

The author of Hebrews goes on to graphically describe some of the atrocities that the *called out ones*, God's *ecclesia*, have suffered for their faith in Messiah throughout history:

Women received back their dead, raised to life again. Others were tortured and refused to be released, **so that they might gain a better resurrection.** 36 **Some faced jeers and flogging, while still others were chained and put in prison.** 37 **They were stoned; they were sawed in two; they were put to death by the**

sword. They went about in sheepskins and goatskins, destitute, persecuted and mistreated – 38 the world was not worthy of them. **They wandered in deserts and mountains, and in caves and holes in the ground**, (Hebrews 11:35-38, NIV). [Bold and underline is by the author, solely for emphasis]

The author of Hebrews concludes Chapter 11 by stating that these believers, although suffering much for their faith in the Messiah, entered not into the Promised Land, because God had a better plan:

These were all commended for their faith, yet none of them received what had been promised. 40 **God had planned something better for us so that only together with us would they be made perfect**, (Hebrews 11:39, 40, NIV). [Bold and underline is by the author, solely for emphasis]

In Chapter 12, the author of Hebrews cites a unique verse indicating that the *called out ones* potentially will suffer (to the point of shedding blood), and he commences to tell the *ecclesia* one of the reasons why:

In your struggle against sin, **you have not yet resisted to the point of shedding your blood.** 5 And you have forgotten that word of encouragement that addresses you as sons: "My son, do not make light of the Lords' discipline, and do not lose heart when he rebukes you, 6 because **the Lord disciplines those he loves, and he punishes everyone He accepts as a son**." 7 **Endure hardship as discipline**; God is treating you as sons. For what son is not disciplined by his father? 8 **If you are not disciplined (and everyone undergoes discipline), then you are illegitimate children and not true sons**. 9 Moreover, we have all had human fathers who disciplined us and we respected them for it. How much more should we submit to the Father of our spirits and live! 10 Our fathers disciplined us for a little while as they thought best; but God disciplines us for our good, that we may share in his holiness. 11 **No discipline seems pleasant at the time, but painful. Later on, however, it produces a harvest of righteousness and peace for those who have been trained by it**, (Hebrews 12:4-11, NIV). [Underline and bold is by the author, solely for emphasis]

The author has provided a small clue in these scriptures to reveal partly why Christians (during that intensified period of tribulation) will more than likely experience greater persecutions before the Lord returns. But, once again, this will be discussed in greater detail in another chapter. Nevertheless, it appears that the author of Hebrews is making some very boldly inspired statements concerning the suffering and hardship that awaits the *ecclesia*, even more so than exists today. He confirms this fact in Hebrews 13:13, which reaffirms the statements he had made before concerning the Christian's sharing in the same sufferings that Jesus, Himself, bore:

Let us, then, go to him outside the camp, **bearing the disgrace he bore**. 14 For here we do not have an enduring city, but we are looking for the City that is to come, (Hebrews 13:13, 14, NIV). [Underline, bold by the author, solely for emphasis]

In the Book of James, it immediately continues where the book of Hebrews left off, concerning the trials and tribulations that are (and will increasingly continue) befalling the Christian:

Consider it pure joy, my brothers, whenever you face trials of many kinds, (James 1:2, NIV).

Once again, the same attitude that Paul had (one of rejoicing in his suffering) is identical to James'. James goes on to say, in great detail (as had Paul) what purpose these trials will eventuate:

> Because you know that **the testing of your faith develops perseverance**. 4 Perseverance must finish its work **so that you may be mature and complete**, not lacking anything, (James 1:3, 4, NIV). [Underline and bold is by the author, solely for emphasis]

The entire Book of James, for that matter, deals specifically with the enduring of trials and tribulations; but, more importantly, he explains the results. These also will be discussed in greater detail.

In 1 Peter, the author picks up where James left off and discusses in great detail the results of suffering. In 1 Peter, we see the author exhorting the Christian to not be found retaliating during these sufferings because there not only is a special purpose for them, he specifically states that the Christian was called for this very same purpose:

> **To this you were called, because Christ suffered for you, leaving you an example, that you should follow his steps**. 22 "He committed no sin, and no deceit was found in his mouth." 23 When they hurled their insults at him, He did not retaliate; when he suffered, he made no threats. Instead, he entrusted himself to him who judges justly, (1 Peter 2:21-23, NIV). [Underline and bold is by the author, solely for emphasis]

Once again, we will allow a sneak preview of why this suffering must occur as the author again reiterates that our attitude should be just like that of Jesus, be willing to face death as He did:

> Therefore, since Christ suffered in his body, arm yourselves also with the same attitude, **because he who**

has suffered in his body is done with sin, (1 Peter 4:1 NIV). [Bold and underline is by the author, solely for emphasis]

In the following verse, we see Peter specifically telling the Christian that this suffering to come should not catch us by surprise:

Dear friends, do not be surprised at the painful trial you are suffering, as though something strange were happening to you, (1 Peter 4:12, NIV).

Once again, we remind the reader that this entire chapter has been devoted to citing those scriptures that specifically point out that the truly committed Christian must (and will) suffer for the name of Jesus Christ.

In 2 Peter, the author doesn't dwell too much on the suffering aspect, but does exhort Christians to ensure (their) election by adding to their faith those qualities (goodness, knowledge of the word of God, self-control, perseverance, godliness, brotherly kindness and love) to prevent blindness and the forgetting that we have been cleansed from sin. As James said, *As the body without the spirit is dead, so faith without deeds is dead*, (James 2:26, NIV).

Much of 2 Peter also deals with the judgments due to those that do not believe in Jesus, and the warnings to those that "scoff" as the Lord tarries. 2 Peter ends by once again exhorting the Christian to continue living holy and godly lives, being found spotless, blameless and at peace with Him until *The Second Advent*.

In the Book of 1 John, it discusses the word of life, walking in the light, warnings about antichrists (which are many and even now dwell amid the Christian community), believers being called the Children of God, and the love that we must have for one another. John does find place to remind the Christian that the world (non-believers) will hate us:

> Do not be surprised, my brothers, if the world hates you,
> (1 John 3:13, NIV).

In verse 16, the author makes probably the most astounding statement about sacrificial death in the entire Bible, as he describes the true definition of the word love!

> This is how we know what love is: **Jesus Christ laid**
> **down His life for us; and we ought to lay down our**
> **lives for our brothers**, (1 John 3:16, NIV). [Bold and
> underline by the author, solely for emphasis]

It is interesting to note that another similar verse in the Bible is also numbered 3:16, which probably describes the very same message as it applied to Jesus:

> For God so loved the world, that he gave his only
> begotten Son, that whosoever believeth in him should
> not perish, but have everlasting life, (John 3:16, KJV).

A coincidence? Possibly, but His (God's) omniscient nature, which includes creating the world's numbering system, the stars above and many other unknown facets that encompass this universe, which have not been fully revealed, yet stand ready to unveil the complete and unfathomable glory of God! [There are several books available that the author would recommend to the serious student of God's revelations concerning these topics (stars and numbers), which include E. W. Bullinger's *Number in Scripture* and *Witness To The Stars*]

In the Books of 2 John and 3 John, not much mention is made about suffering and tribulation; although in 2 John, the author does warn the *ecclesia* to be wary of losing what they have worked for. This should be of obvious concern to those who break off their connection to God, thereby incurring the imminent wrath to come.

In the Book of Jude, the main comments here are reserved for the unbelieving angelic beings that are presently bound for judgment on the Great Day, as examples of the fate due to those that believe not. However, the Book of Jude does exhort the *called out ones* to believe that the Lord is coming, and to be wary of "scoffers' who will try to divide them away from the truth.

This particular chapter of our book, once again, has been specifically devoted to reacquaint the reader with the many verses that deal with the subject of suffering, hardship, persecution and tribulations that Christians will experience for holding to the testimony of Jesus Christ. Theorists and scoffers will respond by saying that these instances of affliction were solely accomplished in the persons of Paul and the other apostles in the early days of the *Christian Movement*. Some will say that these afflictions are not to be taken literally, that they merely represent the emotional and psychological trauma being experienced in this fast-paced society we live in. Some would even say that the words spoken of by Christ when He said "pick up your cross and follow me" are merely symbolic of what society today calls "everyday problems." However, we intentionally cited all the passages that deal with suffering, affliction, hardship, persecution and tribulation for two special reasons. Number one, throughout all the books the author has read about the so-called Rapture, whether Pre-Trib, Mid-Trib or Post-Trib, very few have touched on the subject of the sufferings that Christians are destined for. Obviously, if a secret escape to heaven is what theorists believe scripture teaches, then not a single Christian has to worry about facing great tribulation before the Lord returns. However, it almost seems as if they (theorists) feared to tread on these heretofore mentioned subjects in fear of or at the expense of losing an audience that wishes not to be presented a doctrine that calls for these impending horrors; or, that to take such an unpopular position would be cause for expulsion from their respective position in the church community (See John 12:42). Or is it possible that theorists find it more profitable (financially and status wise) to avoid the subject of great tribulation, altogether?

The author is reminded of an incident he had with a pastor of a local church he attended for a short duration. When apprised of the material the author has presented in his book, he agreed with all the evidence, but told the author he couldn't afford to share this with his congregation, solely in fear these truths would frighten his parishioners to the point they would flee his church.

As the author has stated throughout this book, the possibility of the *Christian Church* experiencing great tribulation is not a very popular position to take. However, and this is the second reason, if by chance, theorists, especially Pre-Trib and Mid-Trib advocates are wrong, and the *Christian Church* is not "caught up" to heaven before the Lord returns, it is crucial and essential that the Christian community be spiritually and emotionally prepared for that possibility, rather than resting solely on grace to deliver it from the persecutions that it is destined to experience. True! Christians are saved by grace (unmerited favor), and true, the *called out ones* are chosen from the very basic foundations of the world. However, to assume that this "grace" and "election" provides for the Christian some form of physical immunity from "great tribulation" by the soon-to-come wrath of the satanically imbued Beast, could possibly be the greatest hoax ever perpetrated on today's Christian community. Unfortunately, the author might add, these unproven "Left Behind" Rapture doctrines are being preached by some of the most renowned and well-meaning scholars and evangelists the world has ever known.

This position (that the author takes) is an obvious minority point of view. But if the soothing Pre-Tribulation Rapture view is wrong, then what unexpected trials loom on the horizon for the Christian, especially those new babes in Christ? What incentive or motivation is being provided for those who have chosen rather to coast through their Christian experience by anticipating a secret pre-tribulation escape to heaven? How prepared for tribulation would those Christians be? Those who ignorantly say, "I have no need to fear tribulation, because Jesus is going to deliver me from this earth to heaven at any moment!"

The author will never forget when he came to Jesus on January 5, 1975. Later that year, a well-known scholar of prophesy set a Rapture date for early September of that same year, which caused many (including the author) to anxiously look up for an "any moment" removal from earth to heaven. The author spent that entire day on his knees, praying and singing Psalms to the Lord, looking up towards the clouds to see if he would be able to catch a mere glimpse of the Lord's appearing. The author was in tears throughout the whole day, praying as hard as he could in an effort to more secure his being Raptured at His appearing. The author even called his pastor three or four times throughout the day to see if he was still at home, figuring that if he was still there, the Rapture had not come yet. The author's family had become frightened by his actions, for a while, and then they became angry with him for yelling at them to also kneel and pray. Later their anger turned to laughter, seeing how ridiculous he must have appeared to them. But yet, he silently kept on praying and watching. The Rapture never came. Many years later, he prayerfully and quietly sat at his typewriter, with Bible, concordances and Greek and Hebrew dictionaries in hand, allowing the Holy Spirit to guide him through God's word to reveal His truth, through an in-depth study. As he read and studied God's word, as he dug deep through the Greek and Hebrew translations, God's truth took on a more meaningful experience for the author, one that removed fear and doubts as to whether he will have to experience the greatly intensified times of tribulation spoken in God's word. Whether the author is still alive or not before that appointed time, the love of Jesus, being ministered to him by His Holy Spirit, tells him that he has nothing to fear, regardless!

Dear reader, please go back and read those scriptures about persecution, trials, suffering and those especially that talk about the times of increasing tribulation. Read them again and again, and then ask the Holy Spirit to reveal it to your heart if these were not meant for you and me and all of God's *ecclesia*.

Once again, this book has not been written by this author to bring fear to the Christian, but rather to put the word of God in perspective. The author believes this perspective is truth, a truth that also assures him that whether he is alive on this earth or not, when tribulation begins to increase with greater intensity, God's word has assured him that he will be protected and rescued through God's End-Times Passover!

Chapter 5
TRIBULATIONS IN REVELATION

Before we begin our examination of tribulation mentioned in the Book of Revelation, it must be mutually agreed by the reader and the writer whether this apocalyptic message from Jesus Christ Himself is meant solely for the Christian or, as some theorists purport, it is meant solely for the Jews and/or the genetic descendants of the 12 tribes of Israel. Let's see if there exist any clues in the first few verses that will help us to make that determination.

At the beginning of the Book of Revelation, Chapter 1, verse 1, we see,

> the Revelation of Jesus Christ, which God gave unto him (John), to shew unto his <u>servants</u> things which must shortly come to pass; and he sent and signified it by his angel unto his <u>servant</u> John. [Parenthesis and underline is by the author, solely for emphasis]

Who are the *servants* Jesus speaks of in this verse? Are these *servants* speaking about the Jews who currently live in the Palestinian region we know today as the Jewish State of Israel, as many theorists contend?

Are the messages contained within this great and awesome book intended solely for the descendants of the twelve tribes of genetic Israel? Is this message intended solely for the so-called *Christian Church*, as other theorists claim? Or is this message intended for all of God's people of promise? To find this answer, let's do a brief research on the word *servants* and *bondservants*.

The Greek word for *bondservant* (same word for *servant*) is *doulos* which literally means to be someone's slave or "in bondage." Let's see exactly what W. E. Vine has to say:

A. "DOULOS, an adjective, signifying 'in bondage,' Rom. 6:19 (neuter plural, agreeing with melee, members), is used as a noun, and as the most common and general word for "servant," frequently indicating subjection without the idea of bondage, it is used

(a) of natural conditions, e.g., Matt. 8:9; 1 Cor. 7:21, 22 (1ˢᵗ part); Eph. 6:5; Col. 4:1; 1 Tim.6:1, frequently in the four Gospels; (b) metaphorically of spiritually, moral and ethical conditions: servants (1) of God, e.g., Acts 16:17; Tit. 1:1; 1 Pet. 2:16; Rev. 7:3; 15:3; the perfect example being Christ Himself, Phil. 2:7; (2) of Christ, e.g., Rom. 1:1; 1 Cor. 7:22 (2ⁿᵈ part); Gal. 1:10; Eph. 6:6; Phil. 1:1; Col. 4:12; Jas. 1:1; 2 Pet. 1:1; Jude 1; (3) of sin, John 8:34 (R.V., "bond-servants"); Rom. 6:17, 20; (4) of corruption, 2 Pet. 2:19 (R.V., "bondservants'); cp. the verb douloo.

B. SUNDOULOS, a fellow servant, is used (a) of natural conditions, Matt. 18:28, 29, 31, 33; 24:49; (b) of servants of the same Divine Lord, Col. 1:7; 4:7; Rev. 6:11; of angels, Rev. 19:10, 22:9.

The verb DOULOO means to enslave, to bring into bondage (akin to A, No. 1), e.g., 1 Cor. 9:19, R.V., "I brought (myself) under bondage (to all)," A.V., "I made myself servant," denotes in the Passive Voice, to be brought into bondage, to become a slave or servant, rendered 'ye became servants (of righteousness)" in Rom. 6:18; "being...become servants (to God," ver. 22. See BONDAGE, 8., No.2." (W. E. Vine, *An Expository Dictionary Of Biblical Words,* Thomas Nelson Publishers, pages 1019, 1020)

Doulous is the same Greek word that is used to define the "slaves" in the parable of the king who sent out his *servants* to call those who had been invited to the famed wedding feast found in Matthew 22:1-14. It is the same word used of Paul and his fellow apostles in Acts 16:17, Titus 1:1; 1Peter 2:16, but not necessarily the same word used to describe a fellow-servant (*sundoulous*) of natural conditions (Matthew 18:28). But yet, it has the same meaning that describes Jesus, *Who, being in very nature God, did not consider equality with God something to be grasped, 7 but made himself nothing, taking the very nature of a servant, being made in human likeness,* (Philippians 2:6,7, NIV). [Underline is by the author, solely for emphasis]

According to the above interpretations, it appears that the Book of Revelation is truly intended for those who are Christ's slaves, servants, chosen, elect, etc., in particular, those who have accepted Jesus Christ as Lord and Savior, those who are one of more in a collective group of believers known as true members of God's *ecclesia*. The author is quite certain that most scholars (except dispensationalists), and the majority of those claiming to be born again believers, wholeheartedly agree with and accept the fact that the Book of Revelation was written to God's *ecclesia,* for the purpose of prophesying what takes place before, during and after the Lord returns at His second advent.

Revelation, this great, awesome book, at times extremely difficult to understand by many, has been studied, written about, preached about, revered, purged, deleted, added to, stomped on and cast to and fro these many centuries since its original writing. Many Bible scholars and novice theologians, too, have postulated a myriad of theories and conclusions to its messages. Thousands of books, articles and many other materials have been written about the Book of Revelation, that currently fill thousands of libraries, churches and homes throughout the world, all containing varying interpretations. But, yet, it is not reported that anyone has deciphered and discerned this great book to the degree it can be viewed by mankind with any specific conclusion that would pass canonical muster. But yet, many people (scholars, theologians, Bible students, preachers, evangelists, scientists and even some self-proclaimed prophets, many on the internet, especially) make claim they know the answers to what exactly the entire book entails, and have even formulated specific time frames to the prophecies contained therein.

How arrogant and egotistically perverse for any one person (or persons) to make claim to understanding Revelation in its totality, much less even understanding it in general. Yet, many theories abound, many in recent times, by theorists who conveniently interpret and use certain portions of the Book of Revelation as biblical evidence it contains conclusive proof the *Christian Church* will be secretly caught up to heaven anywhere from three and a half to seven years before *The Second Advent*. Let's examine some of those myths and conclusions many make about the Book of Revelation, and maybe we can glean some information and wisdom from this great book that will provide greater clarification.

First of all, after exhaustively reading and studying the Book of Revelation for over twenty five years, as well as the works of many other (old and recent) authors who have written about the Apocalypse, the author has concluded that it is not a chronologically time frame developed or presented work, as many theorists claim. This should be obvious even to the novice student of the Bible. For example, in Chapter 15, we see in verse 1, *seven angels who had seven plagues, which are the last, because in them the wrath of God are finished*, (Revelation 15:1, NASB). Hal Lindsey, in his book *The Rapture*, states that this verse is definitive proof that in Chapter 15, the seven plagues are over. Yet, in the 16th, 17th and 18th chapters of Revelation we see a variety of plagues and wrath mentioned. We also see in Chapter 21, verse 9, where John still sees *one of the seven angels who has the seven bowls full of the seven last plagues, came and spoke with John to show him the bride, the wife of the Lamb.* If Mr. Lindsey concludes that the seven plagues are over in Chapter 15, why is it that we see the seven bowls still full in Chapter 21, verse 9? This is just one of many such examples of the skewing and twisting of scripture that continues to muddle the theological waters by theorists solely to pad their secret pre-tribulation escape to heaven theories.

If examined carefully, from a chronological perspective, we can see (by virtue of the symbol-laden manner that Revelation is presented) that it is not laid out in any historically dated or sequential fashion; but, rather, what we can see is that the Apocalypse is a series of visions that have been presented to John. Nothing in this book is presented in any dated fashion, as if Chapter 1 represents the beginning of a specific time period and Chapter 2 continues that time chronology all the way to Chapter 22. There is, however, a beginning and an end to it. In the beginning, we see the author (the Lord) addressing John and stating specifically to whom He is addressing these great messages. If we may, let's momentarily jump over to several verses in the last Chapter (22:10-17), where we see John being addressed by an angel, a fellow servant, who tells John to *not seal up the words of the prophecy of this book, for the time is near* (vs. 10). Let's read this group of scriptures carefully, then we will ask a very important question:

Then he told me, "Do not seal up the words of the prophecy of this book, because the time is near. 11 Let him who does wrong continue to do wrong; let him who is vile continue to be vile; let him who does right continue to do right; and let him who is holy continue to be holy." 12 "Behold, I am coming soon! My reward is with me, and I will give to everyone according to what he has done. 13 I am the Alpha and the Omega, the First and the Last, the Beginning and the End. 14 Blessed are those who wash their robes, that they may have the right to the tree of life and may go through the gates into the City. 15 Outside are the dogs, those who practice magic arts, the sexually immoral, the murderers, the idolaters and everyone who loves and practices falsehood. 16 I, Jesus have sent my angel to give you this testimony for the churches. I am the Root and the Offspring of David, and the bright Morning Star." 17 **The Spirit and the bride** say, "Come!" And let him who hears say, "Come*!*" Whoever is thirsty, let him come; and whomever wishes, let him take the free gift of the water of life, (Revelation 22:10-17, NIV). [Bold and underline is by the author, solely for emphasis]

In verses 10 and 11, we see the angel speaking to John about not sealing the words of the prophecy of the book and telling John to let people continue in their ways. In verses 12 and 13, the angel is no longer speaking to John but we do see a parenthetical exhortation directly from the Lord concerning the Christian's reward and the Lord's reiteration of His true nature. Then in verse 14 and 15, we see Jesus continuing an obvious spiritual exhortation concerning the washing of our robes, and about those who never will be allowed access to the "Tree of Life." In verse 16, we see another exhortation from Jesus confirming that it is He who has sent His "angel to testify to you (John and all believers) these things for the churches." This clearly states that from the beginning to the end of this great book, Revelation is intended to be read, adhered to and believed upon by the totality of the *ecclesia*, which is comprised of all believers! This also clearly indicates that the some of the messages paint pictures of events past and many that have not yet been fulfilled! Considering that the Book of Revelation was written about two thousand years ago, and that obviously the *ecclesia* has not been caught up to have that meeting in the air with Jesus Christ, there is no way that we could currently see the church in heaven, even if were to concede that it were the Bride of the Lamb. This fact brings up a very important and extremely interesting aspect in a verse of scripture cited so far, which is found in verse 17. Let's read it again:

> **The Spirit and the bride say**, "**Come**!" And let him who hears say, "**Come**!" Whoever is thirsty, let him come; and whoever wishes, let him take the free gift of the water of life. (Revelation 22:17, NIV). [Bold is by the author, solely for emphasis]

This scripture should be of extreme importance to Pre-Tribulation escape theorists, in particular, those who advocate the theory that the *Christian Church* will be caught up before the so-called Great Tribulation and goes to heaven to be with the Lord to participate (supposedly as the bride) in the great wedding mentioned in Revelation 19:7, 8. If we are to accept their theory that the *Christian Church* already has escaped the tribulation because the word "church" is not mentioned after Chapter 3:22, as Lindsey, Walvoord, et al claim, how can they conclude that the *Christian Church* is seen as the Bride in Revelation 22: 17. If the exhortation in this particular verse is spoken in context as part of John's concluding narrative, which (at the time John wrote Revelation) was an exhortation to the *ecclesia* currently on earth, how can theorists explain the Bride being mentioned in Revelation 22:17? More importantly, if the warning by the angel (at this juncture) to John is a message intended for the *Christian Church*, why is it we see in verse 17 the spirit and the *bride* (supposedly the church) extolling this "Come" exhortation to the *bondservants,* whom we now know are none other than God's *ecclesia*? Are theorists telling us that at this juncture (when John was writing down the visions of the Book of Revelation) that the *Christian Church* (supposedly the bride) was already in heaven?

The first three chapters are the beginning of the Revelation narrative, prior to John's deliverance of the letters to the seven churches, and prior to the beginning of John's visions, which don't begin until Chapter 4. The ending of the Revelation narrative is found to continue again at Revelation 22:8, where John states that he is *"the one who heard and saw these things* (vs. 8)." From verse 8 to verse 21, John is not experiencing visions anymore; he is now providing the concluding narrative of the accounts of all the visions he saw. In his final message (vs. 10-21), John is not documenting the end of history of the world, as if all these things had already come to pass. He is now concluding the narrative of the Book of Revelation (including several exhortations by Jesus in verses 12, 13, 15); and the conclusion of this narrative includes a message **from the spirit and the bride** to the *ecclesia*, which say **"Come."** If this narrative includes and sees the spirit and the bride (which theorists postulate is the church) exhorting the Christian bondservants to "come," how can theorists conclude that the *Christian Church* is the Bride of the Lamb? Are theorists claiming that part of the *Christian Church* (as the Bride) was already in heaven when the angel gave John the visions, and was then extolling them the message to come and partake the water of life for those who thirst (who are members of the church) to "Come?" The verse immediately before this profound statement (*And the spirit and the Bride say come*) clearly tells us to whom this message is intended for:

> I Jesus have sent mine angel to **testify unto you these things in the churches**. I am the root and the offspring of David, and the bright and morning star.17 **And**

the Spirit and the bride say, Come. And let him that heareth say, Come. And let him that is athirst come. And whosoever will, let him take the water of life freely, Revelation 22:16-17, KJV). [Bold and underline is by the author, solely for emphasis]

Once again, if the message contained in the Book of Revelation is intended for the *bondservants* (another name for those who comprise the *ecclesia*), and the *Christian Church* is supposed to be seen by theorists in the book only through Chapter 3, and then raptured between the end of Chapter 3 and before the beginning of Chapter 5, how can the Bride (supposedly the *Christian Church*) already be seen (supposedly in heaven) alongside the Spirit in verse 17 of Chapter 22, urging the *Christian Church* to "Come"? How can we see the *ecclesia* (supposedly the Bride) being spoken of in this verse, which is the ending part of John's narrative in the Book of Revelation?

Also, for those who claim that the *Christian Church* is the City of God, how can this city (supposedly the church) be viewed as being in heaven and at the same time *called out ones* are on earth looking for a city that is to come down from heaven (Hebrews 13:14)? As we stated before, the Bride of the Lamb is not the *Christian Church*, but rather, it is the Holy City of God, New Jerusalem, the present dwelling of God, which will descend when He returns, as it is so beautifully stated in Hebrews 13:14:

> For here we do not have an enduring city, but we are looking for **the City that is to come**, (Hebrews 13:14, NIV.) [Bold and underline is by the author, solely for emphasis]

If the wrath, plagues, vials and all the other horrors prophesied in the Book of Revelation (after Chapter 3) are painting only a picture of punishment due solely for the unsaved, and, as theorists contend, will also include a *special wrath* program for Jacob's descendants and/ or unrepentant Jews, those members of the tribe of Judah from the genetic Israel nation, then Christians should rip Revelation out of the Bible and toss it to the wind. Why would they need to read it if it didn't pertain to them? If, however, the totality of Revelation is intended for the *called out ones*, who are in fact joint heirs in the promises made to faith-believing Israel, it is then the most important message of our day. It is a message that should quicken our hearts not to fear, but to rejoice in the knowledge that God will not only rescue His "bondservants," but protect them from the wrath that will rain on *all* of those who rejected His gift of salvation. If a pre-tribulation escape to heaven appears remote or unlikely, the *called out ones* need not be saddened; rather, they should be rejoicing as did Paul, Peter, Stephen and the millions of other bondservants who "ran the good race" and brought many more lost souls to the fold with an attitude of boldness!

The totality of the Book of Revelation, as stated earlier, is an awesome array of symbolic clusters that provide much insight to past, present and the future, and of tribulation, judgments and visions of God's wrath. Unfortunately, too many scholars and theorists (in vain attempts) have tried to pinpoint times and dates, persons and places and events with little success in consistency and continuity. Since there is no mutually agreed doctrine concerning the book of Revelation by the totality of Christendom, it is safe to conclude that no one person (or doctrinal camp) has proven beyond a shadow of a doubt as to when, where, how and what exactly is going to happen. However, one continuously resounding theme is extolled throughout the Bible: *Therefore keep watch, because you do not know what day your Lord will come,* (Matthew 24:42, NIV). However, in 1 Thessalonians 5, the *called out ones* are reminded that they will not be caught off guard regardless of what happens, especially concerning the Day of the Lord:

> Now, brothers, about times and dates we do not need to
> write to you, 2 for you know very well that **the day of**

the Lord will come like a thief in the night. 3 While people are saying, "Peace and safety," destruction will come on them suddenly, as labor pains on a pregnant woman, and they will not escape. 4 But you, brothers, are not in darkness so that this day should surprise you like a thief. 5 **You are all sons of the light and sons of the day. We do not belong to the night or to the darkness**. 6 **So then, let us not be like others, who are asleep, but let us be alert and self-controlled.** 7 For those who sleep, sleep at night, and those who get drunk, get drunk at night. 8 But since we belong to the day, let us be self-controlled, putting on faith and love as a breastplate, and the hope of salvation as a helmet. 9 **For God did not appoint us to suffer wrath but to receive salvation through our Lord Jesus Christ**, (1 Thessalonians. 5:1-9, NIV). [Bold and underline is by the author, solely for emphasis]

It is at this point that we feel compelled to reiterate the difference between God's *wrath* and the so-called period of great *tribulation*. Theorists contend that the phrase *great tribulation* mentioned in Matthew 24:21, 29 and Revelation 7:14 will include all of God's wrath (vials, bowls, etc.) predicted throughout the Book of Revelation. Therefore, if the church is not appointed to wrath, it therefore must mean it has been caught up to heaven to escape this so-called seven year ordeal. Theorists contend that the entire seven-year duration that supposedly encompasses the so-called Great Tribulation will be filled with God's entire wrath, a wrath they also call the *great tribulation*.

Let's examine these two words closely. First of all, the word *wrath* (according to Webster) means 1: *strong vengeful anger or indignation* 2: *retributory punishment for an offense or a crime: divine chastisement.* Secondly, the word *tribulation* (according to Webster) means: *distress or suffering resulting from oppression or persecution; also: a trying experience.*

71

If we are to understand clearly the words used in the Bible, when God begins to punish the *unjust*, the Bible does not use the word *tribulation* to describe His indignation, it uses the word *wrath*. Rightly written, when God pours out His *wrath* on the *unjust*, He will not be *oppressing* or *persecuting*, or even *trying* (testing) the unrepentant. No! He will be punishing them with a strong and vengeful anger. When the man of lawlessness is trying to beat down the *ecclesia*, he is obviously bent on *oppressing* and *persecuting* the *called out ones*, who will be totally *distressed* and in a great state of *suffering*. In other words, God pours out vengeful wrath on the *unjust* for their disobedience, but the son of perdition oppresses and persecutes the *called out ones* solely because they are God's *ecclesia*! Therefore, to interchangeably use both words *wrath* and *tribulation* (as if they meant the same thing) when speaking about the so-called Great Tribulation, is definite proof that theorists carelessly and erroneously use the words of God to conveniently promote their mythologies. Not only do they promote their secret tribulation escape to heaven mythologies from a foolish exegetical perspective, but also deviate from a sound grammatical perspective.

In verse 9 of 1 Thessalonians 5, it specifically states: *For God did not appoint us to suffer wrath but to receive salvation through our Lord Jesus Christ.* If we are to believe that God's *wrath* (the various plagues, vials, bowls and trumpets mentioned throughout the Book of Revelation) should be interpreted to mean the same thing as the *tribulations* that the *ecclesia* is destined to experience, then we Christians (especially theorists) have failed to interpret God's *wrath* (and words) correctly. Verse 9 specifically states that we are not destined for wrath; however, throughout the Bible, a myriad of scriptures state that Christians *will* experience *great tribulation*. The various plagues, vials, bowls and trumpet judgments are not (nor ever were) intended for God's *called out ones*, but rather, for the unbeliever.

Theorists keep pounding and pounding their bully pulpit beliefs that there will be a seven year period of wrath called *The Great Tribulation*, and they envision all of the plagues, vials, bowl judgments they see throughout the entire book of Revelation as being prevalent throughout that so-called Great Tribulation period. They base this seven year period on their interpretation of Daniel 9:24-27, which ostensibly predicts that the Beast will strike a covenant for seven years with the geopolitical leadership of national Israel (whom they identify solely as the Jews from the Jewish State of Israel). Then (after three and a half years of peace and safety) the Beast (or antichrist) breaks the covenant and begins to wreak havoc solely on Jews for three and a half years before Jesus returns at *The Second Advent*. They believe that since this seven year period is designed solely to punish the Jews for turning their back on God, then there is no way the *Christian Church* can be seen on earth during those seven years; therefore, it will have been caught up to heaven, participating in a great wedding, while all hell breaks loose here on earth. Sadly, theorists deny God's glory by not believing He has the power to protect His preaching *ecclesia* even if there was a full seven-year period of wrath, (See 2 Peter 2:9).

Nonetheless, there is no scriptural evidence whatsoever that the *ecclesia*, God's *called out ones*, will be removed from earth immediately before the man of lawlessness commences to war against the *called out ones* of God. On the contrary, as the author believes he has presented sufficient scripture to negate this premise, God's *ecclesia* will remain on earth, gloriously preaching the gospel of Jesus Christ, while experiencing the intensified persecutions by the man of lawlessness and his anti-Christian forces, until *The Second Advent*!

If the scriptures clearly state the *called out ones* will remain on earth during this horrific period, theorists somehow can't get their stories straight concerning this matter, because they keep pounding their pulpits incessantly that the *ecclesia* is already in heaven before the so-called Great Tribulation. Yet, in Revelation 7:14 they see (and identify) a group of *saints* arrayed in white robes who supposedly came out of *that* so-called Great (seven year) Tribulation period. On one hand they claim these saints in 7:14 were raptured to heaven (that's how they came out of great tribulation) and on the other hand they confuse their adherents when they continue their mythologies by stating these tribulation saints spoken of in Revelation 7:14 are those Jews (or other gentiles who didn't make it in the Rapture), but rather were converted to Christ during the so-called Great (seven year) Tribulation. Theorists can't have it both ways. Either the saints (and all *called out ones* are saints) in Revelation 7:14 are on earth during their so-called Great Tribulation period, or they are in heaven. Actually, they are wrong on both counts. The mention of saints in 7:14 is not picturing a scene in heaven solely because these saints are before the throne of God. Most certainly they serve Him day and night in his temple; but this service is an earthly scene because they are serving Him who is *dwelling among* them on earth. What we see in Revelation 7:14 is identical to what we see in Matthew 25:31-34, which is clear proof that it's an earthly scene:

> When the Son of man **shall come** in his glory, and all the holy angels with him, **then shall he sit upon the throne of his glory**: 32 And before him shall be gathered all nations: and he shall separate them one from another, as a shepherd divideth his sheep from the goats: 33 And he shall set the sheep on his right hand, but the goats on the left, (Matthew 25:31-34, KJV). [Bold and underline is by the author, solely for emphasis]

This is an earthly scene, not a heavenly one. Theorists insist this is a heavenly scene primarily because it is quoted in the Book of Revelation. As we demonstrated in Chapter 13 (*A Thousand Years*) in our first book, regarding Revelation 20:4, we explained who John truly saw seated on the throne. It was not the souls of those who were beheaded because of their testimony for Jesus, and because of the word of God, and did not worship the beast. What we saw was Christ sitting on His throne, experiencing the moment when all (sole) judgment was given to him!

Revelation 20:4 speaks solely about the vindication of these souls who have been martyred throughout history, not their resurrection. Those we see in Revelation 7:14 are the totality of all the risen saints, after *The Resurrection*, standing before the throne of God. This is an earthly scene. Revelation 7:14 is speaking about the entirety of *called out ones* who throughout history also experienced great tribulation at the hands of antichristian forces. This is proven by the fact mentioned in a preceding verse in this Chapter, verse 9:

> After this I beheld, and, lo, **a great multitude, which no man could number,** of all nations, and kindreds, and people, and tongues, stood before the throne, and before the Lamb, clothed with white robes, and palms in their hands, (Revelation 7:9, KJV). [Bold and underline is by the author, solely for emphasis]

Who comprises this great multitude, which no man could number of all nations and kindreds and people and tongues? Who stood before the throne, and before the Lamb, clothed with white robes, and palms in their hands, that are mentioned in Revelation 7:9? Are they only those who repented due to God's wrath during the so-called Great Tribulation, as many theorists purport? It surely is not talking about the 144,000, which are identified in verses 3 to 8 as coming from the twelve tribes of Israel. This great multitude in verse 9 is identified as coming from every nation, tribe, people and language, and it is a throng so large no man could number. Verse 14 answers the question:

> And I said unto him, Sir, thou knowest. And he said to me, these are they which **came out of great tribulation,**

and have washed their robes, and made them white in
the blood of the Lamb, (Revelation 7:14, KJV). [Bold and
underline is by the author, solely for emphasis]

Revelation 7:14, does not state that those who washed their robes and
made them white in the blood of the Lamb came out of *The Great
Tribulation*, but out of *great tribulation*. There is no article before *great
tribulation* in this verse. The saints in 7:14 are not a select portion
of God's *ecclesia* in heaven that supposedly were Raptured seven
years before the Lord returns to earth. Nor are they a select group of
the *ecclesia* that came out of great tribulation (implying Rapture or
departure to heaven after death) before or during the so-called *Great
Tribulation*. Revelation 7:14 is painting a picture of all of the righteous
saints that have died (or were martyred for Christ) throughout history.
It also includes those who will be alive and awaiting the *Parousia* of
Christ, who will be changed (along with those who sleep in Christ)
and caught together to have a meeting in the air with the Lord, to
escort Him back to earth, and will be standing before His glorious
throne on earth! Those in white garments (in Revelation 7:14) are
all of those who throughout history have suffered and endured
great persecutions for their belief in a coming savior. Regardless of
the persecutions or tribulations these *called out ones* experienced
throughout history, they placed their faith and trust in their Messiah!
This particular vision John the revelator saw is a picturing all of God's
children, who throughout history died and or suffered for (and in)
their faith of their savior. This speaks of the redeemed throughout
history who are now standing before the throne of their Messiah,
Jesus Christ, our Lord and our God!

Verse 17 (of Revelation 7) clearly states that these (in white robes)
will be led to *springs of living waters*, the very same "living waters"
we see in Revelation 21:6 (*the spring of the water of life*) and in Ezekiel
47:1-9, which provides the *fruit* (which) *will serve for food and their
leaves for healing*. This is the same "fruit" spoken of in Revelation

22:2, of which "the water of life" in verse 1 provides irrigation to *the tree of life, bearing twelve crops of fruit, yielding its fruit every month, and the leaves of the tree are for the healing of the nations.* This is talking about the Holy City of God and the Tree of Life described in Revelation 22:19, that warns that anyone who adds anything to this book will lose their share: *And if anyone takes words away from this book of prophecy, God will take away from him his share in the tree of life and in the holy city, which are described in this book*, (Vs. 19). This is the same Holy City of God we see that comes down to earth at *The Second Advent*, as spoken in Revelation 22:1-3. This is a scene on earth, not one in heaven!

> Then I saw a new heaven and a new earth, for the first heaven and the first earth had passed away, and there was no longer any sea. 2 I saw the Holy City, the New Jerusalem, **coming down out of heaven** from God, prepared as a bride beautifully dressed for her husband. 3 And I heard a loud voice from the throne saying, "**Now the dwelling of God is with men, and he will live with them.**" They will be his people, and God himself will be with them and be their God, (Revelation 21:1-3, NIV).

As we presented in Chapter 15 (*Jesus Christ Is God*) of the first *The End Times Passover* book, the same picture painted in Ezekiel, Chapters 40 through 48, is not one of a restored Jewish geopolitical nation called Israel in the Palestinian region in the Middle East, as theorists postulate. This is the prophetic picture of the *true* Promised Land, the New Holy City of Jerusalem! The new home of all the *called out ones*, spending an eternity with God! The following two chapters in Ezekiel describe the apportionment of territories to Holy Israel in the true Promised Land, New Jerusalem, the soon-to-come earth-based dwelling of God:

> This is the land you are to allot as an inheritance to the tribes of Israel, and these will be their portions,"

> declares the Sovereign LORD. 30 "These will be the
> exits of the City: Beginning on the north side, which is
> 4,500 cubits long, 31 the gates of the city will be named
> after the tribes of Israel. The three gates on the north
> side will be the gate of Reuben, the gate of Judah and
> the gate of Levi. 32 "On the east side, which is 4,500
> cubits long, will be three gates: the gate of Joseph, the
> gate of Benjamin and the gate of   Dan. 33 "On the
> south side, which measures 4,500 cubits, will be three
> gates: the gate of Simeon, the gate of Issachar and the
> gate of Zebulun. 34 "On the west side, which is 4,500
> cubits long, will be three gates: the gate of Gad, the gate
> of Asher and the gate of Naphtali.35 "The distance all
> around will be 18,000 cubits. "And the name of the city
> from that time on will be: **THE LORD IS THERE**,"
> (Ezekiel 48:29-35, NIV). [Bold, caps and underline is
> by the author, solely for emphasis]

Once again, if read in context of what the Old Testament prophecies
portray, what we are seeing in Ezekiel 37 through 48 is a picture
of *The Resurrection* and the beginning of the eternal reign of
Jesus Christ on earth. This is not a picture of a country restored
solely for Jews by Jesus (before His return) in the Middle East
community of Palestine, today being called the Jewish State of
Israel. God did not set His sanctuary in the State of Israel in
1948! God does not have His tabernacle there! These chapters
in Ezekiel describe in detail exactly what is seen fulfilled in the
last two chapters of Revelation. Therefore, what we are seeing
in Chapter 7 of Revelation is not a gathering of a select group of
(Great Tribulation) martyrs before the throne of God in heaven,
but rather, it's a gathering of all of the *called out ones* (who washed
their garments and made them white in the blood of the Lamb)
before the throne of God in the New Jerusalem, the Holy City of
God, right here on earth:

Now <u>the dwelling of God is with men</u>, and he will live with them, they will be his people, <u>and God himself will be with them</u> and be their God. 4 He will wipe every tear from their eyes. There will be no more death or mourning or crying or pain, for the old order of things has passed away, (Revelation 21:3, 4 NIV). [Underline is by the author, solely for emphasis]

Nowhere in Chapter 7 is it mentioned that this scene occurs in heaven. What we are seeing here is but one of the visions that John saw, but nowhere does John imply that this scenario should be viewed in heaven. Even if we were to place this vision in a chronological order (which we don't believe is the case), the preceding vision that John had seen involved the sealing of the 144,000, which is an obvious earthly scene: *Do not harm the land or the sea or the trees until we put a seal on the servants of our God*, (Revelation 7:3, NIV). These white-robed *called out ones* are not the Raptured *Christian Church* or *tribulation saints* in heaven, but rather, they are all of God's children from history (who by faith trusted in the returning Messiah) and who are standing before His glorious throne, on earth!

In this group is included a myriad of *called out ones* who were martyred throughout history and those who are immediately martyred preceding the Lord's return. The martyrs did not die due to God's wrath, but rather, they "*overcame him* (Satan) *by the blood of the Lamb and by the word of their testimony; they did not love their lives so much as to shrink from death*, (Revelation 12:11, NIV). These also are not Jews who were converted to Jesus by virtue of God inflicting a vengeful wrath; these represent *a great multitude that no one could count, <u>from every nation, tribe, people and language,</u>* (Revelation 7:9, NIV). This numberless throng includes all of those who died believing in the Messiah before He arrived (the first time) in the person of Jesus Christ, all of those who died after Jesus was resurrected and ascended to heaven, and it will include all of the *called out ones* who will be martyred during the reign of the man of lawlessness. When Revelation 7:14 says that "These are they who have come out of *great tribulation*; there is no article before *great tribulation*. It is not speaking about a specific group of people (supposedly only Jews or *tribulation saints*) who were so severely tormented by God's wrath (until they repented) during a seven-year period of tribulation, as theorists claim. But, rather, they are those who throughout all of history (including those who did experience martyrdom for believing in the Messiah) washed their robes white by believing in the Lamb of God; those who paid for their sins by the shedding of His blood, and by the word of their testimony.

Also (and extremely important), are we to believe that there is a difference between those who were martyred for Christ throughout history and those who will be martyred during the so-called times of great tribulation that will ensue immediately before He returns? Are we to believe that those who have been martyred throughout history, such as the prophets and patriarchs, and Paul, Stephen, Peter, et al, did not wash their robes white in the blood of the lamb? Only those martyred during the so-called seven-year Great Tribulation period receive white garments?

Theorists make claim this throne scene in Revelation 7:14 surely could not include those martyred throughout history before Jesus paid the price for sin at Calvary, claiming redemption was not fulfilled before this time. Who is Jesus Christ, if not the Messiah foretold by all the prophets from Abraham up to John the Baptist? The entire Old Testament is filled with prophecies of the coming Messiah. All faith believers, from Job, Abraham to Moses to David and all the prophets knew and foretold about the coming Messiah, resurrection glory and the true Promised Land, which is the Holy City of God! The entire Chapter of Hebrews 11, especially, speaks about the faithful who were seeking a better country, a heavenly city that was to come, which would be fulfilled through Messiah. Certainly, most of national Israel failed to recognize what the prophets of old were prophesying about. Most did not recognize their anticipated Messiah in their midst in the person of Jesus Christ. He is the same Messiah that the great faith-believing cloud of witnesses (in Hebrews 11) was placing their faith in.

Once again, there is no article seen before the words *great tribulation* in either Revelation 7:14 and Matthew 24:21. Therefore, theorist cannot postulate that this is speaking about a specific (seven year) period of time, immediately before the Lord's return. Revelation 7:4 speaks about *all* of those who washed their robes white in the blood of the Lamb, throughout history! Before the Lord returns, tribulation will increase like never before, especially based on the fact that Satan will be loosed for a short season. Knowing that his time is short, he will give his power to the man of lawlessness to persecute and kill as many of God's *called out ones* as he can, in one last desperate attempt to thwart God's plan of rescuing those whose faith and trust lay in their Messiah!

Does this not tell us that many *called out ones* have been placing their lives on the line throughout history for the Messiah, and that many more will indeed be martyred for believing in the Christ, as times of tribulation will continue to intensify immediately before *The Second Advent*? Does this not also tell us that many Christians, who find themselves fearful and squeamish about the possibility that they also may be martyred for Christ, have reasons to question the degree of their commitment to Jesus Christ, our Lord and our God? Have we truly committed ourselves to the reality that (in the very near future) we may be faced with the possibility and the occasion of having to choose between life and death, for Christ? Unfortunately, a great throng of Christians are basing their 'blessed hope' solely on a soothing secret pre-tribulation escape to heaven doctrine that speaks only about being rescued from intensified persecutions at the hands of the great *man of lawlessness* before Christ returns. If, by even the remotest chance, the secret pre-tribulation Rapture theory is not a scriptural fact, what will these worrisome Christians do? Are they spiritually, emotionally and physically prepared to stand up and be counted? Or will they, like the apostle Peter did, deny Christ once, twice, maybe even three times? Will they crumble under the pressure of having to make such a major decision in an effort to avoid such great tribulation? Are you prepared to surrender all, even your life, for Christ?

What Church Escapes Tribulation?

The author would like state, at this point, that it appears that the seven churches mentioned in the Book of Revelation are symbolic composites of the differing personalities, doctrinal precepts and ecumenical diversities that have been evident in and continue to portray the Christian community throughout history. There probably exists a greater and deeper meaning in the letters of exhortation to these respective churches. Nevertheless, the messages contained therein surely can be applied to any existing congregation that professes an allegiance to God. But, suffice it to say, the author will merely share the initial messages he gleaned from reading them.

Since we don't see at this juncture of Revelation the churches being removed yet, the only logical conclusion we can make is that the following exhortations are intended for members of God's *ecclesia*, the *called out ones* of Jesus Christ, regardless of their respective denominations. If each of these seven churches represents a specific congregation of the past, now existing or that will be present during the period of great distress, the Christian community then is presently at a loss for discerning which specific denominations are to receive the messages that are contained in the first three chapters. The author will make no attempts to identify which named church can be compared to any existing denomination. Many churches today make claim that theirs is the Church of

Philadelphia (the one that escapes "the hour of trial"); however, it is yet to be proven that any such denomination is walking in the total holiness, purity and courage that God requires of it or as the apostles strived for. Nevertheless, the author believes these profound messages of exhortation to these seven churches are applicable to any denomination that claims to be part of the body of Christ.

In the letter to the angel of the church in Ephesus, we see a group that has worked hard, persevered and tolerated not the wicked men who claimed to be apostles. They endured hardships for the name of Jesus and did not grow weary. However, they have forsaken their first love, which was that youthful newfound love for God that required no reward. Just being in love with Him was sufficient (See Jeremiah 2:2); and, with the increase of lawlessness, men's hearts grew cold, (See Matthew 24:12). The warning here is that failure to repent will result in the removal of their Lampstand. By the way, the word "Lampstand" here means "one of the seven Churches" (Revelation 1:20).

In the letter to the angel of the church in Smyrna, we see the Lord exhorting this group that there are some members who cling to legalistic customs (they say they are Jews and are not) which the Lord sees as originating from satanic influences. To the true believer (those who are being afflicted and are impoverished), Jesus reminds them that they are rich, in the sense that they belong to Him. But nevertheless, He continues to offer them assurance, although the devil will put some of them in prison to test them, suffer persecution and even death. But, Jesus reminds them that being faithful, <u>even to the point of death</u>, will result in those *called out ones* receiving the crown of life.

To the angel of the church of Pergamum, the Lord acknowledges that although the *called out ones* are in the world (which is ruled by Satan, the prince of the power of the air), they are holding true to the name of Jesus <u>in the face of death</u>. Yet the Lord also knows that some in this congregation still hold to certain forms of idolatry and customs that go contrary to the nature of Christ. His exhortation (to him who overcomes) is to continue to hold on and they will receive some of the hidden manna. W. E. Vine says, "the hidden manna is promised as one of the rewards of the overcomer (Revelation 2:17); it is suggestive of the moral excellence of Christ in His life on earth, hid from the eyes of men, by whom He was 'despised and rejected' the path of the overcomer is a reflex of His life." However, "the hidden manna" appears to signify more of an aid to the *ecclesia* during times of tribulation. George Eldon Ladd, in his, *A Commentary of The Revelation of John*, cites verses from Exodus 16:32-34 that paint a possible explanation of the preserving aspect of manna for Israel:

> Hidden manna: Probably John's thought is drawn to the manna because of the allusion to Balaam in whose time Israel was being fed with manna. Hebrew tradition held that a pot of manna was preserved in the ark (Exod. 16:32-34; Heb. 9:4), and when the temple was destroyed, Jeremiah (11 Macc. 2:4ff.) or an angel (Apoc. Baruch 6:5-10) rescued the ark with the manna, and they were miraculously preserved until the messianic times, when the manna would become once again food for God's people. John uses the idea metaphorically to indicate admission of the messianic feast, which is elsewhere called the marriage supper of the Lamb (19:9). The manna is referred to as hidden, perhaps because it was hidden in a pot of gold and 'laid up before God" (Exod. 16:23); or else because it is thought of as hidden now in the presence of God but destined to be revealed in the messianic age. (George Eldon Ladd, *A Commentary of The Revelation of John*, Eerdmans, Pub. Co. Grand Rapids, MI 1972)

More importantly, the hidden manna is a perfect picture of how Jesus Christ will provide preservation during perilous times, Him being "the bread of life." In Revelation 23, the redeemed are seen eating from the tree of life, bearing twelve crops of fruit, but no mention of manna is made, much less "hidden manna." Therefore it could make sense to identify the "hidden manna" mentioned to the church in Pergamum as the living Word of Christ, through and in the person of the Holy Spirit. While the unbelieving world is fraught with fear as to how it will survive, and making them prime candidates to receive the mark of the Beast, the *called out ones* will not need to acquiesce to the mark because the Lord will provide the *ecclesia* with both a spiritual and tangible sustenance through "the hidden manna."

It could very well be that during this time of great crisis and persecution, the need for food will not be a factor for the *called out ones*, but merely the word of God will suffice. The author believes that one of God's words provide for us confirmation concerning this aspect. E. W. Bullinger presents a revelatory fact about this heavenly bread, in his book, *Number In Scripture*. In his studies, concerning the cardinal number 1, he states that words which are mentioned only once in the Bible convey a more profound meaning than those mentioned twice, three times, etc. One of those words mentioned only once in the Bible, he says, is the word *daily* (Gr. *epiousios*, coming upon us), which is found in the Lord's Prayer. He says when we pray "gives us this day our *daily* bread," the word *daily* is not conveying our request for God to provide us our daily nourishment of food (which comes from the earth), which He already provides on a daily basis; but, rather, it conveys the receiving of the word of God (from above) on a daily basis:

> We must expect this peculiar word of the Lord Jesus
> to have such a fullness in it that no one English word
> is able to express it. It qualifies the word "bread." It is

this bread, which is *espiousios, i.e., coming upon us*. It is not the bread which perisheth, but the heavenly bread which *cometh down* from heaven (John vi.32, 33), even Jesus the living Word of God. For "man doth not live by bread only, but by every word that proceedeth out of the mouth of the Lord doth man live." **In other words, it is not the bread which *cometh up* from the earth which we ask our Father in this prayer, but it is the bread which *cometh down* from heaven, even Christ, the living word**, and the scriptures, the written Word. By these alone, we truly live." (E. W. Bullinger, *Number In Scripture*, page 76). [Italics by Bullinger; bold and underline is by the author, solely for emphasis]

Therefore, being in constant communion with (the word of) God, as walking in the spirit with the Lord at all times, appears will be the most important key to ensure that which will sustain the *called out ones* during the approaching times of great tribulation the *ecclesia* will face before *The Second Advent*. God provides great insights to His words, especially to the persons who diligently seek the deeper things of God.

Those who *overcome* (Gr. *nikao*, which means "mightiest prevail") will also receive a white stone with a new name written on it, known only to him who receives it. Ladd states that in the ancient world, white stones had a variety of uses, one signifying acquittal by jury (the black stone signifying condemnation) and the other usage was as a ticket of admission to a public festival, which here could be symbolizing admission to the messianic feast, which we believe the Bible clearly states will be held on earth.

To the angel of the church of Thyatira, the Lord acknowledges that this type of congregation is preserving in deeds, love, faith and service (that you are now doing more than you did at first); however, He says that a tolerance still exists for false religiosity and immoral customs. Those who still abide by these ways will suffer loss of children, but the Lord exhorts those who do not engage in these teachings, but remain in faith to Him, will not have to endure some of the impending trials. He exhorts the true believers to hold on to what they have (their faith solely in Jesus) until He comes. Those that abide in Him, and do His will until the end, will be given authority over the nations.

To the angel of the church in Sardis, the Lord is seen admonishing this congregation for its complacency. He rebukes them to "wake up!" This church is symbolic of many in the Christian community who weekly clock in for an hour or two and are content with the minimal involvement they feel is required to maintain their church membership status. But the Lord here exhorts these so-called church members to strengthen what little remains of their faith in God, and do the works He has ordained. He says that if they don't wake up, His coming will catch them by surprise as the thief does to those who know not what time he comes. Yet, the Lord acknowledges that a few people have not soiled their garments, and these will walk with Him because they overcome the trials and tribulations during this awesome period. The Lord says he will never erase those names from the Book of Life because they have proven worthy during the time of trial.

To the angel in the church of Philadelphia, the Lord acknowledges this congregation as being faithful to the name of Jesus, even though their outward strength has dwindled from the persecutions. These are the *called out ones who* have endured patiently throughout their existence, keeping the command of the Lord. He tells them that they will not be victimized by the "hour of trial" that is going to come on the whole world for testing. He exhorts them to continue to hold on to what they have (faith in the Lord Jesus Christ) so no one will take their due reward, the crown of life. To those that overcome, the Lord will write on them the name of God and the name of His City, New Jerusalem, making them pillars in the Temple of God. Here we see the Lord "sealing" the true believers and granting them residency in New Jerusalem, which is coming down from heaven, from where our God, Jesus Christ, will forever more dwell with mankind on earth (Hebrews 13:14).

It is interesting to note that in the Lord's message to the Church of Philadelphia, which is on earth, Jesus is promising this church that those who overcome He will write on them the name of God and the name of the city of His God, the New Jerusalem, which is coming down from heaven. Here, Jesus is telling these church (of Philadelphia) members that,

> Him that overcometh will I make a pillar in the temple of my God, and he shall go no more out: and I will write upon him the name of my God, and the name of the city of my God, which is new Jerusalem, which cometh down out of heaven from my God: and I will write upon him my new name, (Revelation 3:12, KJV).

Are we to believe that Jesus is telling these overcomers that they have to wait 1000 years later before they are made a pillar in the Holy City of God, as theorists interpret Revelation 20:4 and Revelation 21:1-3? Moreover, if *the name of the city of my God, which is New Jerusalem,* is written on the overcomers (which are obviously members of the *ecclesia*), and if New Jerusalem is the bride (which theorists claim is the church) isn't it odd that the name of the Bride is written on members of the church?

To the angel in the church of Laodicea, we see the Lord admonishing this congregation for their lackadaisical attitude toward Jesus, claiming to be rich in material wealth and not having any need for the saving grace of Jesus. The Lord here is showing this congregation that, without Christ, God sees a person as being wretched, pitiful, poor, blind and naked. The Lord sees that these who have confidence in material goods are neither hot nor cold in their relationship with Him; therefore, He will spew them out of His mouth. But yet, the Lord counsels them that if they will buy gold refined in the fire, white garments to cover their nakedness and salve to put on their eyes to see, they can become rich in Christ. The salve is obviously the oil representing the Holy Spirit, the white garments representing the salvation provided by Christ through His shed blood, and the refined gold a reminder that we need not fear the assaying trials *called out ones* will go through. This is a symbolic sign of the purification process that the *ecclesia* is going through, and will more so during the increasing times of tribulation. This is an evident eventuality, as we see in verse 19, where the Lord is telling the *called out ones* that His rebukes and disciplining action are a result of His love.

So far, we have avoided the subject of purification and purging because it will be covered in greater detail later on; however, we are spiritually quickened to provide a brief clue to this aspect of God's overall redemption plan. In 1 Peter 4:1, we read:

> Therefore, since Christ suffered in His body, arm yourselves also with this same attitude, **because he who has suffered in his body is done with sin. As a result, he does not live the rest of his earthly life for evil human desires, but rather for the will of God**, (1 Peter 4:1, NIV). [Bold and underline is by the author, solely for emphasis]

This verse becomes even more meaningful during the times of increasing tribulation, as we will see later on. At this juncture (in our search for scripture that addresses tribulation of the *ecclesia*), we will momentarily leave the Book of Revelation. However, in a future chapter, we will examine this book in greater detail to help identify scripture that definitely sees the church (or believers) experiencing great tribulation from the Satanically-empowered Beast before *The Second Advent* of Jesus Christ. We will concede to theorists that the word "church" is not seen in the remaining chapters of Revelation; although, in Revelation 22:16, we see a parenthetical exhortation from Jesus once again stating that the entire book of Revelation is a testimony for the *churches*:

> I, Jesus, have sent my angel to give you this testimony
> for the churches. I am the Root and the Offspring of
> David, and the bright Morning Star, (Revelation 22:16,
> NIV).

This basically concludes our search through the New Testament for scripture that addresses trials and tribulations that clearly identify the *ecclesia* as recipient. As long and laboriously as it has been to read these chapters concerning the topic of "tribulation," we felt it was necessary to cite these tribulation-related passages (very few theorists expound on this subject) to remind the *called out ones* that although a secret pre-tribulation escape to heaven is a favored doctrine, should the remotest possibility that the secret Rapture-to-heaven of the *ecclesia* will not be in store for believers, the reader cannot complain that the word of God did not forewarn His *called out ones* that "*.... we must through much tribulation enter into the kingdom of God*, (Acts 14:22, KJV)."

Chapter 6

THE PURPOSE FOR TRIBULATION!

In the last few chapters, we covered extensively those scriptural passages that deal with tribulation, trials, persecutions, etc., for the purpose of familiarizing our reader to a subject that many theorists choose to avoid while they build their secret pre-tribulation escape to heaven scenarios. Obviously they fail to address the subject of tribulation because it is their contention that the *Christian Church* will not experience persecution, in their staunch belief it will be removed from earth to heaven during the so-called Great Tribulation. Therefore why even bother. But, God's word clearly tells us that we must experience much tribulation to enter the Kingdom of God.

After reading all of these verses concerning tribulation, the reader is probably tossing hands in the air and hopelessly lamenting, "Why become a Christian? Who needs all that suffering?" Life is bad enough as it is, why program us to a belief system that includes having to accept the fact that horrors loom before those that believe in Jesus Christ?" Agreed! There is much validity in those questions, if viewed solely from a secular or humanist perspective. True! Why become a Christian if the only thing immediately in store is trials and tribulations, persecutions from non-believers, which may include family, friends, fellow church members and neighbors, and the distinct possibility that we might even end up having to die for the cause? "Besides," say many Christians, "I thought that once I accepted Jesus Christ as my Lord and Savior, I wasn't going to have to suffer any longer as I did in the past, but rather, as a new Born Again believer, the next thing in store for me is an any-moment Rapture to heaven to be with Jesus Christ, at least for a 7-year period of time before He returns back to reign on earth!"

These questions and comments are valid, if a secret pre-tribulation escape to heaven is what the Bible clearly teaches. But if a pre-tribulation escape is not in store for the *called out ones*, then what purpose is served by the *ecclesia* having to experience great tribulation?

Let's read two significant verses in the Bible to help us set the tone for this chapter. First, in John 3:16, Jesus is telling Nicodemus (and all mankind, too) that, *For God so loved the world that He gave his one and only Son that whoever believes in Him shall not perish but have everlasting life*, (NIV). This one verse encapsulates the totality of God's purpose for mankind and the manner in which He accomplished His reunification program for His creation.

Most Christians know the basic history of Adam and Eve, their fall in the Garden of Eden, their separation from God and the chronology thereafter. We then see in the Old Testament where God chose a special person (the Hebrew Abraham) and a group of people (Israel) as His entity to reveal Himself and to fellowship with His creation once again, as He had with Adam and Eve. But many of the chosen descendants of Abraham rebelled against the laws and rulers He had provided for their own protection, and heeded not His words sent forth through His prophets. But yet (by virtue of His omniscient nature), God had a plan of reunification with His *called out ones* from the very beginning of time, knowing full well that redemption would be needed. He chose to step down from His majestic abode in heaven and took the form of man, offering Himself (in the person of Jesus of Nazareth) as a propitiatory sacrifice to pay for the sins of the world. All He asks is that, by faith, we should believe in the person of Jesus Christ so as to not perish, but have eternal life and fellowship with the Creator of all things.

Throughout history, God continues to reach out to mankind to accept this gift of salvation, but His creation continues to rebel, thinking of itself as a god, rather than accepting this precious gift. The natural man, skeptical and not understanding the things of God, laments: "If man is fallen, why doesn't God simply wave His Almighty hand and remove all evil and restore His creation to Himself. Why doesn't God simply speak (as He did when all things were created) and bring in everlasting peace?" The answer is found in 2 Peter 3:9, the second significant verse, which reads:

> The Lord is not slow in keeping His promise, as some understand slowness. He is patient with you, **not wanting anyone to perish, but everyone to come to repentance,** (2 Peter 3:9, NIV). [Bold and underline is by the author, solely for emphasis]

True! Those who have already come to the Lord by faith know and understand the reality of the Gospel. They know that the only way anyone can become reconciled to God is by faith, and by believing that Jesus Christ paid the price for their fallen state. But millions have yet to see (or accept) this reality. Even more so, as the Day of the Lord approaches, mankind in general and even many of those *called out ones* (who should be trusting in Jesus for all things) are being seduced by power, money, prestige, greed, lust and the satisfying of self, rather than seeking meaning for the true purpose of life. Rather than seeking reunification and fellowship with God (which was His original plan and purpose for mankind), humanity has charted its own course, a course of self-destruction:

> The God who made the world and everything in it is the Lord of heaven and earth and does not live in temples built by hands. 25 And he is not served by human hands, as if he needed anything, because he himself gives all men life and breath and everything else. 26 **From one man he made every nation of men, that they should inhabit the whole earth**; and he determined the times set for them and the exact places where they should live. 27 **God did this so that men would seek him and perhaps reach out for him and find him**, though he is not far from each one of us. 28 'For in him we live and move and have our being.' As some of your own poets have said, 'We are his offspring.' 29 **Therefore since we are God's offspring, we should not think that the divine being is like gold or silver or stone – an image made by man's design and skill.** 30 In the past God overlooked such ignorance, **but now he commands all people everywhere to repent.** 31 For he has set a day when he will judge the world with justice by the man he has appointed. He has given proof of this to all men by raising him from the dead, (Acts 17:24-31, NIV). [Underline and bold is by the author, solely for emphasis]

Two important verses in this group of scriptures to note of their importance include verses 27 and 31. Verse 27 states that God established times and places so men would seek Him, and perhaps reach out and find Him, even though He is not far from each one of us. Verse 31 states that God has set a *day* when He will judge the world with true justice in the person of Jesus Christ, and He has proven this to all mankind by raising Jesus Christ from the dead.

Here is the purpose of life! God has allowed mankind to follow in its own footsteps, if for no other reason than to prove to it that without a personal relationship with God it is doomed to fail the human experience! Throughout the Bible, we see God forever exhorting mankind to return to Him, but yet, there is continued rebellion. But as we have seen, God does not give up on His creation, but continues to draw it back to Him through the agency of the Holy Spirit, and those who now believe. The most important task of those that now believe is to preach the gospel of the Kingdom of God so no one shall perish. But as we can see by the Book of Revelation, many will not turn to God regardless of the sanctifying power of the word of God, nor will they turn back from the results of the horrific atrocities that will befall unbelievers when God's wrath is poured out.

"But," the Christian says, "If I believe now, and I'm doing the work of a true Christian, is it also necessary for me to endure tribulation?" "Of course not," say theorists. "God is not a cruel God. He will Rapture you to heaven for seven years and spare you from all these things." Unfortunately, many Christians (and their leaders) still do not understand God's ways. Unfortunately, this escapist mentality is extremely prevalent in the evangelical community because theorists have expounded on it for so long, and so often, that they fail to see what God truly has in store for His *ecclesia*. Unfortunately, the Christian (leadership) of today has lost sight of what God wants to accomplish with His *called out ones* during the intensified period of tribulation that will precede *The Second Advent*. Although it appears that God will accomplish many more tasks during and through the remainder of history, one of those tasks will be to bring many more people to His Kingdom before He pours out His wrath, and He will accomplish this goal by using His *called out ones* like never before.

How? Let's go back to the time (in Acts 26:1-29) when Paul was incarcerated and was brought before King Agrippa, which paints (through one of Paul's ordeals) a perfect example of Christian testimony that resulted in people coming to repentance and receiving salvation. The author is including the entire chapter in order that the reader may experience one of the greatest testimonies and sermons (along with Stephen's in Acts Chapter 7) of all time:

> Then Agrippa said to Paul, "You have permission to speak for yourself." So Paul motioned with his hand and began his defense: 2 "King Agrippa, I consider myself fortunate to stand before you today as I make my defense against all the accusations of the Jews, 3 and especially so because you are well acquainted with all the Jewish customs and controversies. Therefore, I beg you to listen to me patiently. 4 The Jews all know the way I have lived ever since I was a child, from the beginning of my life in my own country, and also in Jerusalem. 5 they have known me for a long time and can testify, if they are willing, that according to the strictest sect of our religion, I lived as a Pharisee. 6 **And now it is because of my hope in what God has promised our fathers that I am on trial today**. 7 This is the promise **our twelve tribes are hoping to see fulfilled** as they earnestly serve God day and night. **O king, it is because of this hope that the Jews are accusing me.** 8 Why should any of you consider it incredible **that God raises the dead**? 9 I too was convinced that I ought to do all that was possible to oppose the name of Jesus of Nazareth. 10 and that is just what I did in Jerusalem. On the authority of the chief priests I put many of the saints in prison, and when they were put to death, I cast my vote against them. 11 Many a time I went from one synagogue to another to have them punished, and I tried to force them to blaspheme. In my obsession against them, I even sent to foreign cities to persecute them. 12 On one of these journeys I was going to Damascus with

the authority and commission of the chief priests. 13 About noon, O king, as I was on the road, **I saw a light from heaven**, brighter than the sun, blazing around my companions and me. 14 We all fell to the ground, and I heard a voice saying to me in Aramaic, 'Saul, Saul, why do you persecute me? It's hard for you to kick against goads.' 15 Then I asked, 'Who are you, Lord?' '**I am Jesus, whom you are persecuting**,' the Lord replied. 16 'Now get up and stand on your feet. **I have appeared to you to appoint you as a servant and as a witness of what you have seen of me and what I will show you.** 17 I will rescue you from your own people and from the Gentiles. **I am sending you** 18 **to open their eyes and turn them from darkness to light, and from the power of Satan to God, so that they may receive forgiveness of sins and a place among those who are sanctified by faith in me**.' 19 So, then, King Agrippa, I was not disobedient to the vision from Heaven. 20 First to those in Damascus, then to those in Jerusalem and in all Judea, and to the Gentiles also, **I preached that they should repent and turn to God and prove their repentance by their deeds**. 21 That is why the Jews seized me in the temple courts and tried to kill me. 22 But I have had God's help to this very day, and **so I stand here and testify to small and great alike**. I am saying nothing beyond what the prophets and Moses said would happen – 23 that the Christ would suffer and, as the first to rise from the dead, would proclaim light to his own people and to the Gentiles." 24 At this point Festus interrupted Paul's defense. "You are out of your mind, Paul!" he shouted. "Your great learning is driving you insane." 25 "I am not insane, most excellent Festus," Paul replied. "What I am saying is true and reasonable. 26 the king is familiar with these things,

and I can speak freely to him. I am convinced that none
of this has escaped his notice, because it was not done in
a corner. 27 King Agrippa, do you believe the Prophets?
I know you do." 28 Then Agrippa said to Paul, "**Do
you think that in such a short time you can persuade
me to be a Christian**?" 29 Paul replied, "Short time or
long – **I pray God that not only you but all who are
listening to me today may become what I am, except
for these chains**, (Acts 26:1-29, NIV). [Underline and
bold is by the author, solely for emphasis]

The author believes with all his heart that when tribulations become
more intense than they are now, a myriad of Christians will be
brought before various officials and other governmental authorities
throughout the world to proclaim the Gospel of Jesus Christ. Like Paul
our declarations of faith before these governing bodies will be similar
testimonies that will have the very same results: bring more people
to the knowledge of God's saving grace before the Lord's return! For
those theorists who contend there will be a secret pre-tribulation
escape to heaven, seven years before Christ returns, this last phase
of history would then make any preaching of the gospel a virtual
impossibility. Theorists who see only semi-converted Jews or genetic
Israelites as being those persecuted, tortured, thrown in prisons, or
even killed during the end times, miss one of God's greatest displays
of witnessing and testimony that God's *ecclesia* could possibly be
involved with. Let's read again what is stated in Matthew 24:

> **Then you will be handed over to the persecuted and
> put to death, and you will be hated by all nations
> because of me**. 10 At that time **many will turn away
> from the faith** and will betray and hate each other,
> 11 and **many false Prophets will appear and deceive
> many people**. 12 Because of the increase of wickedness,
> the love of most will grow cold, 13 but he who stands

firm to the end will be saved. 14 **And this gospel of the kingdom will be preached in the whole world as a testimony to all nations, and then the end will come**, (Matthew 24:9-14, NIV). [Underline and bold is by the author, solely for emphasis]

This is the same message that we find in Mark's account of tribulation at the hands of the antichristian forces. However, in Mark's account, we read about the beautiful power that the Holy Spirit will display through the Christian at that time:

> You must be on your guard. You will be handed over to the local councils and flogged in the synagogues. **On account of me you will stand before governors and kings as witnesses to them**. And the gospel must first be preached to all nations. 11 **Whenever you are arrested and brought to trial, do not worry beforehand about what to say. Just say whatever is given you at the time, for it is not you speaking, but the Holy Spirit**, (Mark 13:9-11, NIV). [Underline and bold is by the author, solely for emphasis]

This intensified period of tribulation immediately before *The Second Advent* will see some of the boldest evangelizing ever seen in the history of mankind. Matthew 24:14 clearly states, *and this gospel of the kingdom will be preached in the whole world as a testimony to all nations, and then the end will come*! Theorists, who merely see Jews as finally being converted through tribulation and or God's wrath during this period of time, miss the point. The tribulation at the hands of antichristian forces is not God's punishment or wrath for past transgressions. It is an opportunity for *called out ones* to make one final stand for Jesus, resulting in many unbelievers turning to God before the Lord's return. The great "testing" to come about during this period is not to see who can withstand the most *pain-*

until-you-repent; but, rather, this testing through persecution will be to see who will remain faithful to Jesus and the power of His word to bring as many more people to the Kingdom of God before His return. The *man of lawlessness* will be keenly (and diabolically) aware of this effort by *called out ones*. Henceforth, he will pull out all stops to silence the *ecclesia*. Satan, knowing that his time is short, will do everything in his power to destroy Christians throughout the world. The fact that the Christian will be boldly preaching the gospel during this intensified period of tribulation is proof that the Holy Spirit could not possibly be seen as being removed before this period of time. This intensified tribulation will result in one of the most glorious manifestations of the power of the Holy Spirit that has ever been seen. Even though scripture (in Daniel 12:7) records that the power (the missionary undertaking) of God's holy people will eventually be shattered, shortly before the Lord's return, the intended works of the Holy Spirit through the saints (Daniel 12:3) will result in millions of people converting to Jesus Christ. Many of these *called out ones* will be martyred, but many also will be alive to see *The Second Advent* of Jesus Christ. Here then we have one of the main purposes for not seeing the *Christian Church* removed before *The Second Advent.*

It boggles the mind to see how theorists can argue for the removal of the *Christian Church* (and the Holy Spirit as well), and then see people heretofore uncommitted to Jesus Christ, all of a sudden turning to the Lord due to persecutions from the Beast (and or God's wrath) and then suddenly proclaiming the gospel of Jesus Christ. If anything, it appears that those who have trusted and depended on their wealth and material goods (rather than God) will be more inclined to bow before the *man of lawlessness* when pressure is applied to them. If unbelievers have suddenly noticed that a myriad of Christians have been secretly Raptured from the face of the earth along with the Holy Spirit, the author is inclined to believe that their loyalty and allegiance will be more to the Beast system than to Jesus Christ.

But yet, those true believers who patiently endure these trials will obviously be so convinced that Jesus will eventually rescue them, that they will joyously stand up for their savior under any circumstances. There will be many who will say they believe, and actually will call themselves *Christian* at that time (See Daniel 11:34), but will not have the power of the Holy Spirit working in them. In John 12:42, we see a perfect example of those who profess to believe in the Lord; however, they still cling to those things that they feel will bring them the security and the glory they seek for themselves:

> Yet at the same time many even among the leaders believed in him. But because of the Pharisees they would not confess their faith for fear they would be put out of the synagogue; 43 **for they loved praise from men more than praise from God,** (John 12:42, 43, NIV). [Bold and underline is by the author, solely for emphasis]

Matthew 24:9-14 and Mark 13:9-11 are portions of scriptures that are echoed in Luke 12:4, 5 and Luke 21:12-19; however, in Luke 21:12-19, we specifically see that *called out ones* will not experience these end-time tribulations as punishment from God, but rather, to be witnesses to the unsaved:

> But before all this, **they will lay hands on you and persecute you.** They will deliver you to synagogues and prisons, and you will be brought before kings and governors, and all on account of my name. 13 **This will result in your being witnesses to them.** 14 But make up your mind not to worry beforehand how you will defend yourselves. 15 For I will give you words and wisdom that none of your adversaries will be able to resist or contradict. 16 **You will be betrayed by parents, brothers, relatives and friends, and they will put some of you to death.** 17 All men will hate you because of me.

18 **<u>By standing firm you will save yourselves,</u>** (Luke 21:12-19, NIV). [Bold and underline is by the author, solely for emphasis]

In verse 15, we see once again the power of the Holy Spirit working as never before, providing the *called out ones* with words and wisdom that none of their adversaries will be able to resist. Even though this experience will be reason for great sorrow (especially in the knowledge that some friends, family, and even fellow church members will betray us), the Lord exhorts us not to worry beforehand because not a hair on our head will perish, even though some of us may have to die.

What a glorious period that will be. Not necessarily to experience death, but, if one has to face death, the author can envision no greater honor than to stand up and preach the gospel of Jesus Christ, to be found faithful to Jesus, to face death squarely in the eye and say "*O Death, where is thy sting?*" Then, to look at our Savior's face and have Him say, "Well done, good and faithful servant" as He hands us our *stephanos*, the martyr's crown of life! What great glory for God! To realize that, like Stephen, our death might possibly result in another person's salvation has to be the ultimate Christian experience:

> While they were stoning him, Stephen prayed, "Lord Jesus, receive my spirit. 60 Then he fell on his knees and cried out, "**<u>Lord, do not hold this sin against them</u>**, (Acts 7:59, 60, NIV). [Bold and underline is by the author, solely for emphasis]

In verse 60, we see where Stephen, in his last dying breath, was praying for God to forgive his enemies, a prayer the author believes God honored. Here we see a glorious picture of the disciple Stephen, preaching the word of God to the Sanhedrin, unto death, looking up to heaven and surrendering his God-breathed, life-giving spirit back to the Lord. The Greek word for *crown* is *stephanos*, and the author believes the word of God states that those who witness for the Lord in that period of time will receive a greater reward. Is this willingness to die for the Lord's glory being a "super macho Christian" as brother Hal Lindsey states? If so, then that is what the author is. If wanting to serve Jesus with such zeal and fervor is wrong, then the author stands convicted. If being a member of God's *ecclesia* means that the *called out one* has to *shrink* back from the face of death, then all that Christ performed on the cross has gone for naught.

In Revelation 12:11, it describes a loud voice in heaven speaking about those who were willing to give up their lives to preach the gospel of Christ. This is not describing solely those who will be martyred during the end times. It describes those who throughout history overcame the accusatory powers of Satan and times of great tribulation through the blood of the Lamb:

> They overcame him by the blood of the Lamb and by the word of their testimony; **they did not love their lives so much as to shrink from death**, (Revelation 12:11, NIV). [Bold and underlines is by the author, solely for emphasis]

Back in Philippians 3:10, we see a clue from Paul's attitude toward death that should be the attitude of all Christians:

> **I want to know Christ** and the power of his resurrection **and the fellowship of sharing in his sufferings, becoming like him in his death,** 11 and so, somehow, to attain to the resurrection from the dead, (Philippians. 3:10, 11, NIV). [Bold and underlines is by the author, solely for emphasis]

Was Paul being a "super macho Christian?" If so, then the author finds no shame whatsoever in being identified with Paul, Stephen, Peter and all the other *called out ones* who laid their lives down so others can have eternal life.

As the author concludes this important chapter, please indulge him to share a very personal message. On many occasions, one of the sermons that the author preached in various churches during his brief ministry as an evangelist, he used an extremely graphic example of how he saw himself drowning in a pool of filth before coming to Christ. He described a gory scenario that included them picturing a giant vat filled with decaying dead animals, mixed amongst rotten meat, mingled with live venomous spiders, scorpions and snakes, all floating atop a pool of bodily waste material, generating the most odoriferous stench imaginable. He used this graphic example in order for the audience to get a more profound picture of how decrepit the author felt about himself before turning to the Lord. He told his audiences how he once was down in the bottom of that vat, bound by alcohol, drugs, and illicit sex, almost to the point of suicide because he could not see any way out of the devil's trap. But, after it was explained to him that Jesus Himself became sin in order for all of us to have eternal life, when he finally turned his life over to Christ, he told his audiences that he could actually see Jesus Christ diving head first into the vat, becoming all of its content, just so the author could be set free. This was the only way the author could make his audience see and feel how the author felt as he turned his life over to Jesus. Make a mental picture of this scenario. Picture Jesus diving head first into that abysmal stench. Not only becoming all of the individual filth *you* have personally committed throughout your entire life, but also becoming the putridity of all of mankind's combined sins throughout history. This thought simply boggles the mind. But, yet, that's exactly what Christ did. He willingly leaped head first into humanity's vat of sin, not only drowning in it, but also becoming the despicability of humanity's waste.

The author has often wondered why Jesus Christ cried out, *My God, my God, why hast thou forsaken me,* (Matthew 27:46)? Was it because the physical pain was too much for him to endure? Maybe that was a part of it. Death by crucifixion is known to be one of the most painful and heinous ways to kill a person. However, the author believes in his heart that the agony and despair Jesus Christ felt at that moment was due primarily because our sinless Lord was not only experiencing the sting of sin, feeling the horror and the anguish of the sins of all mankind consuming his entire human persona, He was also experiencing a separation from God for the very first time!

No Mr. Lindsey, we aren't talking "super macho Christian" here. We're talking about being eternally grateful for salvation. Eternally grateful for being rescued before the author experienced a physical and senseless death no one would wish on his worst enemy. Not only did Jesus Christ rescue the author from dying a disgraceful death, alone and separated apart from friends and loved ones, He actually brought the author back from among the physically dying and spiritually dead and into new life. How God could have such grace and mercy to not only restore this former decrepit soul back to life, but to even choose him to do this work (writing this book) is a mystery that will remain unsolved by this author until he sees Jesus Christ face to face.

Therefore, being eternally grateful for this salvation, if the Lord tells the author that "not a hair on his head will perish," knowing that he will soon be spending an eternity with his savior, then dying a physical death for Jesus, as He was willing to die for the author and all of mankind, is not a thing to fear:

> Since the children have flesh and blood, he too shared in their humanity so that by his death he might destroy him who holds the power of death – that is, the devil – 15 **and free those who all their lives were held in slavery by their fear of death**, (Hebrews 2:14, 15, NIV). [Bold and underline by author, solely for emphasis]

Chapter 7
CONCERNING THE APOSTASY!

According to the belief held by proponents in their secret pre-tribulation escape to heaven theory, the *Christian Church* will not have to endure any form of persecution before *The Second Advent*. Instead, it will be "caught up" to meet the Lord in the air and then whisked up to reside safely in heaven during a time of great tribulation that supposedly will last between three and a half to seven years. The *Christian Church*, then, supposedly returns with Christ after this a period of great tribulation on earth, which supposedly will include the punishing of the Jacob's descendants (Jews) unto repentance. As their theory goes, the *Christian Church* will be Raptured (1 Thessalonians 4:16, 17) before this awesome period they call *The Great Tribulation*. Hal Lindsey contends that the Rapture takes place somewhere between 1 Thessalonians 4:16 and 2 Thessalonians 2:1, where it speaks about the coming of the Lord at His Second Advent after the seven years of tribulation have expired.

Lindsey and other theorists claim that what is spoken about in 1 Thessalonians 4:16-17 (the dead in Christ are raised first and those who are still alive at that time are "caught up together" to be with the Lord in heaven), and what is spoken about in 2 Thessalonians 2:1-3 (that day, the coming of the Lord, will not come until the rebellion occurs and the man of lawlessness is revealed), is supposedly describing two separate events, ostensibly separated by a seven-year period of time. One question the author would ask theorists, at this juncture, is, "If Paul is informing the *called out ones* in 1 Thessalonians 4:16-17 that they will be caught together with those who sleep in Christ to be with the Lord to heaven before the Great Tribulation, why is it necessary for Paul to reassure the *ecclesia* (in 2 Thessalonians 2:1-3) that *The Second Advent* of the Lord will not happen until *after* the rebellion and the revealing of the man of lawlessness?" If (as theorists' scenarios go) the *called out ones* are supposed to be in heaven before the apostasy and the man of lawlessness will be revealed, why is it necessary that the *Christian Church* be informed about this aspect, a prospect that it would take for granted if indeed it supposedly will be returning with the Lord from heaven at *The Second Advent*?

Theorists claim that 1 Thessalonians 4:16-17 addresses solely the Pre-tribulation Rapture that is supposed to happen seven years before *The Second Advent* and that 2 Thessalonians 2:1-3 pertains only to *The Second Advent* of Christ. They claim that Paul (in these two letters) is discussing two different events. Rather than enter this debate again, we will ask the reader to go back and reread Chapter 7 (*He Comes With His Holy Ones*) of our first book for explicit clarification.

The author believes that scripture clearly conveys that both letters to the Thessalonians were written by Paul solely to encourage the *ecclesia* about *The Second Advent*. In the first letter, Paul discusses *the resurrection* (which theorists call The Rapture), which is the fact that the dead in Christ will be raised first and those *called out ones* who are still alive and waiting will immediately be caught together with them to meet the Lord in the air, and then be with Him forever. In the second letter, Paul's main message concerns *the timing* of *the resurrection* and the Lord's return and, he states emphatically, that this cannot happen until *"the rebellion and the man of lawlessness is revealed."*

Let's examine this apostasy aspect. First of all, what causes this rebellion? Who does the rebelling? And what do these apostates rebel against? These are very important questions, which the author will attempt to answer.

Firstly, at the beginning of the second letter to the Thessalonians, Paul is seen boasting about the *"perseverance and faith in all the persecutions and trials"* that the Thessalonians are enduring. Here, Paul is acknowledging to them (and to all of the *ecclesia*) that to stand up for God will result in much tribulation. Since the time of Christ's resurrection, ascension and subsequent outpouring of the Holy Spirit (which sealed the down payment on God's redemption program), the single most important requirement for the *ecclesia* has been to preach the Gospel and believe in the Lord Jesus Christ by faith and *"Thou shalt be saved,* (Romans 10:9, KJV)." Throughout the beginning of time, and even more so since the resurrection of Christ, it has been Satan's primary mission to hammer a wedge between the believer and God. This historic war has been waged from the time of Adam and Eve and continues to this very day. However, during the last days (when tribulation will increase exponentially, leading to Christ's return), the battle will intensify as never before. One of the missions (if not the primary one) of Satan (during this period) will be to try even harder to separate as many believers as he can from their faith in the Lord Jesus Christ, because he knows his time is short. The increased times of persecutions to be unleashed by the Satanically-imbued *man of lawlessness*, during this period of great tribulation, will be primarily for that purpose. It is not designed for God to punish a special group of people (supposedly Jacob and his descendants) for turning their backs on Him, and much less for inflicting enough pain on Jacob's descendants so that they will eventually buckle under it and repent. One of the main purposes for the increased time of tribulation at the hands of the man of lawlessness is for God to purify and separate His *ecclesia* from the unrepentant. This is why during this period of persecution we will witness the greatest evangelizing season in history, a time of reckoning where all of humanity (including Christians) will have to finally choose their allegiance between God and Satan, regardless of the consequences that may befall them!

Many in the *Christian Church* today believe that when they accepted Jesus Christ as Lord and Savior they now have immunity from persecution and a safety net in what theorists call The Rapture. They believe that by merely accepting Jesus Christ in their hearts, everything in their Christian journey from now on will be one smooth ride to heaven. The debate between those who believe that *"once saved, always saved"* continues to this very day. The author will not enter this debate other than to say scripture clearly says two things about this issue. One is found in Romans 8:1, 35-39, which basically states that nothing can separate us from the love of Christ. However, even though He will always be committed to loving us, can we say the same thing about Him, regardless of the horrendous circumstances that await the *ecclesia* before *The Second Advent*? Therefore, the proverbial question begs to be asked: Can a person lose their salvation after coming to Christ?" The answer is "Yes!" In Hebrews 6:1-6, the author provides the following warning:

> Therefore let us leave the elementary teachings about Christ and go on to maturity, not laying again the foundation of repentance from acts that lead to death, and of faith in God, 2 instruction about baptisms, the laying on of hands, the resurrection of the dead, and eternal judgment. 3 And God permitting, we will do so. 4 **It is impossible for those who have once been enlightened**, who have **tasted the heavenly gift,** who

have shared in the Holy Spirit, 5 who have tasted the goodness of the word of God and the powers of the coming age, 6 **if they fall away, to be brought back to repentance, because to their loss they are crucifying the Son of God all over again and subjecting him to public disgrace**, (Hebrews 6:1-6, NIV). [Underline and bold is by the author, solely for emphasis]

Verse four is very important, in that it clearly states that even those who have tasted the heavenly gift (which is the power gifts from the Holy Spirit), they can fall away into a state of apostasy. However, as the Bible states in 1 John 1:9-10, *"If we confess our sins, he is faithful to forgive us our sins and purify us from all unrighteousness. If, however, we claim we have not sinned we make Him out to be a liar and His word has no place in our lives."* It should be obvious to all true believers that to claim there is no sin in us is to not only call the Lord a liar, but it would also find us denying the power of the Holy Spirit, which convicts us of sin. Here is where the Christian comes perilously close to committing the unpardonable sin spoken of in Matthew 12:31 and Mark 3:29:

And so I tell you, every sin and blasphemy against the Spirit will not be forgiven. 32 Anyone who speaks a word against the Son of Man will be forgiven, but anyone who speaks against the Holy Spirit will not be forgiven, either in this age or in the age to come, (Matthew 12:31,32, NIV).

What is blasphemy? This is an issue that has been debated for centuries. However, W. E. Vine provides a sound understanding of blasphemy, when he stated that, "As to Christ's teaching concerning "blasphemy" against the Holy Spirit, e.g., Matt. 12:32, that anyone, with the evidence of the Lord's power before His eyes, should declare it to be Satanic, exhibited a condition of heart beyond Divine illumination and therefore hopeless. Divine forgiveness would be inconsistent with the moral nature of God. <u>As to the Son of Man, in his state of humiliation, there might be misunderstanding, but not so with the Holy Spirit's power demonstrated</u>." (W. E. Vine's, *An Expository Dictionary of Biblical Words*, Page 124, Thomas Nelson Publishers) [Underline is by the author, solely for emphasis]

Can our salvation be lost or taken away without our acquiescence? The author believes the answer is a resounding no! In Romans 8:35-39, it emphatically states that nothing can separate us from the love of God, which is in Christ Jesus. He will forgive those who seek His forgiveness. However, during the time of tribulation (and even today), many that profess to believe in the Lord Jesus Christ *will* rebel and *will* turn away from their faith in Christ! During these times of trials and testing, many will renounce Jesus Christ as Lord and savior merely to survive tribulation at the hands of anti-Christian forces. For example, in Luke 8:4-8, we read about the parable of the sower, which perfectly describes the degree of effectiveness the word of God has on mankind. In verses 11 through 15, Jesus gives the disciples the exact meaning of the parable so there will be no misunderstanding:

> This is the meaning of the parable: The seed is the word of God. 12 Those along the path are the ones who hear, and then the devil comes and takes away the word from their hearts, so that they cannot believe and be saved. 13 Those on the rock are the ones who receive the word with joy when they hear it, but they have not root. **They believe for a while, but in the time of testing they fall away**. 14 The seed that fell among thorns stands for those who hear, but as they go on their way they are choked by life's worries, riches and pleasures, and they do not mature. 15 But the seed on good soil stands for those with a noble and good heart, who hear the word,

retain it, and by persevering produce crop, (Luke 8:11-15, NIV). [Bold and underline is by the author, solely for emphasis]

This parable is identical to the one in Matthew 13:1-9, which is interpreted in verses 18 through 23, and Mark 4:1-9, and verses 13 through 20. However, in Matthew's and Mark's account, we see how much of a crop is produced by the "good soil" man, "yielding a hundred, sixty or thirty times what was sown."

This message of sowing and reaping is immersed throughout the New Testament, including the parable of the talents (Matt. 25:14-30 and the ten Minas (Luke 19:11-27). Let's briefly look at Matthew 25:14-30:

Again, it will be like a man going on a journey, who called his servants and entrusted his property to them. 14 To one he gave five talents of money, to another two talents, and to another one talent, each according to his ability. Then he went on his journey. 16 The man who had received the five talents went at once and put his money to work and gained five more. 17 So also, the one with the two talents gained two more. 18 But the man who had received the one talent went off, dug a hole in the ground and hid his master's money. 19 After a long time the master of those servants returned and settled accounts with them. 20 The man who had received the five talents brought the other five. 'Master,' he said, 'you entrusted me with five talents. See, I have gained five more.' 21 His master replied, 'Well done, good and faithful servant! You have been faithful with a few things; I will put you in charge of many things. Come and share your master's happiness!' 22 The man with the two talents also came. 'Master,' he said, 'you entrusted me with two talents; see, I have gained two more.' 23 his master replied, 'Well done, good and faithful servant! You have been faithful with a few things; I will put you in charge of many things. Come and share your master's happiness!' 24 Then the man who had received the one talent came. 'Master,' he said, 'I knew that you are a hard man, harvesting where you have not sown and gathering where you have not scattered seed. 25 So I was afraid and went out and hid your talent in the ground. See, here is what belongs to you.' 26 His master replied, 'You wicked, lazy servant! So you knew that I harvest where I have not sown and gather where I have not scattered seed? 27 Well then, you should have put my money on deposit with the bankers, so that when I returned I would have received it back with interest. 28 Take the talent from him and give it to the one who has the ten talents. 29 **For everyone who has will be given more, and he will have an abundance. Whoever does not have, even what he has will be taken from him**. 30 **And throw that worthless servant outside, into the darkness, where there will be seeping and gnashing of teeth**, (Matthew 25:14-30, NIV) [Underline and bold is by the author, solely for emphasis]

We all know that a person is saved by grace, not of works, that any one should boast. This merely implies that we didn't have to work to receive the gift of salvation. However, throughout the entire Bible, we see that God has *chosen* (Acts 13:48) and *called out* from among the world, a people (*ecclesia*) for a specific purpose. These people (*ecclesia*) who have been *called out from* (*ecclesia*) the world have not been called out to escape the tribulation of the world; but, rather, to be a major influence (if not an integral part) in the fulfillment of God's overall plan of redemption!

Therefore, the degree of effectiveness that the word of God has on the individual believer, as evidenced in the parable of the sower, will have much to say about who will turn away from God during *great persecutions* that will intensify immediately prior to the Lord's return! Let's examine Luke, Chapter 8.

There appears to be four types of people who are referred to in the parable of the sower. There is the *path* group, those who hear the message about the kingdom, but don't understand. The *rocky places* group, those that hear the word and receive it with joy, but have no root; henceforth, the word lasts for a short time and, then, when trouble or persecution comes, because of the word, they quickly fall away. Then there is the *thorns* group, those who hear the word, but the worries of this life and the deceitfulness of wealth choke it, making it unfruitful. Then, there is the *good soil* group, the ones who hear the word and understand it. And, as Luke 8:15 states, *"But the seed on good soil stands for those with a noble and good heart, who hear he word, retain it, and by persevering, he produces a crop, (Luke 8:15, NIV)."*

One of the greatest phenomena being experienced in evangelical circles today is the massive rallies and crusades that feature dynamic preachers extolling the gospel of Jesus Christ. At these events, many are moved to a so-called *conversion* by the charisma of the speakers and the great emotional swell that springs up from the crowds. The author believes that many are sincere when they come to the forefront and truly surrender their hearts to the alter call. But have they really surrendered all to follow Christ? Have they made a commitment to pick up their cross and give up everything, even their life to do his will? The author believes that many are caught up more so with the swell of emotional and euphoric experience produced by the theatrics of the event, and possibly experience a brief moment of remorse. But, for the most part, many have not really made a true commitment to the totality of the Christian walk. While many enjoy the healing, forgiveness and the blessings contained within Christianity, most are not prepared to surrender everything and make Jesus the Lord and Master of their lives. They love the blessings, but are unwilling to pick up their cross!

The author remembers an experience of this sort while attending a Baptist Bible conference in Hume Lake, California, back in 1956. The author can still hear the preacher belting out those oft heard words: "You have to repent, you have to accept the blood of Jesus, you have to be saved or you're going to Hell!" The author can still remember going up to the altar, getting down on his knees and pouring out his soul, tearfully asking God to forgive him for his sins. However, after he came back to his hometown, after momentarily feeling a beautiful peace in his heart, the memory of the event would soon become an isolated part of his youthful past. The author never attended another event like that again until January 5, 1975, at a small Assemblies of God Church in Montebello, California. It was there that he was again led to Christ by a youthful pastor named David Tanner. Since then, the author's life in Jesus has grown at a consistent pace, albeit filled with much strife and life-altering challenges. Was the author truly saved back at Hume Lake when he accepted Christ in 1956? Or was he saved on January 5, 1975? The author does not truly know. However, the important aspect to this story is not when the author was saved, but rather when did the word of God take hold of him and begin producing fruit?

The Bible specifically states that we (*called out ones*) were chosen in Him before the creation of the world to be holy and blameless (Ephesians 1:4) and that we were also predestined to be conformed to the likeness of His Son that he might be the firstborn among many brothers. And those (*called out ones*) He predestined, He also called; those He called, He justified; those He justified, He also glorified (Romans 8:29, 30). These scriptural verses assure the author that God has chosen him and has *called him out* from the world for a purpose.

But, should the author ever reject this calling (as Judas, one of the Lord's original apostles did), then he doesn't believe that he can rest solely on his church membership to assure him a spot at the great reunion God has in store for His true disciples!

It appears then that the only sin that God cannot forgive is when the *called out ones* blatantly reject the calling by Holy Spirit, which is an act of blasphemy against almighty God. All other sins He forgives, if they come to the throne of grace and confess them to Him. But how will the author (and the total professing community of Christians) react when these horrific times of increased tribulation come upon us? Those represented as the *pathway* group evidently have not understood the word of God, and it would appear that they would have a difficult time holding firm during this period if they know not how to live by the word of God. Those of the *rock* group will also have difficulty, because they have no root (although they believe for a while); but, in the time of extreme testing (as prophesied in Matthew 24:5-12), many will definitely fall away! Those of the *thorn* group appear headed for an even greater time of trouble because their hopes lie in wealth, which deceitfully seduces their need for security. But, more importantly, they are choked from life's worries, riches and pleasures - and they do not mature! The *good soil* group, those with a noble and good heart, however, hear and retain the word of God and, by persevering, produce a crop! If we were to view these four groups of people (the *pathway* group, the *rock* group, the *thorn* group and the *good soil* group) existing during the time of tribulation, which group would we most likely see coming through great tribulation more or less unscathed.

In the Book of Revelation, where it speaks about the letters to the seven angels of the seven churches (which could represent varying degrees of the Christian walk, throughout history), it appears that the *pathway* group is not mentioned; the *rock* group could very well be applied to the church in Ephesus, *you have forsaken your first love,*

(Revelation 2:4); the *thorn* group could very well be applied to the church in Laodicea, *You say, 'I am rich; I have acquired wealth and do not need a thing*, (Revelation 3:17); and the *good soil* group could very well be applied to the church of Philadelphia, *Since you have kept my command to endure patiently, I will also keep you from the hour of trial that is going to come upon the whole world to test those who live on the earth*, (Revelation 3:10). The author is not proposing a new theory here, but rather, demonstrating how these verses blend harmoniously with each other, and how God's word appears to be providing us with an overall theme concerning the attitude (and walk) that should be manifested in all professing Christians, especially those of the *good soil* group!

Theorists contend that the *apostasy* mentioned in 2 Thessalonians 2:4 does not apply to the *Christian Church* because it will have been secretly *caught up* from earth to heaven before the increasing times of great tribulation. They contend that the *apostasy* here should be applied to the so-called "Roman Church" or other humanistically oriented religious groups, which will be more prevalent during this time. But, if they apply these theories solely to these groups, or to unbelieving Jews, how can they see someone fall away from something they never had, which is true faith in Jesus Christ?

Throughout history, satanic forces have waged a spiritual warfare against God and His people, and they continue to this very day. However, as the end times approach the world, as we know it today, these battles will increase tremendously. While many in the evangelical community continue to reach out for the lost through much commercialism and theatrics, Satan's power is being felt with greater measure because he knows his time is short. A quick cursory glance in the daily newspaper, and through radio and television reports, we can see Satan intensely pumping the bellows of his furnace of deception, hatred, violence and chaos, which, unfortunately (due to the incessant exploitation of these maladies by media) has also numbed much of Christendom throughout the world, thereby fanning the flames of apostasy as never before. These flames are reaching greater heights and, unfortunately, we see way too many Christians falling into one of these four groups by virtue of their spiritual malaise. Far too many Christians have become part of the *"pathway"* group, those who hear but don't understand. Many are those who walk with the *"rocky places"* group, those who hear and accept with joy but have no root to resist during times of trouble. Most of today's Christians can be found among the *"thorns"* group, those who hear the word of God; however they are being choked by worries, riches and pleasures. Thank God for those of the *"good soil,"* whom the author believes are the ones which will be primarily responsible for bringing more lost sinners into the Kingdom of God, especially during the last days!

True, we do have an *apostasy* period now; however, as Paul states in 2 Thessalonians 2:3, the fulfillment of the final rebellion (by those who profess to be walking with God) will occur in massive proportions immediately before the Lord's Second Advent! Let's examine a group of scriptures that speaks directly to this period of time:

> But mark this: **There will be terrible times in the last days**. 2 People will be lovers of themselves, lovers of money, boastful, proud, abusive, disobedient to their parents, ungrateful, unholy, 3 without love, unforgiving, slanderous, without self-control, brutal, not lovers of the good, 4 treacherous, rash, conceited, lovers of pleasure rather than lovers of God – 5 **having a form of godliness but denying its power. Have nothing to do with them.** 6 They are the kind who worm their way into homes and gain control over weak-willed women, who are loaded down with desires, 7 **always learning but never able to acknowledge the truth**. 8 Just as Jannes and Jambres opposed Moses, so also these men oppose the

truth – men of depraved minds, who, as far as the faith is concerned, are rejected. 9 But they will not get very far because, as in the case of those men, their folly will be clear to everyone, (2 Timothy 3:1-9, NIV). [Underline and bold is by the author, solely for emphasis]

Here we see a perfect example of the people who fit the *"thorn"* group. The key to this group of scriptures is found in verse 5, which bears repeating: *"Having a form of Godliness but denying its power!"* Here we see a group of so-called 'church' people who mouth religious precepts, make claim to being God-fearing and righteous. However, when it comes to living and walking a life of faith in Christ, they struggle between true faith verses money, power and their own glories, which will include the overindulgence of worldly pleasures. Throughout history, and now more recently, many well-known people of the cloth have been excommunicated from their church groups, or convicted of crimes that go against the will of God. Sadly, many who have once been enlightened, if they fall away, it will be impossible to be brought back to repentance, because to their loss they are crucifying the Son of God all over again and subjecting him to public disgrace, (Hebrews 6:4-6, NIV). This sad fact will become more pronounced as the day of wrath draws nigh. In verses 10 through 17, however, we see the author describing so beautifully the *"good soil"* group.

> You, however, know all about my teaching, my way of life, **my purpose, faith, patience, love, endurance,** 11 **persecutions, sufferings** – what kinds of things happened to me in Antioch, Iconium and Lystra, the persecutions I endured. Yet the Lord rescued me from all of them. 12 **In fact, everyone who wants to live a godly life in Christ Jesus will be persecuted,** 13 **while evil men and imposters will go from bad to worse, deceiving and being deceived**. 14 But as for you,

continue in what you have learned and have become
convinced of, because you know those from whom you
learned it, 15 and how from infancy you have known
the Holy Scripture, which are able to make you wise for
salvation through faith in Christ Jesus. 16 All Scripture
is God-breathed and is useful for teaching, rebuking,
correcting and training in righteousness, 17 so that
the man of God may be thoroughly equipped for every
good work, (2 Timothy 3:10-17, NIV). [Underline and
bold is by the author, solely for emphasis]

The key to this group of scriptures is found in verse 12, which also
deserves repeating: *"In fact, everyone who wants to live a godly life in
Christ Jesus will be persecuted!"* Therefore, it appears that during the
end times, two major groups of confessing Christians will exist in
the world: those who will turn away from their faith in God during
horrendous times, and those who will knowingly face persecution
for the testimony of Jesus. God is no respecter of men. He either is
for you because you believe in the saving grace of Jesus Christ, or He
is against you because you have rejected His gift of salvation. It is
obvious from the examples we have given so far that the first three
groups (the *pathway*, the *rocky places* and the *thorns*) will not be
found enduring times of great tribulation. Instead, they will be giving
in to horrific pressures (including the mark of the beast), while those
people who have decided to trust in Jesus (even if it means being
executed) will inherit the fulfillment of the Kingdom of God when
the Lord returns.

It should therefore be concluded that a "falling away" is to be seen
from the beginning of time; however, its massive culmination will
be seen during the persecutory reign of the man of lawlessness. If, as
theorists contend, the antichrist (or Beast) is known to exist three and
a half years before his true nature is revealed (2 Thessalonians 2:3),
and has subtly implemented his 666 program, where no one can buy

or sell without the mark, it is therefore evident that enduring for Jesus Christ will require a greater amount of faith and commitment than ever before, which will be obviously lacking in the *pathway, rocky places* and *thorn* groups, but not in the *good soil* people of Christ!

Hal Lindsey and others see this apostasy as being a single event (which can be measured in a day's time); however, as scripture reveals, the "apostasy" should not be viewed in a timely event-like fashion, but rather, as an escalating swell of rebellion toward Jesus Christ! There is no set magical day seen here in 2 Thessalonians 2:3; but, rather, it will be a rapidly and increasing fulfillment of a defection and revolt against God's saving grace. Sides will be chosen! Those who are Christ's will stand up and be counted! Those who are not truly committed (unto to death) for Christ, will align themselves with the man of lawlessness and accept the mark of the Beast. Many professing Christians will even join the Beast as he makes war on the *called out ones* until he has overpowered and killed many of them (Daniel 7:21; 11:32-35; 12:7). However, part of the *ecclesia* will come through this ordeal unscathed, having been protected by God's End Times Passover program! Those that remain will get to see their dead brethren in Christ rise first as they themselves will be caught together with them to greet and have a meeting with the Lord in the air, then escort Him back to earth in all His glory, as He returns to judge those who believed not, then to reign with Him on earth forever and ever.

As the author stated earlier, these that remain are not the so-called "tribulation saints" in the sense that they were *left behind* after the so-called Rapture and eventually repented due to tribulation and or God's wrath. These are all of those *called out ones* who will be on earth during the reign of the man of lawlessness and will eventually overcome him by faithfully preaching the Gospel to the glory of Jesus Christ, even unto death! Yes! Many will be martyred but many will also pass through the tribulation of antichristian forces unscathed! These will not be semi-converted Christians or Jews who accept salvation resulting from God-inflicted-punishment-until-you-repent. These will be the *called out ones* of Christ, God's *ecclesia*, who will be victorious in the greatest spiritual warfare ever witnessed by mankind. These will be God's Christian Soldiers who will be preaching the gospel to the end, even if it means giving up their lives so others can live in eternity with Jesus Christ, our Lord and our God!

Chapter 8
ONWARD CHRISTIAN SOLDIERS!

We can see in scripture that Christians will indeed experience great tribulation (as they have throughout history), but with increased intensity immediately before the Lord returns. We have seen this fact through the word of God in the Gospels, the letters to the Romans, and the epistles to the different churches. We have seen that the *ecclesia* (true believers and followers of the Lord) will not be secretly "caught up" to heaven before Jesus Christ returns to rule and reign His eternal kingdom on earth. We see many who profess to be Christians unfortunately buckling under the societal and financial pressures that exist today. Unfortunately, many Christians will fall away from their faith in Christ and will literally crumble and fall apart more so when the man of lawlessness is revealed, through the power of Satan. We see that a special group of people, who care not for their own lives, will make one last stand for the testimony of Jesus Christ. Some unbelievers will convert to the Lord during this time, but it will not be due to God's wrath; but, rather, by the last great outpouring of the Holy Spirit, and the spiritual message of Jesus Christ delivered by some of the bravest souls ever to exist. We say brave, not in the sense of being strong in flesh and might, but rather, brave in the sense that they are trusting in Jesus to eventually bring them through this crisis.

How, then, do these brave souls accomplish the task? How do these committed individual believers prevail through this great period of distress? We examined the Bible in the beginning of this book, to help us identify where the subject of tribulation addresses the Christian. Now, we will also examine it to identify scripture that not only shows us how God will implement his End Times Passover, but also, what God expects the *called out ones* to do during this period as an integral part of His overall redemption program. Let's first examine the Gospels to see what Jesus had to say to the *called out ones* about their conduct, especially as the Day of the Lord draws nearer to the end.

After Jesus was baptized in water by John the Baptist, (Matthew 3:16), we see the power of the Holy Spirit descending upon Him. There is absolutely no way that people can be an effective vessel for the Lord unless they first believe by faith, repent, and seek the power gifts of the Holy Spirit. It is a well-known fact throughout Christendom that in order to gain access to the Kingdom of God, and to also be used by God, a person has to experience what is known as the "born again" phenomena (see John 3:5-8). Immediately upon accepting Jesus Christ as Lord and Savior (see Romans 10:9-10), the new man in Christ will usually experience immediate temptation; but, by the grace of God, and by resisting the devil's attacks (James 4:7), the Christian can be loosed from the devil's slanderous and diabolical ploys. Thereafter, the Christian's main mission is to lead others to Christ by preaching the gospel of the Kingdom of God (Matthew 4:17), which was the very first thing Jesus did after receiving the Holy Spirit and subsequent temptation by the devil.

At this point in time, it is very important to note that the preaching of the gospel and being a teacher of the word do not necessarily go hand in hand; at least not immediately after conversion. In the Book of Acts, we see where it took Paul (although indwelt with power gifts from the Holy Spirit) approximately 17 years before he was able to teach the message as effectively as he did when he wrote the second letter to the church at Corinth, (See 2 Corinthians 12:1-10). This does not mean that Paul was not effective in his testimony during this time. Many people were converted because of his bold witness and testimony of how Jesus Christ changed his life. However, it wasn't until later on that Paul (in mature growth) was able to provide the disciples with the incisive teachings of Christ. This also does not negate the fact that Jesus *can* work great miracles through new babes in Christ. He has, He does and will continue to do so. However, like all of God's processes of life, there is to be experienced a metamorphosis by each individual Christian that cannot always be harvested before its time. When Jesus left the disciples as He ascended to heaven, His last message in Acts 1:1-8 plainly states, that when the power gifts of the Holy Spirit come upon them, they are to be witnesses to the ends of the earth. What is a witness? Does a witness in a courtroom trial teach things about the law? Does a witness go about "rightly dividing the word" of God? No! A witness gives testimony about what has been individually experienced.

The main responsibility for Christians (new ones especially) is not to stand on the mountaintop and indiscriminately begin quoting scripture; but, rather, to share a testimony of what God has individually performed in their lives. When He gave His disciples the "great commission" in Acts 1:1-8, Jesus didn't use the word *preach*, which is the word derived from the Greek word *euangelizo*, from where we get the word "evangelize." He said, "You will be my *witnesses.* Although many Christians after maturing will be sent by God for the specific purpose of preaching and teaching the word of God, the implication we see from Jesus in this passage refers to our individual tasks of sharing what God has performed in our lives as a testimony to His glorious works, power and saving grace. The precise meaning of the word *witness*, however, does carry a much greater response from the individual, because it requires a serious commitment, one possibly resulting in death!

The word *witness* in the Greek is *martus* or *martur*, where W. E. Vine states: "whence, Eng., martyr, **one who bears witness by his death,** denotes one who can or does aver what has been seen or heard or knows; it is used (a) of God, Rom. 1:9; 2 Cor. 1:23; Phil. 1:8; 1 Thess. 2:5, 10 (2nd part); (b) of Christ, Rev. 1:5, 3:14; (c) **of those who witness for Christ by their death,** Acts 22:20; Rev. 2:13; Rev. 17:6, (d) of the interpreters of God's counsel, yet to witness in Jerusalem in the times of Antichrist, Rev. 11:3; (e) in a forensic sense, Matt. 18:16, 26:65; Mark 14:63; Acts 6:13; 7:58; 2 Cor. 13:1; 1 Tim. 5:19; Heb. 10:28; (f) in a historical sense, Luke 11:48; 24:48; Acts 1:8, 22; 2:32, 3:15; 5:32; 10:39, 41; 13:31; 22:15; 26:16; 1 Thess. 2:10 (1st part); 1 Tim 6:12; 2 Tim. 2:2; Heb. 12:1, **"(a cloud) of witnesses," here of those mentioned in Chapt. 11, those whose lives and actions testified to the worth and effect of faith, and whose faith received witness in Scripture;** 1 Pet. 5:1." (W. E. Vine, *An Expository Dictionary of Biblical Words*, Page 1237, Thomas Nelson Publishers) [Underline and bold is by the author, solely for emphasis]

In Acts 22:20, we see Paul alluding to the martyrdom God's children would experience when he made his remorseful remarks as he confessed to Jesus his complicity in the death of the disciple Stephen, *"And when the blood of your **martyr** Stephen was shed, I stood there giving my approval and guarding the clothes of those who were killing him."* In the New American Standard Bible version, the word used for "martyr" is "witness," however, they both mean the same thing: *martus,* **one who bears witness by his death!** [Bold and underline is by the author, solely for emphasis]

As 1 Thessalonians 4:16, 17 states, many *called out ones* will still be alive when Jesus returns. The dead in Christ will be raised first and those who are alive and waiting for the Lord's return will be "caught" together with them to greet and have a meeting with the Lord in the air, as He makes His descent to planet earth. Until that time, the Lord exhorts us to reach out to the entire world and lead the lost to His Kingdom.

Jesus' first remarks after being baptized and tempted by the devil, and subsequently returned to Galilee (thereby fulfilling the prophecy of Isaiah 9:1, 2), are probably the most important ones ever uttered: "REPENT, FOR THE KINGDOM OF HEAVEN IS NEAR!" It is these same words that He wants *called out ones* to echo in everything we do and say. God very easily could snap His fingers and restore everything to His liking; however, He wants His creation to come to Him voluntarily. The word *repent* means "a change of mind," which is what God wants. He wants His creation to change their minds from their worldly ways and come to Him voluntarily, because we love Him, not because we have to or have been forced to do so!

In Matthew 5:11, 12, we once again see Jesus reminding His *ecclesia* that *called out ones* will suffer as a result of following Him; but, He also tells us that these persecutions and insults will result in rewards! Henceforth, the battle wages on and the individual Christian must be of the business of putting on spiritual battle gear, unlike any the world has ever known. In Ephesians 6:10-18, the apostle Paul provides the Christian with the keys for this preparation:

> Finally, be strong in the Lord and in his mighty power. 11 Put on the full armor of God so that you can take your stand against the devil's schemes. 12 **For our struggle is not against flesh and blood, but against the rulers, against the authorities, against the powers of this dark world and against the spiritual forces of evil in the heavenly realms.** 13 **therefore put on the full armor of God, so that when the day of evil comes,**

you may be able to stand your ground, and after you have done everything, to stand. 14 Stand firm then, with the belt of truth buckled around your waist, with the breastplate of righteousness in place, 15 and with your feet fitted with the readiness that comes from the gospel of peace. 16 In addition to all this, take up the shield of faith, with which you can extinguish all the flaming arrows of the evil one. 17 take the helmet of salvation and the sword of the Spirit, which is the word of God. 18 **And pray in the Spirit on all occasions with all kinds of prayers and requests. With this in mind, be alert and always keep on praying for all the saints,** (Ephesians 6:10-18, NIV). [Underline and bold is by the author, solely for emphasis]

While Christians will experience much persecution and great tribulation in the latter days, there has been spiritual warfare from the beginning of history. However, immediately before *The Second Advent*, it will increase with greater intensity as has never been seen by mankind before. But God's *called out ones* will be able to withstand the onslaught, more so during this most horrific season.

There are five elements involved in God's spiritual armament for Christians, elements that go contrary to military standards, as the world understands. Number one is the *belt of truth*. The word "belt" used here is "gird," or in the Greek, *perizonnumi*, which literally means to be dressed for service. This means that the Christian is to be ready for service when the truth is known. What is the truth but what the Lord states in John 14:6, *"I am the way and the truth and the life. No one comes to the father except through me."* While the military man wraps himself with a holster belt to house his weapon, the Christian wraps himself with the belt of truth, which holsters the word of God.

Secondly, the Christian is seen putting on the *breastplate of righteousness* as the second line of defense while engaging in spiritual warfare. The Greek word for breastplate is *thorax* and, according to W. E. Vine, is seen metaphorically as *righteousness* in this verse. In 1 Thessalonians 5:8, we see it used to describe the *righteousness* found in faith and love. The physical heart (right beneath the left breast) is the power source of the human body, pumping life-giving blood to the millions of arteries that sustains it. How appropriate that this heart should be protected by a breastplate made not of cold, hard steel; but, rather, made of faith and love found only in Jesus Christ. It should be noted that the Israelites were well aware of this concept through the prophet Isaiah. In Chapter 59:15-17, the prophet clearly states that the Lord Himself is the provision for salvation, and *that* through *His* righteousness, not our own:

> Truth is nowhere to be found, and whoever shuns evil becomes a prey. The Lord looked and was displeased that there was not justice. 16 he saw that there was no one, and he was appalled that there was no one to intercede; so his own arm worked salvation for him, and his own righteousness sustained him. 17 **He put on righteousness as his breastplate, and the helmet of salvation on his head; he put on the garments of vengeance and wrapped himself in zeal as in a cloak**, (Isaiah 59:15-17, NIV). [Underline and bold is by the author, solely for emphasis]

In Matthew 6:33, we see Jesus reminding His *called out ones* not to worry about their lives, what they will eat or drink, or about their bodies and what they shall wear, but rather, *"seek first his kingdom and his righteousness and all these things will be given to you as well."* The message here is that during times of warfare, both spiritual and bodily, as the Christian puts on the breastplate of righteousness, that of faith and love found only through Jesus Christ (not our own), then shall the believer find protection in time of need. As Christians put on the *"belt of truth and the breastplate of righteousness,"* they are firmly planted in readiness to preach the gospel of peace. In addition to all this, the third piece of spiritual equipment that needs be used by the Christian is the *"shield of faith."* The Greek word for shield is *thureos*, which, according to W. E. Vine, formerly meant a stone for closing the entrance of a cave; therefore, a shield, large and oblong, protecting every part of the soldier. The word is used metaphorically of faith, Ephesians 6:16, which the believer is to take up "in (*en* in the original) all" (all that has just been mentioned), i.e., as affecting the whole of his activities."

Whereas, the shield has long been known as a military piece of equipment to ward off incoming missiles from enemy forces, in Ephesians, we are told by the apostle Paul that the Christian's shield is faith in Jesus Christ, who through His almighty power is able to extinguish the flaming arrows of the evil one. We are told in James 4:7 that as we resist the devil, he will flee us. However, even though we are often weak in resisting temptations, the Lord's protective powers are still in force and will protect the *called out ones* during times of trials. In 2 Peter 2:4-9, he reiterates that the Lord can (and has always been able to) rescue the believer:

> For if God did not spare angels, when they sinned, but sent them to hell, putting them into gloomy dungeons to be held for judgment; 5 if he did not spare the ancient world when he brought the flood on its ungodly people, but protected Noah, a preacher of righteousness, and seven others; 6 if he condemned the cities of Sodom and Gomorrah by burning them to ashes, and made them an example of what is going to happen to the ungodly; 7 and if he rescued Lot, a righteous man, who was distressed by the filthy lives of lawless men 8 (for that righteous man, living among them day after day,

was tormented in his righteous soul by the lawless deeds he saw and heard) – 9 **if this is so, then the Lord knows how to rescue godly men from trials and to hold the unrighteous for the day of judgment, while continuing their punishment**, (2 Peter 2:4-9, NIV). [Underline and bold is by the author, solely for emphasis]

Here we see the *called out ones* donning their spiritual uniform, which includes the belt of truth in the knowledge that the only way humanity can be reconciled to the Father is through His Son, the Lord Jesus Christ. We also see the Christian being protected by the Lord's breastplate, which is (His) righteousness, that of faith and love. The third part of this spiritual uniform is the "shield of faith," which is provided by God as a result of submission to this truth, which results in the righteousness of His faith. As the Christian "believes," the automatic "shield of faith" is provided by God, which results in protection from the fiery darts of Satan.

Now we see the fourth part of the Christian arsenal for spiritual warfare, that being the "helmet of salvation." The Greek word for "helmet" is *perikephalaia* which (according to Vine) comes "from *peri*, around, and *kephale*, a head. It is used figuratively in Ephesians 6:17, with reference to salvation, and in 1 Thessalonians 5:8, where it is described as "the hope of salvation." The head is not to be regarded here as standing for the seat of intellect; the word is not used elsewhere in scripture. In Ephesians 6:17, salvation is a present experience of the Lord's deliverance of believers as those who are engaged in spiritual conflicts. In 1 Thessalonians 5:8, the hope is that of the Lord's return, which encourages the believer to resist the spirit of the age in which he lives." (W. E. Vine, *An Expository Dictionary of Biblical Words*, Page 543, Thomas Nelson Publishers)

It is interesting to note that W. E. Vine also agrees here that the "hope of salvation" mentioned in 1 Thessalonians 5:8 is viewed as the hope of the Lord's return, which will include the being "caught" aspect of *The Second Advent*. However, Vine does not venture to say that the "hope" is solely the fulfillment of the act of being "caught up." We will later be discussing the "blessed hope" of Titus 2:13 in greater detail.

But as we can plainly see, the obvious reference to the "helmet of salvation" is the reality that those who accept Jesus Christ as Lord and Savior are "covered" by God's salvation. It is said in Romans 10:9, 10 that "if you confess with your mouth (which is part of the head) that Jesus is Lord, and believe in your heart (which is seen as being protected by the breastplate of righteousness) that God raised Him from the dead, you will be saved!" It further states that it is with your heart that you believe, and it is with your mouth that you confess and are saved!

So here we see that the true Christian warrior is the individual that puts on "the belt of truth," that being that Jesus is the only way to the Father; the "breastplate of righteousness," which is the protective force that comes from the Lord's faith and love for us; the "shield of faith," which protects us from the fiery darts of Satan; and "the helmet of salvation," which is the "hope" of the Lord's soon return to reign as King of kings and Lord of lords. Finally, the fifth aspect of Christian military arsenal is the *"sword of the Spirit,"* probably the most important part of spiritual equipment for the Christian journey, more so, as the days grow shorter.

As the Christian soldier dons the spiritual accouterments, and readies the body as a living sacrifice for the preaching of the gospel, out of the spiritual sheath comes forth the sword of the spirit, which is the word of God! The word *sword* (in the Greek, according to Vine) has two distinct meanings. The word for *sword* in Ephesians 6:17 is *machaira*, which is "a short sword or dagger," whereas the word for "sword" in Revelation 1:16, 2:12, 16; 19:15, 21, is *rhomphaia*, a weapon of larger size. The word *rhomphaia* is used in Revelation to describe the Lord's judicial acts in the outpouring of His wrath on unbelievers. The word *machaira*, from where we get the word *machete*, is a short sword or dagger, and hereby implies that the Christian, through the power of the Holy Spirit, is to preach the word of God, and thereby provoke the conscience of mankind. It does not imply the presence of the physical or military-style power that only the Lord will generate. True, many Christian soldiers have been used by God in the performance of His almighty power to realize military-style miracles (David slaying Goliath with his slingshot, as one example). However, the message being conveyed in Ephesians 6:17 is that the Christian, especially in the latter days and times of tribulation, will be seen preaching the gospel of Jesus Christ, and not engaged in physical combat against the armies of the Beast. True, the Two Witnesses in Revelation 11:1-14 are seen performing great feats (power to shut up the sky so that it will not rain, turning water into blood and striking the earth with every kind of plague); however, it appears that they alone will have this type of power, while the remaining believers will be limited to evangelizing in the traditional manner. In these verses (Ephesians 6:14-17), we see the Christian soldier moving forward in life, carrying the message of Jesus Christ to all mankind with the "sword of the Spirit," (the little sword or dagger), whereas the Two Witnesses (for three and a half years) and especially the Lord at His Second Advent, will yield the much larger and awesome sword (*rhomphaia*) of prophesying the impending wrath and judgment of God.

It bears repeating (as stated in an earlier chapter) that the Christian nature is not one of retaliation, nor will it include one of waging war alongside Christ when he returns, as Hal Lindsey asserts in his book, *The Rapture*, page 19. Here, Mr. Lindsey quotes Revelation, Chapter 19, in an attempt to prove that the *Christian Church* is already in heaven, where he sees it supposedly experiencing the marriage and wedding supper, and supposedly returning as the "armies" (vs. 14) that come with Him when He returns to judge the earth." True, the *ecclesia* will be involved in the administrative Judgment process *after* the Lord returns. However, scripture does not identify the *Christian Church* as being part of the armies the Lord uses to wage war! Mr. Lindsey very conveniently omitted two verses (10 and 13 of Chapter 19) to make it appear as though the Bride (which he believes is the *Christian Church*) is now saddled upon white horses and is following the Lord as part of His war-waging entourage. As we pointed out in a previous chapter, the *ecclesia* is not seen as part of the Lord's armies in Revelation 19. Neither should the *called out ones* be viewed in a human militaristic sense; but rather, as an army of soldiers whose weapon is the word of God and whose main responsibility is to preach the gospel of Jesus Christ. The Christian is never encouraged to fight, retaliate or militarily force people or nations to abide in God or in His ways. Although many Christians have served in the military and have engaged in physical battle in a myriad of wars throughout history, the military branches they patriotically served under were armies of various nations, not God's army. God could very well have supported these various nations at one time or another, but they were not God's armies in the sense that the war was between the *Christian Church* verses other nations or other religions. On the contrary, the Christian is exhorted to turn the other cheek. In Matthew 5:38-48, we see Jesus specifically stating what kind of attitude Christians should have towards others, especially our enemies:

> You have heard that it was said, 'Eye for eye, and tooth for tooth.' 39 But I tell you, do not resist an evil person. **If someone strikes you on the right cheek, turn to him the other also.** 40 And if someone wants to sue you and take your tunic, let him have your cloak as well. 41 If someone forces you to go one mile, go with him two miles. 42 Give to the one who asks you, and do not turn away from the one who wants to borrow from you. 43 You have heard that it was said, 'Love your neighbor' and hate your enemy.' 44 But I tell you: **Love your enemies and pray for those who persecute**

<u>you</u>, 45 that you may be sons of your Father in heaven. He causes His sun to rise on the evil and the good, and sends rain on the righteous and the unrighteous. 46 If you love those who love you, what reward will you get? Are not even the tax collectors doing that? 47 And if you greet only your brothers, what are you doing more than others? Do not even pagans do that? 48 Be perfect, therefore, as your heavenly Father is perfect, (Matthew 5:38-48, NIV). [Underline and bold is by the author, solely for emphasis]

More on turning the other cheek later in another chapter, but it is important that we interject this group of scriptures to remind the Christian that being a soldier for Christ does not entail physical or militaristic retaliation. Instead, it requires the preaching of the gospel of Jesus Christ in faith and love, in His righteousness, through His spiritual sword (which is the word of God) and under His protective shield and breastplate of righteousness. All He asks of us is to put on the "belt of truth," and be ready to do His will. All the spiritual accouterments for this warfare are given freely to the Christian, and its reloading power comes as we abide in Him through the spiritual agency of the Holy Spirit.

In Ephesians 6:18, Paul adds the finishing touch to the appropriating of these elements by stating that our source of ammunition comes when we pray in the Spirit on all occasions with all kinds of prayers and requests. He goes on to say that *"With this in mind* (knowledge of God's provisions), *be alert and always keep praying for all the saints."* The word for "alert" in the Greek is *agrupneo*, which (according to W. E. Vine) means, "to be sleepless (from *agreuo*, to chase, and *hupnos*, sleep). It is used metaphorically, to be watchful, in Mark 13:33; Luke 21:36; Ephesians 6:18; and Hebrews 13:17. The word expresses not mere wakefulness, but the watchfulness of those who are intent upon a thing. The main connotation is that of being "spiritually" awake and not necessarily going without sleep. In Mark 13:33, it states to *"be on guard! Be alert! You do not know when that time will come!"* In Luke 21:36, it states to *"Be always on the watch and pray that you may be able to escape all that is about to happen, and that you may be able to stand before the Son of Man!"* The Greek word for "alert (*agrupneo*)" is used as "watch" in Hebrews 13:17, as it describes the need for Christians to obey and submit to their elders (Gr. *hegeomai*, guides): *"They keep watch over you as men who must give an account."* The Greek word *"agrupneo*, alert" henceforth, is meant to convey an ever watchfulness of spiritual residency with (and in) the Lord through prayer! As the Day of the Lord approaches, and as appears that Christians are destined for times of great tribulation, during the reign of the Beast, then the putting on of God's armor is required even more so! In Romans 12:14-21, we see the apostle Paul exhorting the Christian concerning this period of time, and the effect it will have on the unbeliever:

> Bless those who persecute you; bless and do not curse. 15 Rejoice with those who rejoice; mourn with those who mourn. 16 Live in harmony with one another. Do not be proud, but be willing to associate with people of low position. Do not be conceited. 17 Do not repay anyone evil for evil. Be careful to do what is right in the eyes of everybody. 18 If it is possible, as far as it depends on you, live at peace with everyone. 19 **Do not take revenge, my friends, but leave room for God's wrath, for it is written: "It is mine to avenge; I will repay,"** says the Lord. 20 On the contrary: "If your enemy is hungry, feed him; if he is thirsty, give him something to drink. **In doing this, you will heap burning coals on his head**." 21 Do not be overcome by evil, but overcome evil with good, (Romans 12:14-21, NIV). [Underline and bold is by the author, solely for emphasis]

In verse 20, we see that in our kindness to the enemy, those acts will in themselves cause the unbeliever to repent. The word for "coals" in the Greek (according to W. E. Vine) is *anthrax*, signifying retribution by kindness, *i.e.*, that, by conferring a favor on your enemy, you recall the wrong he has done to you, so that he repents, with pain of heart." This truth was known by the Israelites from the book of Proverbs:

> If your enemy is hungry, give him food to eat, if he is thirsty, give him water to drink. 22 In doing this, you will heap burning coals on his head, and the Lord will reward you, (Proverbs 25: 21, 22, NIV).

The key in verse 21 is, as we feed and give drink to the thirsty enemy, a repentance results, which is rewarded by the Lord. Once again, in Romans 12:19-21, we see Paul exhorting the Christian not to retaliate by taking revenge, leave room for God's wrath. On the contrary, Paul exhorts the Christian to not be overcome by evil but to overcome evil with good.

There is, unfortunately, a strong backlash mounting within the Christian community against the heathen world. Some even finding justification to act in a non-Christian manner all the while quoting scripture. We see a mounting force by many, even amongst the evangelical community, under the misinterpretation of scripture that promulgate and support military buildups, political doctrines and personalities in the name of anti-communism and anti-terrorism. True, Communism and terrorism are anti-Christian acts and philosophies the world would be better off under Christian-oriented leadership. However, two wrongs don't make a right. It is no more Christian to blow up abortion clinics than it is to perform abortions. It is no more Christian to kill a person by the electric chair than it was for that individual who took a person's life. It is no more Christian to bomb another country solely because it fired the first strike. But yet, in its human weakness, and its lack of faith in God to avenge the wrongs, mankind continues to retaliate against aggressive entities. Nation against nation, brother against brother, husband against wife, neighbor against neighbor, and we continually find ourselves using religious rhetoric to justify our actions. But that is not what God intended then, nor does He today.

Many professing Christians will experience eye-opening realities as troubles mount; many will acquiesce to the socio-political pressures of today's world, some to the point of accepting any lies (the mark of the beast?) in order to survive. But, it will be the true, born-again, Holy Spirit-gifted Christian that will be used by God during this awesome period approaching mankind. It will be those valiant soldiers of the cross, those who arm themselves with the "belt of truth," those who put on the "breastplate of righteousness," those who have "fitted feet with the readiness that comes from the gospel of peace," those who take up the "shield of faith" to extinguish the flaming arrows of demonic forces, those who take the "helmet of salvation" and the blessed hope thereof, those who take the "sword of the Spirit," which is the word of God, those who maintain alertness and watchfulness by abiding in Jesus Christ through prayer and supplication. It is these faithful ones that God will use to proclaim the gospel of Jesus Christ to the world, more so as the Day of the Lord draws nigh. And it will be these *chosen ones*, the *elect*; these *called out ones*, the *ecclesia*, those that will "shrink not" during times of major trials and temptations at the hands of antichristian forces, even unto death. It is these that will receive a crown of righteousness at the Second Advent of Jesus Christ. It is these, who *"being confident that He that began a good work in them will carry it on to completion until the day of Jesus Christ,"* (Philippians 1:6, NIV). It is these that will be "pure and blameless until the day of Christ." (Philippians 1:9). It is these that *by the power that enables Him to bring everything under control, will transform our lowly bodies so that they will be like His glorious body,* (Philippians 3:12). It is these (along with those who have already died in Christ) that will be "caught together" with those that remain alive at the last trump to meet and greet the returning Lord at His Second Advent. It is these that will sit on thrones alongside Jesus Christ to rule with Him on earth forever and ever. Many are those who mouth the word of Jesus but believe not in His overall redemptive plan. Many are those who say, "Yes! I'm a Christian" but choose not to put on the full armor of God. Many are those who hang onto their salvation solely by their belief and hope in a secret pre-tribulation escape to heaven, and by merely clocking in at local churches, or by tuning to their favorite evangelist on media.

Many who still fear the consequences of joining God's true army will be legion. Many Christian soldiers will travail in far away regions, parts known only to God and those they minister to, soldiers whose names will never be seen or heard of in public light, but solely by the great record keeper of the Lamb's Book of Life. Many a Christian soldier will don spiritual uniforms, fearing not for their own safety or life, in quest of bringing the message that Jesus Christ died on the cross to pay for their sins. These are the true soldiers of the cross! These are the ones who are prepared to give up everything and follow Christ, even unto to death! Are you ready to make such a commitment? Are you ready to pick up and carry your cross, regardless of the cost?

> If anyone comes to me and does not hate his father and mother, his wife and children, his brothers and sisters-- **yes, even his own life**--he cannot be my disciple.27 **and anyone who does not carry his cross and follow me cannot be my disciple**, Luke 14:26,27, NIV). [Bold, italics and underline is by the author, solely for emphasis]

Onward Christian soldiers!

Chapter 9
"AND LEAD US NOT INTO TEMPTATION"

In the previous chapter, the Christian soldier dons the spiritual equipment for end times warfare, which includes the "belt of truth," the "breastplate of righteousness," the "shield of faith," the "helmet of salvation," and the "sword of the spirit, which is the word of God." This is the true battle regalia the Christian soldier should be adorned with to combat today's persecutions, as well as the one that will be required during those times of great tribulation that loom in the immediate horizon. Yet, it is also obvious that within the word of God, the redemptive assurance for *called out ones* is fulfilled primarily through prayer. The subject of prayer requires a volume of books; but, in this chapter, we will focus only on that great prayer that the Lord Jesus Himself urged us to pray at all times: THE LORD'S PRAYER! Let's read it from Matthew 6:9-13:

> This is how you should pray: 'Our Father in heaven, hallowed be your name, 10 your kingdom come, your will be done, on earth as it is in heaven. 11 Give us today our daily bread. 12 Forgive us our debts, as we also have forgiven our debtors. 13 **And lead us not into**

> **temptation**, but deliver us from the evil one, (Matthew
> 6:9-13, NIV). [Bold and underline is by the author,
> solely for emphasis]

We are convinced beyond a shadow of doubt that this great prayer
was specifically intended by the Lord for Christians to pray, more
so as the last days appear imminent. This prayer specifically
makes requests for the present heavenly kingdom to come down
to earth, that the complete state of holiness that exists in God's
present dwelling place in the heavens will identically be here on
earth, where God will eventually (and finally) dwell amongst
mankind as was His original plan back in the Garden of Eden.
This prayer also includes a request for sustenance (both physical
and spiritual), the bread representing food and Christ Himself;
and for the constant forgiveness needed for our daily sins, as
we should also forgive daily those who have sinned against us.
The final aspect of this great prayer addresses the issue of the
Christian seeking help to not fall into temptation, and to be
delivered from the clutches of the evil one, that fallen angelic
being known to everyone as Satan. The Greek noun for the "evil"
one (according to *W. E. Vine) is *poneros* (in the adjectival form),
which is describing his very nature; "akin to *poneros*, labor, toil,
denotes evil that causes labor, pain, sorrow and malignant evil."
Poneros is used to describe Satan in Matthew 5:37, 6:13; 13:19, 38;
Luke 11:4 (in some texts); John 17:15; Eph. 6:16; 2 Thessalonians
3:3; 1 John 2:13, 14; 3:12; and 5:18, 19. No more identification
on the subject of evil is warranted, necessary or desired. (* W. E.
Vine, *An Expository Dictionary of Biblical Words*, Thomas Nelson
Publishing, Page 380)

A complete study on the Lord's Prayer alone would warrant reams
of paper; however, the aspect concerning "temptation" is the one
we will focus our attention on. The word "temptation" in the Greek
is *peirasmos*, which (according to W. E. Vine) means "trials with

a beneficial purpose and effect (a) of "trials" or "temptations," Divinely permitted or sent, Luke 22:28; Acts 20:19; Jas. 1:2; 1 Pet. 1:6; 4:12, RV., "trial" (AV., "to try) 2 Pet. 2:9 (singular); Rev. 3:10, RV., "trial" (AV. "temptation) in Jas. 1:12, "temptation" apparently has meanings (1) and (2) combined, and is used in the widest sense; (b) with a good or neutral significance, Gal. 4:14, of Paul's physical infirmity, "a temptation" to the Galatians converts, of such a kind as to arouse feelings of natural repugnance; (c) of trials of a varied character, Matt. 6:13 and Luke 11:4, where believers are commanded to pray not to be led into such forces beyond their own control." Vine goes on to state that *peirasmos* is also applied to Matthew 26:41; Mark 14:38; Luke 22:40, 46, **where they are commanded to watch and pray against entering into temptations by their own carelessness or disobedience; in all such cases God provides "the way of escape,"** 1 Corinthians 10:13 (where PEIRASMOS occurs twice)." (W. E. Vine, *An Expository Dictionary Of Biblical Words*, Page 1129, Thomas Nelson Publishers) [Bold and underline is by the author, solely for emphasis]

Vine also offers other examples of how the Greek word *peirasmos* is used of "trials definitely designed to lead to wrong doing, temptation, Luke 4:13, 8:13, 1 Tim. 6:9," and also the example "of trying or challenging God, by men" spoken of in Hebrews 3:8. The word *peirasmos* is the noun, which comes from the Greek word *peira*, a trial, and the Greek word *peirazo*, the verb for "try". It is also the verb (*peirazo*) which is used for the word "test" in Mark 8:11; Luke 11:16; Acts 5:9 and 15:10, where we see examples of the Lord's authority being "tested" by the Pharisees," (W. E. Vine, *An Expository Dictionary Of Biblical Words*, Page 1129, Thomas Nelson Publishers)

However, our main concern in this chapter is with the word "temptation" as it relates to the Lord's prayer and its application to the *ecclesia*, especially in these troubled times (and those) that will increase even more so when the man of lawlessness is revealed. The Lord's Prayer states: *"And lead us not into temptation, but deliver us from the evil one."* The question one must ask, as we read this verse, is "Does the Lord now lead us into temptation?" "Is God responsible for the everyday trials and temptations that are being experienced by Christians on a daily basis?" These are very important questions, to say the least. The Bible clearly states that mankind was born with a sinful nature resulting from the first man's (Adam's) rebellion toward God (Romans 5:12), and the wages of that rebellion will (and continues to) result in death, (Romans 6:23). Paul recognized this more than anyone else and spoke at great length about the anguish of sin controlling the human species, and also who is the only person that can solve this dilemma (Romans 7:7-25):

> What a wretched man am I! Who will rescue me from this body of death? (Romans 7:24, NIV)

He provides the answer in the following passage:

> Thanks be to God – through Jesus Christ our Lord. (Romans 7:25, NIV)!

There is a continual struggle going on between good and evil, and the only known escape is through the forgiving power found in the atoning blood shed by Jesus Christ at Calvary. All Christians know that; but, why then, do we still continue to sin? Is that why we still suffer? Are we suffering as a result of sin? Is that why we are going through trials? Are we being punished for our daily sins? If we weaken during times of temptation and submit to them to the degree that we find ourselves continuing to do those things we know we shouldn't do, is it our fault? These are important questions that we will attempt to answer.

The word *peirasmos* is connected to the word *peira*, which (according to W. E. Vine) means "a making trial, an experiment, is used with *lambano*, to receive or take, in Hebrews 11:29, rendered 'assaying,' and verse 36, in the sense of 'having experienced of (akin, to assay, to try, had trial," [W. E. Vine, *An Expository Dictionary Of Biblical Words*, Page 1167, Thomas Nelson Publishers]. It is interesting to note that the word *peira* means *an experiment*, while also connoting an *assaying*. Much has been written about Christians being tested (as if by fire) by the great assayer, the Lord Jesus Christ. Webster's New World Dictionary defines 'assay' as "the analysis of an ore, alloy, drug, etc., to determine the nature, proportion, or purity of the ingredients." Could this mean that the Christian's temptations are really an experiment, a test to see how much we can endure, and only those who overcome these trials will pass the test and enter the Kingdom of God when the end comes?

Since accepting Jesus Christ as his personal Lord and Savior on January 5, 1975, the author has been growing strong in the knowledge of God's word and understanding more clearly His will. The author learned that by constant prayer and by studying the word, God's nature and His will for us are revealed more clearly each passing day. The author has experienced a greater degree of faith than ever before, having learned how to use God's power to overcome obstacles. But yet, the author finds himself making mistakes and acquiescing to various temptations that all humans are bombarded with. The Lord has given the author the strength to finally abstain totally from alcohol and other drugs, and God has given the author most of all an inner peace he never knew was possible. But yet, like all humans, still in the flesh, the author has yet to bring his body and soul into complete submission, and he will never see that day until Jesus Christ returns to complete the totality of His redemption plan. In the meantime, like all Christians, we continue to war against rulers, authorities and powers of this dark world:

> ...For our struggle is not against flesh and blood, but against the rulers, against the authorities, against the powers of this dark world and against the spiritual forces of evil in the heavenly realms, (Ephesians 6:12, NIV).

So, what about temptations? Does God place them on us? Does the Devil? Or are they merely the results of the sowing and reaping aspect inherent in the sinful nature of our fallen state? In the Lord's Prayer, we are exhorted to ask the Father to "lead us not into temptation," it being inferred by some that the Father in fact might be leading us into negative situations. But is He really dangling the carrot of sin and leading us into *temptation*, or is there a specific purpose for the *trial* or *experiment* of that moment?

The word for *lead* (according to W. E. Vine) is the Greek word *eis*, the primary preposition which means *to* or *into* (indicating the point reached or entered) and *phero*, a primary word meaning *to bear, carry, bring forth*. In other words, the word *lead* (in both accounts of the Lord's Prayer found in Matthew 6:13 and Luke 11:4) is *eisphero*, which literally means *to bring something forth into a certain point*. It is obvious that at the time of judgment, the Lord will be solely responsible for executing His wrath on unbelievers. However, during the more intense tribulation period, many will receive divine protection by the hand of God, whomsoever He chooses! It appears then that those who constantly have this prayer on their lips will obviously be walking in the Spirit as the Lord instructed us to do. As mankind is being led towards the final hour, God specifically tells us to pray that we fall not into that temptation, the great trial that will befall all of mankind. In Acts 17:20, we see the same word used when a group of Epicurean and Stoic philosophers began to dispute with Paul over the message he was "...*bringing* (eisphero) to them, which was *"strange ideas to our ears."* In Luke 5:18, 19, we see the same word being used to describe the incident where a paralytic was taken to the top of a roof and then was lowered in front of Jesus for healing, because they couldn't *"bring* (eisphero)*"* him through the door due to the large crowd. The word *eisphero* is also used in 1Timothy 6:7 in the NIV which reads, *"For we brought* (eisphero) *nothing into the world, and we can take nothing out of it."* [Parenthesis by the author, solely for emphasis]

These three examples clearly indicate that *eisphero* literally means to "bring forth" and, as it is applied in the Lord's Prayer, it obviously indicates that the Lord will have a hand in the temptations we experience. However, as it is applied to the increased period of temptation during times of intensified tribulations, it is very clear that those who are calling out the name of the Lord (Romans 10:13), with genuine faith and with the Lord's Prayer on their lips, will be divinely protected. Those who *walk* (Gr. *peripateo,* occupy) in the Spirit, those who have genuinely accepted Jesus Christ as Lord and Savior, redeemed by the blood of the lamb of God, will be doing His will, which includes a constant reciting of that plea He exhorted us to pray. It is ironic that the word *eisphero* is also the very same word used in Hebrews 13:11-12 which states that:

> The high priest carries (eispheros) the blood of animals into the Most Holy Place as a sin offering, but the bodies are burned outside the camp. And so Jesus also suffered outside the city gate to make the people holy through His own blood, (NIV). {Parenthesis by the author solely for emphasis]

When Christians say this prayer, *"and lead* (eispheros) *us not into temptation,"* they know that the judgment comes at the hands of the Lord, who is closing the final chapter of the world as we know it, through fire. However, those who are His children, His *called out ones,* will be in constant prayer, asking forgiveness for daily sins, repeatedly asking for His mercy – which He will provide! When the

Lord says, *Behold, I come like a thief! Blessed is he who stays awake and keeps his clothes with him, so that he may not go naked and be shamefully exposed* (Revelation 16:15), He is not addressing a group of people who are idly sitting by comfortably in the belief that they need only to join a church and thereby have assurance of salvation by sheer virtue of membership alone. God is a merciful God, and He alone decides who is truly sincere about their Christian commitment. However, the scriptures throughout indicate that, although we have been bestowed the gift of salvation, through grace and unmerited favor, many people will be surprised to find that God also is looking for an *ecclesia* that is actively walking in the spirit and doing the will of God, even if it means experiencing persecution unto death! There is no implying here that people have to be perfect in the sense of achieving holiness through their own righteous acts. Unfortunately, though, much of Christianity is guilty of "*having a form of Godliness but denying the power* (2 Timothy 3:5)," *always learning but never able to acknowledge the truth* (vs. 7). The verse, which states "*These people honor me with their lips, but their hearts are far from me. They worship me in vain; their teachings are but rules taught by men,*" is a lashing out by Jesus in Matthew 15:8 which was intended for the Pharisees of His time. However, the same can be said of many Christians who have joined various religious bodies, yet once having obtained membership, they use it as a license to appropriate grace as irresponsibly as one uses their overdrawn bank card. Not that the Lord won't forgive our daily sins (seventy times seven if necessary); however, this lack of reaching out to God (by not constantly walking in the spirit) can be stifling to the spiritual growth required to do His will, especially as the Day of the Lord's return draws nearer.

The author is thoroughly convinced in his heart that the *ecclesia* will go through intensified tribulation before the Lord returns, not because of any doctrines developed by theorists through self-interpreting the word of God; but, because the word of God explicitly states that the *called out ones* will experience persecutions, will endure many greater trials than being evidenced today, and the only available escape will come from God's divine *passing over* His people in the same manner He has throughout history. In these imminent end times, true *called out ones* need a Passover that can only be appropriated through a constant abiding in Him (and His Spirit) through prayer.

Many a day (in past times) the author spent hours before the throne of Grace, asking the Lord to deliver him from the insidious abuse of alcohol. He praises God even today that He was slow to anger and long-suffering. However, had the author reached out to Him with greater measure, had he resisted the Devil much earlier in life, God could have used him to reach even more people with the Gospel than he has so far. The author doesn't discount God's grace, he doesn't discount His long-suffering, and he also knows that He makes all things work for the good to those who love Him and who have been called according to His purpose (Romans 8:28). That past alcoholic crisis period has shown the author to be more loving and patient towards others and their respective weaknesses. But how foolish he feels in the realization that the power of God was always there for the asking, but he lacked faith! Yes! Even as a Christian, he lacked faith. When he came to the realization that nothing is more important than his relationship with Jesus Christ, not his job, not family, not money, not status, not so-called friends, not even his own life, not anything except for his walk with Christ, then is when he saw the Holy Spirit begin a greater work than he ever imagined! Then, and only then did he feel the power of God begin to create a new work, which resulted in having all these things added back to him in greater measure. Unlike Job, who committed no crime that warranted his afflictions, the author spent the majority of his life seeking self-indulging pleasure and earthly glory and fame and was paying a heavy price for it, before surrendering to the love, grace and mercy the Lord provides to those who vigorously seek Him. The price the author paid for his past indiscretions was not punishment meted out by a vindictive God. The price was an automatic reaping of the wages of sin the author himself sowed! Even now, the author has yet to reach the physical and spiritual perfection that his soul cries out for. But he is running the race, using every ounce of spiritual and physical energy he can muster to be found doing the will of God. And he does accomplish his daily tasks, regardless of the ever-recurring physical and emotional pains he experiences daily (resulting from many past indiscretions) by being constantly in His word so that he may be thoroughly equipped for every good work. But this is not enough. The author and all Christians need to be found in constant prayer, including the Lord's Prayer, which he silently repeats daily, being the last words to come from his mouth and heart when he retires at night.

When the word *eisphero* (to bring forth or lead) is used, it includes someone or something that is bringing the subject forth. In the case of the Lord's Prayer, it appears that the Lord here is controlling the temptation. However, this prayer tells us to pray that giving in to that temptation need not be the case, and God will provide an escape because He answers the prayer. Those who are walking in the Spirit will have this particular prayer answered in a positive manner. And these prayers cannot be answered unless there is a profound fellowship with Christ, regardless of the cost or sacrifice of worldly pursuits and creature comforts.

The second part of that particular verse follows the two-pronged request. Not only to not be led into temptation, but that we *called out ones* also may be delivered from the evil one during the intensified period of tribulation that will prevail at the hands of the man of lawlessness during the last days! The Greek word for *deliver* is *rhuomai*, which means to *draw to oneself*, akin to Gr. *eruo*, to drag, where we see a picture of the Lord literally "dragging" the Christian unto Himself. This is a deliverance that does not convey the physical redemption of our bodies (1 Corinthians 15:54) and the overall *salvation* (Gr. soteria, salvation), spoken of in Acts 4:12, that is fulfilled at His Parousia. But, rather, it's a *rescue* (Gr. *sozo*, deliverance) act where the Christian is physically and temporarily protected from danger and suffering. The prayer herein implies that during times of persecution the Christian is not seen as being removed (or snatched) from earth up to heaven. But, rather, being divinely rescued from the onslaught of the devil's wickedness and persecutions, more so as the *ecclesia* finds itself victim to the diabolical wiles of the man of lawlessness. The same message is found in Revelation 3:10, in God's message to the church in Philadelphia, where it states that "Since you have kept my command to endure patiently, I will also *keep* you (Gr. *tereo*, kept from) the hour of *trial* (Gr. *peirasmos*, temptation) that is going to come upon the whole world to *test* (Gr. *peirazo*, to make proof of) those who live on earth. That "great testing" is to include all who live on earth, and all who *endure* (Gr. *bastazo*, bearing under hardships) for His name's sake will be *kept* (Gr. *sozo*, safe, well) from the "hour of trial," which will be testing men's faith in Jesus Christ. On one hand, God is "bringing forth (*eisphero*)" the trial and, on the other hand, He states that those who call upon the name of the Lord, those who are constantly walking in the spirit, those whose lips are found praying the Lord's Prayer will be *guarded* (*tereo*, kept from) during the trial itself! Obviously, this does not mean that we are to be found repeating the Lord's Prayer 24-hours (non-stop) per day. However, as we are confronted with times of peril, there is nothing else that one could better do than to reach out to our Lord by reciting this magnificent prayer!

In James 1:12, it states, 'Blessed is the man who perseveres under trial (Gr. peirasmos, temptations), because when he has stood the test (Gr. dokimos, found approved), he will receive the crown (Gr. stephanos) of life that God promised to those who love Him." This, of course, speaks about the daily trials that Christians are experiencing today, but more so will be applied to the true, faith-believing, spirit-walking Christian during the time that the "man of lawlessness" seeks to purge and destroy the world of believers, (Revelation. 13:5-7).

However, in the following verse (James 1:13), we see a statement that appears to contradict this very premise. It states,

> "When tempted, no one should say 'God is tempting (Gr. peirazo, testing) me.' For God cannot be tempted (Gr. apeisasto, cannot be tempted) by evil, nor does He tempt (Gr. peirazo, test) anyone; but each one is tempted (peirazo, tested) when by his own evil desire, he is dragged away and enticed. Then after desire has conceived, it gives birth to sin; and sin, when it is full-grown, gives birth to death."

What we see here could be misconstrued as a major contradiction of scripture; however, it is evidently clear that the temptation spoken of in James 1:12, 13 is not necessarily talking about the "great trial" that will befall mankind during times of great tribulation, but it speaks about the acquiescing or giving in to life's flesh-oriented temptations, which are trials in and of themselves. These trials (giving in to alcohol, drugs, elicit sexual desires, anger, hate, jealousy, sin ad nauseam infinitum) automatically result in destruction. This destruction is not necessarily direct vindictive punishment from God for the sin itself; but, rather, it's an in-built destruction that comes from sowing negativity and eventually reaping the consequences. The results (pain, anguish, sickness and even death) do not necessarily come from a trigger-happy God who is up in Heaven, shotgun in hand, waiting for individuals to stumble so He can have a reason to blow them away. The results from sin are automatically built into the nature of His fallen creation and do not necessarily require any immediate action on God's part. It is the author's belief that one of God's most immutable laws (if not the most) is that whatever a man sows, this he will also reap, (Galatians 6:7). No matter what a person does in life (whether good or bad) there is a natural cause and effect system that God has created in mankind that is inescapable!

There is a big hue and cry from many evangelicals that the AIDS (Acquired Immune Disease Syndrome) epidemic is God's way of punishing the homosexual community for its lewd and lascivious lifestyle. Although homosexual activity is loathsome to God, this disease is engulfing this community not so much because God is in heaven, ready to pour out His immediate wrath on it. God's temporal cause-and-effect nature (the sowing and reaping effect He built within mankind) automatically takes effect. This same principle applies to the usage of drugs and alcohol, and to those who let anger, jealousies and hate control their lives. This sowing and reaping aspect built within mankind is possibly one of God's most immutable laws, regardless of grace. Although we can be forgiven for these sins, and eternal salvation can still be claimed, temporal punishment for those sins is still required. However, when the perpetrators of these activities repent, and turn to God for forgiveness, a healing process can take place. When we give in to these temptations (even though they are diabolically placed before us), the result is sin, which causes death. But when we are confronted with these temptations, and turn to God's strength (and grace), the power of the Holy Spirit can help heal, recover and *restore* (Gr. *sozo*, deliver) us to health from these temporal afflictions.

In Matthew 8:25, when the disciples in the boat were being threatened by the storming waves, they cried out, *"Lord, save (sozo) us. We're going to drown!"* Here we see temporal deliverance from danger. This word *sozo* is the same word used in Mark 13:20, where we see Jesus discussing the times of great tribulation, stating that *"If the Lord had not cut short these days, no one would <u>survive</u> (Gr. sozo, be rescued, temporarily delivered from). But for the sake of the elect (Gr. ekloge,* the chosen ones), *He has shortened them."* Once again, the word here for "save" is *sozo*, meaning a temporal deliverance; whereas, the overall *salvation*, the total redemption of believers, which is finalized at the Lord's Parousia (arrival and presence), is the *soteria*, the spiritual and eternal deliverance granted immediately by God to those who accept His conditions of repentance and faith in the Lord Jesus Christ. *Sozo* does not imply "a-removal-from-earth-to-heaven-rescue" from the present dangers (as theorists contend in their secret Pre-Tribulation escape to heaven theories); but, rather, *sozo* represents a temporal rescuing and protection *from* these dangers. The *salvation* (Gr. noun *soteria*, salvation) from God was established (or purchased) when Jesus paid the price at Calvary and has been appropriated for those who believe and do the will of the Father. However, its overall realization and completion is not fulfilled until the Lord returns after the times of intensified tribulation!

The final topic of this chapter embodies the "temptation" suffered at the hands of Satan himself. The Devil is called the "tempter" in Matthew 4:3 and 1 Thessalonians 3:5. The word "tempter" here is *peirazo*, the very same word used for "test or tester." The same person who tested Jesus in the desert (after fasting forty days and forty nights) is the very same individual we see being spoken about in 1 Thessalonians 3:5. In the preceding verse, Paul is telling the church at Thessalonica that he wished he could be with them, but sent Timothy instead to help strengthen and encourage them in their faith, during their *trials* (Gr. *thlipsis*, tribulations): *"You know quite well that we were destined for them. In fact, when we were with you, we kept telling you that we would be persecuted* (Gr. *thlipsis*, tribulation)." Paul goes on to say that these persecutions have been, and will continue to come, from the hand of the tempter. Paul was showing concern for the church, fearing that in *"some way the tempter might <u>have tempted</u>* (Gr. *peirazo*, tested) *you and our efforts might have been useless,* (1 Thessalonians 3:5, NIV)." The devil is "testing" people's faith daily. He capitalizes on our imperfect nature and constantly lies (he being the father of lies, John 8:45) to discredit the saving grace of God. He is the secret power of lawlessness (2 Thessalonians 2:7), which plagues the whole world, he being the Prince of the Power of the Air, (Ephesians 2:2). He will continue to test and persecute the *ecclesia* in his invisible capacity until he is loosed for a short season, at which time he will unleash his supernatural powers through the person of the Beast (or anti-Christ), giving him the power to openly wage war on the saints (the *ecclesia*), which will include all who have faith in Christ. He is the great "tempter" now, and in those increased times of great and intensified tribulation will be an even greater menace, having given great power to the man of lawlessness to openly persecute those who hold to the testimony of Jesus Christ, (Rev. 12:11, 17).

Hearts Pure As Gold

It is a well known fact that Jesus, besides experiencing death at Calvary, went through many trials and temptations (Luke 22:28), as did Paul (Acts 20:19), as will God's *ecclesia* (James 1:2), today, and more so when the man of lawlessness is revealed. But will these trials befall the *called out ones* because they have brought them upon themselves, or will they be divinely permitted for a specific reason?

As most Christians believe, once a person comes to Christ, they are henceforth "saved" and are entitled to all the benefits due to all members of His *ecclesia*. Most Christians believe one of those benefits is a secret escape to heaven seven years before (or immediately before) the 42 months the beast dictates world affairs, and the subsequent outpouring of God's wrath on mankind before *The Second Advent*. Part of this belief is an irrefutable fact, as the scriptures bear witness. But yet, the author has presented much scripture in the last six chapters that specifically state God's *ecclesia* will experience intensified tribulation before Jesus returns. Yet, theorists and their adherents believe that the *Christian Church* cannot be seen as experiencing any further trials, and they will continue to challenge and deny any such notion. They believe that there is no way that God would allow the *Christian Church* go through any persecutions or any form of tribulation, and this is why they have concocted their soothing secret escape to heaven mythologies. Rather than being painfully honest and candid about what the *Christian Church* is truly going to experience, they conjure up these fanciful and appeasing doctrines, primarily to gain for themselves profit and glory. For what other reason would they withhold the truth from God's *ecclesia* ? Scriptures abound that specifically state the *called out ones* will experience even greater trials as the Day of the Lord gets closer. What theorists and their followers fail to see is that God has a specific purpose for this tribulation, and that purpose is clearly spelled out in scripture. What is God's purpose for allowing His *ecclesia* to go through persecution? One of the main reasons is that God is seeking a church that will be comprised of people with pure hearts; hearts as pure as refined gold, and He Himself is the assayer!

Throughout the Bible, God and His prophets forever speak about a purifying process of the heart that befalls all of His *called out ones*. Many scripture verses make specific reference to this process in metaphor likening it to precious ore being smelted to remove the dross, that scum that forms on the surface of molten metal. But yet, Christian theorists and their adherents continue to claim and believe that if a person has already accepted Jesus Christ as Lord and Savior, no refining process is necessary. However, and according to 1 Peter 4:12-19, it appears that even though thousands upon thousands are repenting of their sins and surrendering their hearts to Jesus, the Bible clearly states that salvation includes a special purging and refining process that will continue to occur until *The Second Advent*, and it will come to pass merely because we are Christians:

<u>Dear friends, do not be surprised at the painful trial</u>
<u>you are suffering, as though something strange were</u>

<u>**happening to you.**</u> 13 But rejoice that you participate in the sufferings of Christ, <u>**so that you may be overjoyed when his glory is revealed.**</u> 14 If you are insulted because of the name of Christ, you are blessed, for the Spirit of glory and of God rests on you. 15 If you suffer, it should not be as a murderer or thief or any other kind of criminal, or even as a meddler. 16 However, if you suffer as a Christian, do not be ashamed, but praise God that you bear that name. 17 <u>**For it is time for judgment to begin with the family of God; and if it begins with us, what will the outcome be for those who do not obey the gospel of God?**</u> 18 And, "If it is hard for the righteous to be saved, what will become of the ungodly and the sinner?" 19 So then, <u>**those who suffer according to God's will should commit themselves to their faithful Creator and continue to do good,**</u> (1 Peter 4:12-19, NIV). [Underline and bold is by the author, solely for emphasis]

This purification concept is difficult for Christians to comprehend, much more so for unbelievers. But, as Peter states, *"do not be surprised at the painful trial you are suffering, as though something strange were happening to you."* While many profess to be people of faith, during the end times (and much to their surprise) their faith will be tested as never before. Christians may not be aware of this fact, and those who are aware have been fearfully or timidly withholding this truth from many of their respective flocks, for nefarious reasons. There is no excuse for theorists who are in the know to withhold this fact from those they have been entrusted to care for, as shepherds of their respective flocks. Yet, they continue to do so, many in fear that their flock will scatter and subsequently cause their church membership and financial donations to decline. The Bible, both Old and New Testament is replete with specific scriptures attesting to the fact of tribulations. But yet, too many church leaders are fearful of providing their parishioners with this truth, primarily in fear of losing members in their respective congregations. Instead they sugarcoat the gospel through soothing mythologies that will bring them praise, accolades and a steady flow of financial donations. Unfortunately, modern-day churches are more concerned about increasing their coffers, their community status, and the stature and grandeur of their church buildings, rather than on the true spiritual growth and maturation needed by their parishioners, regardless of how small its membership.

But God's word clearly states that Christians will experience much tribulation in order to enter the Kingdom of God. The righteous ones of old were very aware that God's people are destined for this testing of faith. For example, In the Book of Job, which encompasses the testing of a person's faith as never before, we see the attitude of a righteous man of God that paints a perfect picture of the type of faith that God seeks in today's Christian:

> Then Job replied: 2 "**Even today my complaint is bitter**; his hand is heavy in spite of my groaning. 3 If only I knew where to find him; if only I could go to his dwelling! 4 I would state my case before him and fill my mouth with arguments. 5 I would find out what he would answer me, and consider what he would say. 6 Would he oppose me with great power? No, he would not press charges against me. 7 There an upright man could present his case before him, and I would be delivered forever from my judge. 8 But if I go to the east, he is not there; if I go to the west, I do not find him. 9 when he is at work in the north, I do not see him; when he turns to the south, I catch no glimpse of him. 10 **But he knows the way that I take; when he has tested me, I will come forth as gold**," (Job 23:1-10, NIV). [Underline and bold is by the author, solely for emphasis]

In Psalms 66:8-10, we see the psalmist praising God for His faithfulness, which includes this same truth of being tested and refined as the smelter refines precious metal:

> Praise our God, O peoples, let the sound of his praise be heard; 9 he has preserved our lives and kept our feet from slipping. 10 **For you, O God, tested us; you refined us like silver**, (Psalms 66:8-10, NIV). [Underline and bold is by the author, solely for emphasis]

However, this refining process is not intended as a means to punish or rid Christians of any remaining sins, as if perfection could come about through their own righteousness; but, rather, it is a smelting process that increases our faith, that which lay in our hearts:

> The crucible for silver and the furnace for gold, **but the Lord tests the heart**, (Proverbs 17:3, NIV). [Underline and bold is by the author, solely for emphasis]

From the beginning of time, God has been more concerned about what resides in mankind's hearts, not the outward appearance as men do (1 Samuel 16:7); the Lord seeks those who are pure in heart, for they will be blessed and see God (Matthew 5:8). He has, from the beginning of time, been searching our hearts, knowing the mind of the Spirit, which intercedes for the *called out ones* in accordance with God's will, (Romans 8:27).

Many of God's chosen people have strayed away. Israel, God's original *ecclesia*, and even those who today call themselves Christians, have backslidden by trusting in their own strength, intelligence, ego and their own form of wisdom, believing them to be godly enough to conduct their lives as they see fit. But God loves His children, He loves those He has chosen from the very foundation of the world, and

He will bring them back through whatever means necessary. He will try His *called out ones*, He will put them through various trials, and He will place them in His smelting pot and refine them. That period of intensified testing and assaying several years before *The Second Advent* will also serve a greater purpose. That purpose is for bringing more people into His kingdom before He pours out His wrath on the rest of mankind.

It is a major portion of theorists' contention that the so-called "Great Tribulation" is specifically designed solely for the Jews, which they call 'the time of Jacob's trouble,' (Jeremiah 30:7). Therefore, they contend the *Christian Church* cannot be on earth during this grievous period. However, after prayerfully scrutinizing the scriptures, this cannot be so. We have presented scripture upon scripture that all the promises that God made to the nation of Israel in the Old Testament are being fulfilled by the entity we call the *Christian Church*. This is not to say that the so-called *Christian Church* is now *spiritual* Israel. As we stated in Chapter 1, what modern day Christians call the *Christian Church* (which they believe did not come into existence until the Day of Pentecost) is the Holy Spirit enhanced entity of faith-believing Israel, His original *ecclesia*, His *called out ones*, who by faith believe in Messiah! A group of scriptures that testifies to this is found in the Old Testament, where theorists contend that the *Christian Church* (or God's chosen people) was never mentioned:

> "Awake, O sword, against my shepherd, against the man who is close to me!" declares the Lord Almighty. **"Strike the shepherd, and the sheep will be scattered,** and I will turn my hand against the little ones. 8 In the whole land," declares the Lord, "two-thirds will be struck down and perish; yet one-third will be left in it. 9 **This third I will bring into the fire; I will refine them like silver and test them like gold.** They will call on

my name and I will answer them; I will say, '**They are my people,' and they will say, 'The Lord is our God,** (Zechariah 13:7-9, NIV). [Underline and bold is by the author, solely for emphasis]

Here we see a reference being made to Jesus' crucifixion and the scattering of the sheep (*called out ones*). Here we see where the one-third remaining will experience a refining process (a testing of one's faith) during the period preceding His Parousia. This refining process is spoken about in 1 Corinthians 3:13-15, the scriptural verses that even theorists agree speaks about the time when Christians will appear before the Judgment Seat of Christ:

> His work will be shown for what it is, because the Day will bring it to light. **It will be revealed with fire, and the fire will test the quality of each man's work.** 14 If what he has built survives, he will receive his reward. 15 If it is burned up, he will suffer loss; he himself will be saved, but only as one escaping through flames, (1 Corinthians. 3:13-15, NIV). [Bold and underline is by the author, solely for emphasis]

It is a fact well known by most Christians that the quality of our individual works will be tested by fire to see if they survive. At that time, on that day, the Lord will bring to light what is hidden in darkness and will expose the motives of men's hearts. At that appointed time (His Parousia, which no man knows the day or hour), all these things will come to pass. If the things that a person did while in the body burn up, he will suffer loss, although he himself will be saved as one escaping through fire. All of these things mentioned so far blend harmoniously with the events spoken about in the Book of Daniel. During that time, as stated in Daniel 11:33-35:

"Those who are wise will instruct many, though for a
time they will fall by the sword or be burned or captured
or plundered. 34 When they fall, they will receive a little
help, and many that are not sincere will join them. 35
Some of the wise will stumble, so they may be refined,
purified and made spotless until the time of the end, for
it will come at the appointed time." [Underline by the
author, solely for emphasis]

How many theorists can make claim they are prepared to instruct the
true wisdom of God to the many, under the specter of persecution by
sword, plunder, capture and fire? How many are prepared to instruct
the many with the true word of God, which clearly states that great
persecutions and trials are in store for the children of God?

In this group of scriptures, we see the similitude spoken of in
Matthew 13:30 where the "tares and the wheat" will be "growing
together," the "wise" will instruct (preach the word of God)
many in the face of persecutions (sword, burned, captured and
plundered). In Daniel 12:10, it speaks about this group of wise
people stating: *"Many will be purified, made spotless and refined,
but the wicked will continue to be wicked. None of the wicked will
understand, but those who are wise will understand."* These wise
ones are the *called out ones* who will be preaching the Gospel,
fulfilling the great commission, *"in all Judea and Samaria to
the ends of the earth,"* (Acts 1:8, NIV). But fear need not be the
case because Jesus will be with His *ecclesia "to the very end of
the age,* (Matthew 28:20, NIV). The greatest evangelizing impact
the world has ever seen, will come about when God's disciples
appropriate the Holy Spirit gifts to their fullest. This period in
history will see God's power being used by His disciples more
so during the increased times of great tribulation; the greatest
evangelizing ever witnessed by mankind will occur during
that time. God's martyrs will not be engaged in military battle

against heathen nations and their respective religions; they will be prophetically proclaiming the Gospel. Not predicting future events, but proclaiming God's will!

However, and much to the surprise and amazement of many theorists and so-called *Christian Church* leaders, there will exist in those days a group so dedicated by their faith in Christ, they will be seen proclaiming the Gospel even unto death. As a result of the many *called out ones* who care not for their own lives, there will be many more people entering the fold than some might suspect would ever do so. And, while many professing Christians today believe they are more faithful than most, they will be shocked to see who many of those frontline soldiers of the cross will be. A myriad of prostitutes, murderers, thieves and every kind of malcontent – even some kings, magistrates, and some rich and mighty people, too - will turn to Jesus at that time, as never before imagined.

Unfortunately, many of the so-called "righteous" *Christian Church* members will fall away, those who find comfort and security in a Pre-tribulation Rapture, money, power, fame and even token membership in their local church. But it is those who are willing to do away with all material wealth and possessions, all of their sophisticated networks of people in high places, all of their ersatz wisdom and knowledge, everything (except for their faith in Jesus Christ), will be found working in the Lord's harvest fields. Many of those who have been burning their fleshly candles at both ends, with every kind of despicable deed that can be imagined, will turn away from sin and unbelief to follow Jesus Christ. Many of these who trust not on the creature comforts that mankind depends on will have no trouble facing death for the Gospel of Jesus Christ. Many of these will be in the group that Jesus spoke of as being, *the last will be first, and the first be last*, (Matthew 20:16, NIV).

Unfortunately, many, who have been deluded into believing that a secret pre-tribulation escape to heaven is on the immediate horizon, will not be *caught up* but will be *caught off* guard when trials and tribulations come upon them; some, even turning to the 666 system, the only way anyone will be allowed to buy or sell in order to exist.

But those who worship not the Beast or his image and receive not his mark on their foreheads or their hands, those who stand firm in their testimony for Jesus, even if it means being plundered or tortured (although many will escape these things), or face execution by being beheaded, these are the ones who will reign forever with Jesus Christ. These are the ones who will sleep in Christ until *The Resurrection*, the second death (The Lake of Fire) having no power over them. Even though tortured and persecuted, many *called out ones* will not be killed, many will stand firm to the onslaught of the man of lawlessness and his minions, broadcasting the Gospel to those yet saved during the most horrific period mankind has ever known. Yet, these Christian solders will bring many others to Christ during this awful period, many receiving protection through God's End Times Passover. These are the ones who will pass through the flames, the ones whose faith-filled works will surpass even death:

> When you pass through the waters, I will be with you; when you pass through the rivers, they will not sweep over you. **When you walk through the fire, you will not be burned; the flames will not set you ablaze**. For I am the Lord, your God, (Isaiah. 43:2, 3, NIV). [Bold and underline is by the author, solely for emphasis]

Many are still fearful of this eventuality. Many die-hard Christians loathe thinking this possibility. Many will continue to believe that now that they have accepted Jesus Christ in their hearts, and who now call themselves *Born Again*, and who now believe they cannot lose their salvation regardless of how they live, sincerely believe they will escape these horrors through a secret escape to heaven scenario that theorists call the Rapture. These theorists love to spew their religious clichés, telling those who scoff at their secret escape mythologies that they are the ones who will be *left behind*. What theorists fail to comprehend is that *they* are the ones who may very well be *caught off guard*, rather than being *caught up* to heaven.

However, if the true hearts of God's *called out ones* can accept the reality that great tribulation is in store for them, and henceforth trust God, regardless of the persecutory horrors that will ensue prior to the Lord's return, those with pure hearts may not experience the brunt of that coming hour.

1 Peter 1:3-7, clearly states that the children of God, His disciples, will be "shielded by God's power until the coming of the salvation that is ready to be revealed in the last time, (vs. 5)" an obvious reference to God's "shield of faith" spoken of in Ephesians 6:16. We are told that in "this (the shielding faith of God) you (the Christian) should rejoice, though now for a little while you may have had to suffer grief in all kinds of *trials* (Gr. *periasmos*, temptations), (Vs 6). These trials have come so that your faith – of greater worth than gold, which perishes even though refined by fire– may be *found* (Gr. *heurisko*, to find oneself, gain, procure, obtain) genuine and may result in praise, glory and honor when Jesus Christ is *revealed* (Gr. *apokalupsis*, appearing), (Vs 7). Verse 7, in particular, indicates that the trials Christians are enduring now, which will intensify exponentially before the appearing of Christ, have a specific purpose: the testing of our faith as the assayer does when he purifies gold in the smelting pot.

In verse 16, of 2 Peter 3, referring to Paul's letters to the churches, Peter tells the ecclesia that they contain some things that are hard to understand, which ignorant and unstable people distort, as they do the other scriptures, to their own destruction. In this particular chapter of this book, the author could be accused of distorting scripture to fit the case he is presenting. However, throughout the entire Bible, it speaks about the Christian's duty to the Gospel of Christ, and the price to expect, which includes trials, temptations, testing, finding ourselves to be approved, standing firm throughout the ordeal, even unto death. Theorists would have us believe in their pet theories that the *called out ones* will escape these things and the Jewish people won't. To continually state and believe that the time of the so-called "Great Tribulation" has been designed solely for them (the Jews, or all of Jacob's descendants) and them alone, for turning their backs on the Lord, is anti-Semitism at its greatest, for *"all have sinned and fall short of the glory of God,* (Romans 3:23, NIV). All need to come to repentance and faith in the saving grace of Jesus Christ.

The author believes that a much greater faith in the saving grace of God is required today, and more so as greater tribulations draw near. How many of us can say today that we are not only prepared to meet the Lord, but are spiritually prepared to suffer for the sake of the Gospel, even unto death? How many of us can say without hesitation that we are *free from the slavery of the fear of death,* (Hebrews 3:15)? How many of us can go to bed tonight and say: "If that's what it takes Lord, here I am, use me so others also can be part of your precious kingdom?"

Some members of the *Christian Church* might not find comfort in this particular chapter; the author found no particular comfort in writing it either, except that the word of God clearly tells him that,

> "he who stands firm to the end will be saved, (Matthew 10:22, NIV)." "Do not be afraid of those who kill the body but cannot kill the soul, but rather, be afraid of the one who can destroy both soul and body in hell, Matthew 10:28, NIV)."

Although the *called out ones* can expect to be betrayed by parents, brothers, relatives and friends, and although they might be included among some of those who might be put to death, because men will hate them for the Gospel of Jesus Christ, *there shall not an hair of your head perish*, (Luke 21:18, KJV)."

Some Christians already have committed their lives unto death, but yet, some are still clinging to the hope of a secret pre-tribulation escape to heaven. It does not appear that such an escape will come about. For those who are still clinging to the hope that they will be spared the torture and physical persecutions, according to Revelation 3:10, it appears that those *called out ones* who are walking in Christ, as is spoken about those belonging to the Philadelphia section of Christianity, will be kept from the hour of trial. But, who, pray tell, can make the claim that their commitment to Christ is faithful enough to place their hearts inside of God's smelting pot, and allow Him to finish the work He has in store for each and everyone one of us?

We will soon know. Millions of professing Christians will be tested. Thousands upon thousands, who make claim that Jesus Christ is their Lord and Savior, will soon be tested as never before. As Satan begins to the pump the bellows to the furnace of chaos, persecution and testing, and the flames of grief and sorrow increase to greater intensity, many which proclaim to know and follow Jesus Christ will find themselves having to examine their hearts as never imagined. Will the heart that rests its hope on the blood pumping mythology of a secret escape to heaven doctrine be able to withstand the cardiac attack of intense tribulation? Or will the returning Christ find a comatose soul whose heart has been clogged by the arterial sclerosis of the Pre-Tribulation escape to heaven doctrine?

The trials, temptations and persecutions are going to increase. Christians will experience great tribulation. This reality should not be viewed as a time of gloom and doom, however; for this will be a period that will immediately precede the most glorious event, ever, especially for all of His *called out ones*, the return of Jesus Christ, our Lord and our God!

> In this you **greatly rejoice**, though now for a little while you may have had to suffer grief in all kinds of trials.7 These have come **so that your faith--of greater worth than gold,** which perishes even though refined by fire-- **may be proved genuine and may result in praise, glory and honor when Jesus Christ is revealed**, 1 Peter 1:6-7, NIV). [Bold and underline is by the author, solely for emphasis]

As we stated in our first book, the Holy Spirit cannot be removed (as theorists contend); but, will be in force with greater measure during that period. As the *called out ones* appropriate this Holy Spirit power with greater determination, and by being in constant prayer (the Lord's Prayer being the perfect example), many unbelievers will repent and will join other Christian soldiers in their quest to bring others into the fold, caring not about their lives, protecting themselves solely with the belt of truth, the helmet of salvation, the breastplate of righteousness, the shield of faith and the word of God as their sword. And even though many will die a physical death, not a hair on their head will *perish*. The Greek word for *perish* is *apollumi*, where the perspective force of the verb implies the completion of the process of destruction. When Christians die a physical death, they don't *perish*, but merely die in the flesh (their soul momentarily sleeping in Christ), then they will be raised in an imperishable body (1 Corinthians 15:51-54) at the last trump, then they will be "caught together" with those who are still alive to meet and greet the Lord in the air, then escort Him back as He descends to earth, where they will reign with Him forever!

The faith of God's *called out ones* will be tested; however, the Lord has assured the *ecclesia* that,

> No temptation has seized you except what is common to man. And God is faithful; He will not let you be tempted beyond what you can bear. But when you are tempted, he will also provide a way out so that you can stand up under it, (1 Corinthians 10:13, NIV).

In other words, as the Christian believer is seen going through the times of greater tribulation than ever before, God will be merciful and provide a way through the temptation, but not necessarily out of it, in the sense of being physically removed from earth to heaven to escape these temptations and persecutions.

Once again, picture the group of disciples on the boat during a great storm, being kept from capsizing or drowning, not being removed from the storm, but rather, being led safely through it by the Lord Jesus Christ. This type of protection, rather than a removal from earth to heaven, we believe, is how God has protected His people throughout history, and His word clearly states that's how He has operated throughout the Bible. As God protected Noah in the great flood, we believe that God will also rescue end-time Christians, while at the same time punishing the unbelievers (2 Peter 2:9). More importantly, we believe the Bible clearly exhorts the *ecclesia* to be found walking and abiding in the Spirit (Ephesians 5:15-21) and to put on the full armor of God (Ephesians 6:10-18), especially as the end draws nearer. God will judge the world before Jesus Christ returns. He will pour out His fiery wrath on the unbeliever; however, as the *called out ones* pray that prayer that Jesus exhorted us to do so in Matthew 6:9-13, we believe God will protect the believer while destroying the man of lawlessness and his minions. Immediately after that, He begins to prepare the new heavens and the new earth (2 Peter 3:13; Isaiah 65:17; Isaiah 66:22), before His eternal reign on earth! Once again, God does not annihilate the earth, but rather He burns up the old heavens (skies) and the earth, and then restructures them to a state of righteous glory, one that He requires in order to dwell among His creation. As Isaiah 66:22 so clearly states:

> For as the new heavens and the new earth, which I will make, shall remain before me, saith the LORD, so shall your seed and your name remain, (Isaiah 66:22, KJV)

With that reality firmly established in God's word, what should be the Christian's response?

> Seeing then that all these things shall be dissolved, what manner of persons ought **ye to be in all holy conversation and godliness,** 12 **looking for and hasting unto the coming of the day of God,** wherein the heavens being on fire shall be dissolved, and the elements shall melt with fervent heat? 13 Nevertheless we, **according to his promise, look for new heavens and a new earth, wherein dwelleth righteousness.**14 Wherefore, beloved, seeing that ye look for such things, **be diligent that ye may be found of him in peace, without spot, and blameless.** 15 And account that the longsuffering of our Lord is salvation; even as our beloved brother Paul also according to the wisdom given unto him hath written unto you, (2Peter 3:11-15, KJV).

Chapter 10
THE PASSOVER LAMB

Our first book *The End Times Passover* [Etymological Challenges to Millenarian Doctrines] was devoted entirely to the refutation of the secret Pre, Mid or Post-tribulation escape to heaven theories. It also attempted to refute millenarianism in all of its various forms. The author believes he presented definitive scriptural proof that Christians should not be looking for a secret Pre, Mid or Post-Tribulation escape to heaven; but, rather, they should be expecting to be here on earth up to the final return of the Lord Jesus Christ.

In our second book, we felt it was necessary to present the clear biblical facts that the *called out ones* are indeed destined to go through intensified tribulation immediately before *The Second Advent*. This second book has been written in hopes that God's *ecclesia* will realize that a totally new attitude and purpose for existence needs to be adopted in order to cope with the impending reality of the End Times. However, the End Times Passover we have been alluding to involves the *true* "blessed hope" of the Christian community, in the sense that God's redemption program includes the "passing over" of His people when He commences to pour out His wrath upon the unrepentant upon His final return.

As the author begins to unveil more specifically God's End Times Passover, he must first present his thoughts and insights to the original Passover. In this chapter, the author will be examining the biblical phenomenon more for the symbolism he has extrapolated from this amazing historical event. While the author may leave himself open to some criticism in the way he interprets the first Passover ritual, this chapter is more of a sermon than a true exegetical scrutiny of this profound message from God. There are many old and new expositors and authors emerging who have conducted extensive studies about the Passover and its cultural and prophetic significance. By no means does this author pretend to be an expert in this field of study. However, as the author studied the entire Passover account, he found various symbols and types that could very well be applied to an effective Christian walk, especially during the End Times. If other Bible scholars have studied this aspect in greater detail, or have written books or material that give greater illumination, the author is eager and open to learn and study this subject even further. However, if the many symbols and types contained in the Passover account reveal deeper insights into God's message to His *ecclesia*, and can be proven and validated by other scriptures, only the Holy Spirit can provide definitive confirmation to the inferences the author herewith presents.

First of all, the scriptures plainly state that many *called out ones* will be alive when the Lord returns (1 Thessalonians 4:15) to "snatch" the *ecclesia* to meet the Lord in the air on His descent to earth at *The Second Advent*. Scripture also clearly states that those who have died (fallen asleep in Christ) will be resurrected and instantaneously changed into immortal bodies, as well as those who are alive and waiting to jointly meet and greet the Lord in the air, to escort Him back to earth (vs. 17). So how does this relate to an *End Times Passover*? What you are about to read in these last three chapters will hopefully fill your heart and soul with the greatest joy you have ever experienced. First, let's examine the original Passover event to help us establish its historical significance, and its possible application to the end times.

When we talk about the miracles that God has performed in past times, the ones most often recognized by the masses include the parting of the Red Sea, the Manna falling from the sky (in the Old Testament), Jesus' raising of Lazarus from the dead, His walking on water, changing water into wine, and the great provision where He broke a few loaves of bread and multiplied the fish to feed over five thousand people, mentioned in the New Testament. We are of the opinion that next to the miracle of Jesus' resurrection, the most magnificent miracle ever performed by God is the one known throughout millions of Jewish homes as The Passover.

As the story goes, the nation of Israel cried out to God to free it from its oppressor, Pharaoh, and deliver that nation from Egypt's bondage, and also to fulfill (as they perceived then) His promise concerning the Promised Land. God responded to Israel's cry and used the great patriarch Moses as His instrument for their rescue. In Exodus 11:1-10, we see where God tells Moses to inform the Pharaoh that if he doesn't loose Israel from its bondage, God will pour out a horrible plague, one that will result in the loss of every person's firstborn, from Pharaoh's own children on down to the slave girl, including all the firstborn of the cattle. Let's review this briefly:

> Now the Lord had said to Moses, "I will bring one more plague on Pharaoh and on Egypt. After that, he will let you go from here, and when He does, he will drive you out completely. 2 Tell the people that men and women alike are to ask their neighbors for articles of silver and gold." 3 (The Lord made the Egyptians favorably disposed toward the people, and Moses himself was highly regarded in Egypt by Pharaoh's officials and by the people.) 4 So Moses said, "This is what the Lord says: 'About midnight I will go throughout Egypt. 5 Every firstborn son in Egypt will die, from the firstborn son of Pharaoh, who sits on the throne, to the firstborn

son of the slave girl, who is at her hand mill, and all the firstborn of the cattle as well. 6 There will be loud wailing throughout Egypt – worse than there has ever been or ever will be again. 7 But among the Israelites not a dog will bark at any man or animal.' Then you will know that the Lord makes a distinction between Egypt and Israel. 8 All these officials of yours will come to me, bowing down before me and saying, 'Go, you and all the people who follow you!' After that I will leave." Then Moses, hot with anger, left Pharaoh. 9 The Lord had said to Moses, "Pharaoh will refuse to listen to you – so that my wonders may be multiplied in Egypt." 10 Moses and Aaron performed all these wonders before Pharaoh, but the Lord hardened Pharaoh's heart, and he would not let the Israelites go out of his country, (Exodus 11:1-10, NIV).

God knew all along that Pharaoh would not listen to the warning (vs. 9) so He commenced to carry out His promise. Before the Lord poured out the awful plague, He told Moses that Israel should prepare itself for this plague in a very unique manner, one which would insure their protection. Let's very carefully read this entire chapter of scripture, which describes the manner by which Almighty God protected Israel from this horrendous plague:

The Lord said to Moses and Aaron in Egypt, 2 "This month is to be for you the first month, the first month of your year. 3 Tell the whole community of Israel that on the tenth day of this month each man is to take a lamb for his family, one for each household. 4 If any household is too small for a whole lamb, they must share one with their nearest neighbor, having taken into account the number of people there are. You are to determine the amount of lamb needed in accordance with what each person will eat. 5 The animals you choose must be year-old males without defect, and you may take them from the sheep or the goats. 6 Take care of them until the fourteenth day of the month, when all the people of the community of Israel must slaughter them at twilight. 7 Then they are to take some of the blood and put it on the sides and tops of the door frames of the houses where they eat the lambs. 8 That same night they are to eat the meat roasted over the fire, along with bitter herbs, and bread made without yeast. 9 Do not eat the meat raw or cooked in water, but roast it over the fire – head, legs and inner parts. 10 Do not leave any of it till morning; if some is left till morning, you must burn it. 11 This is how you are to eat: with your cloak tucked into your belt, your sandals on your feet and your staff in your hand. Eat it in haste; it is the Lord's Passover. 12 On that same night I will pass through Egypt and strike down every firstborn – both men and animals – and I will bring judgment on all the gods of Egypt; I am the Lord. 13 the blood will be a sign for you on the house where you are; and when I see the blood, I will pass over you. No destructive plague will touch you when I strike Egypt. 14 This is a day you are to commemorate; for the generations to come you shall celebrate it as a festival to the Lord – a lasting ordinance. 15 For seven days you are to eat bread made without yeast. On the first day remove the yeast from your houses, for whoever eats anything with yeast in it from the first day through the seventh must be cut off from Israel. 16 On the first day hold a sacred assembly, and another one on the seventh day. Do not work at all on these days, except to prepare food for everyone to eat – that is all you may do. 17 Celebrate the Feast of Unleavened Bread, because it was on this very day that I brought your divisions out of Egypt. Celebrate this day as a lasting ordinance for the generations to come. 18 In the first month you are to eat bread made without yeast, from the evening of the fourteenth day until the evening of the twenty-first day. 19 For seven days no yeast is to be found in your houses. And whoever eats anything with yeast in it must be cut off from the community of Israel, whether he is an alien or native-born. 20 Eat nothing made with yeast. Wherever you live, you must eat unleavened bread." 21 Then Moses summoned all the elders of Israel and said to them, "Go at once and select the animals for your families and slaughter the Passover lamb. 22 Take a bunch of hyssop, dip it into the blood in the basin and put some of the blood on the top and on both sides of the doorframe. Not one of you shall go out the door of his house until morning. 23 When the Lord goes through the land to strike down the Egyptians, he will see the blood on the top and sides of the doorframe and will pass over that doorway, and he will not permit the destroyer to enter your houses and strike you down. 24 Obey these instructions as a lasting ordinance for you and your descendants. 24 When you enter the land that the Lord will give you as he promised, observe this ceremony. 26 And when your children ask you, 'What does this ceremony mean to you?' 27 then tell them, 'It is the Passover sacrifice to the Lord, who passed over the houses of the Israelites in Egypt and spared our homes when he struck down the Egyptians.'" Then the people bowed down and worshipped. 28 The Israelites did just what the Lord commanded Moses and Aaron. 29 At midnight the Lord struck down all the firstborn in Egypt, from the firstborn of Pharaoh, who sat on the throne, to the firstborn of the prisoner, who was in the dungeon, and the firstborn of all the Livestock as well, (Exodus 12:1-29, NIV).

This Old Testament account of the Passover describes a ritual that is still practiced and celebrated throughout Jewish homes all over the world, for what it represented and accomplished: Freedom from slavery! Unfortunately for the majority of Jews (those who still practice the Judaic laws) the true significance of this event has been missed or rejected. Many great Bible scholars (and spirit-filled Christians, alike) have accepted it as possibly the most significant event ever recorded in history, with the exception of Christ's atoning work at Calvary and His subsequent resurrection. The Christian, by virtue of various gifts from the Holy Spirit, has been given the power to understand God's mysteries (Matthew 13:11; Luke 8:10; 1 Corinthians 4:1, 13:2; 14:2); and, the event known as The Passover is probably one of the greatest mysteries ever revealed to believers. Unfortunately, many have not taken the time to study this phenomenon and learn many of its truly inspiring truths.

To better understand how God will provide an End Times Passover (a protective covering from God's wrath), both Christians and Jews have to understand how this historical event relates to the greatest Passover ever, the one where Almighty God sacrificed His own Son to pay the price for our sins. Because unbelieving Jews (and the lost in general) have yet to accept Jesus Christ as Lord and Savior, nor have they experienced the revelatory powers of the Holy Spirit, the ability to understand this reality does not exist in their lives. They have not the power of the Holy Spirit which reveals truth:

> "The man without the Spirit does not accept the things
> that come from the Spirit of God, for they are foolishness
> to him, and he cannot understand them, because they
> are spiritually discerned, (1 Corinthians 2:14, NIV)."

Unfortunately, many Christians themselves do not understand the symbolic aspect or meaning of the Passover, and how it relates to God's overall redemption program. To the biblically learned student of God's word, the Passover ritual spoken of in the Old Testament not only was God's legal and religious requirement to remind His people of their deliverance, it was also God's way of prophetically revealing to all mankind how He would eventually provide a way of escape from persecution and eternal damnation for those who believe in Jesus Christ, God's sacrificial Lamb.

Throughout the Old Testament period, God has provided symbolic clues concerning His eternal plan for mankind. Unfortunately, prior to the outpouring of the Holy Spirit gift of discernment at Pentecost, many of the mysteries of God were sealed. Lack of space prevents us from citing the many symbolic examples used by God that prove He is a consistent and never-changing God: *"But you* (God) *remain the same and your years will never end,* (Psalms 102:27)." This verse, in particular, played a tremendously significant role for the author. This verse, which confirms God's consistency and never-changing nature, actually was the key to the thinking process the author utilized during his research, providing him with an assuredness that the Bible could not be deciphered from a dispensational perspective.

God has known from the very beginning of time (as mankind understands time) what He has (had) in store for His creation. As He unfolds the requirements of His creation, His initial methodology might appear to be one thing and then changed at a later date (as dispensationalists theorize). However, upon extensive study of God's word, it becomes very clear that while God implemented a governance system for national Israel through various memorials, laws, rules and regulations, these very same requirements remain the same forever, albeit they are a type or shadow of things to come. These edicts were given to Israel in a language (of symbolic and traditional ritual) they could understand at that time. However, in His omnipotent nature, The Passover ritual, especially, was in reality a prophecy (through symbolisms) that would be fulfilled in the future through the person of Jesus Christ.

Let's examine Exodus 12:1-11 to see exactly how the Passover meal requirements bear this out. There are twelve requirements involved in the Passover meal, and although they might appear to be insignificant guidelines and mere rituals on how to prepare a simple feast, the symbolism appears to be speaking a greater message, one that every Christian needs to understand how it can apply to their own Christian walk.

As the Lord instructs Moses and Aaron various details concerning these twelve requirements, He begins first by stating when this preparation should take place. God said: "This month is to be for you the first month, the first month of the year. Tell the whole community of Israel that on the tenth day of this month (the month of Abib, or Nisan, after the captivity, which is the first of the Jewish ecclesiastical year, and the seventh of the civil year, which began about the time of the vernal equinox), each man is to take a lamb for his family, one for each household." Therein lays a requirement in the Passover ritual that infers a person's entire household can be saved through their faith and walk with Christ. Although it is an accepted fact by Christians that securing eternal salvation is an individual commitment, in Acts 16:31, we read where the apostle Paul is responding to the jailer's question on what he must do to be saved, and Paul clearly states: "*Believe in the Lord Jesus Christ and you shall be saved, you and your household.*" The author believes that if a Christian man is walking in the spirit, if he is truly following and abiding in the will of Jesus, his wife and family (although they may be weak in the spirit) will partake in the salvation inheritance.

We see a similar example of this in the parable of the watchful servant in Luke 12:35-48. Whether we have been entrusted by God with a spouse, children, employees, even friends and neighbors, the manner in which we minister to them could make a difference in whether they partake in the Kingdom of God. The symbolism of bringing one Lamb for each household could also represent more so the leadership that needs to be provided by the heads of a family, including those who have been entrusted with a shepherd's role in a local congregation, family or business. True, the Lord will judge each individual according to his or her own actions and faith; however, the message in the "one Lamb for each household" indicates that one Lamb is sufficient; one Jesus Christ, one God, is all an entire household needs. That one Lamb, however, requires that there need be only one spiritual leader in each household, and those heads of families not found providing that leadership will be held accountable for many of the indiscretions committed by their flock, (1 Corinthians 8:9; Romans 14:13; Matthew 16:23; Ezekiel 18:30; 42:12). Each individual will be held accountable and share in the responsibility for those that God has entrusted to them. Many a wayward youth have gone astray because shepherds failed to provide the knowledge of God's precepts and the discipline required to build a strong foundation for their children. We see a perfect example of this in Mark 9:42, which states, *"And if anyone causes one of these little ones who believe in me to sin, it would be better for him to be thrown into the sea with a large millstone tied around his neck."* The Greek word for "little" is *mikros*, which means "of persons, with regards to station or age, rank or influence." This word then is describing not just the little children, or merely our own sons and daughters, but anyone great or small that has been entrusted by the Lord to our care. Therefore, the one Lamb for each household here signifies first that we needed only one Lamb (Jesus Christ) to insure true redemption; however, it also paints an important truth that demands faithful, spiritual leadership from all to whom God has entrusted.

Point number two also paints a bigger picture than we imagine. In verse 4 of Exodus 12, the requirement states that *"If any household is too small for a whole lamb, they must share one with their nearest neighbor, having taken account the number of people* *there are."* This requirement paints a magnificent picture of the Christian's responsibility to share Jesus Christ with everyone, but more importantly, with their neighbors. What a sad commentary on the Christian community's lack of involvement that we see so many of our neighbors who are bound by strife, and a myriad of sin. Unfortunately, we choose rather to apply the scripture that speaks about our non-association with the world, rather than reaching out to them with love and the Gospel. The true believer has been assured that the Lord will remember not their sins (Hebrews 8:12). However, many Christians will moan at the Judgment Seat of Christ when they will suffer loss, not for what sins they committed; but, rather, for what deeds they failed to accomplish, those deeds that they have been entrusted to fulfill with the help of Holy Spirit. Like the parable of the talents (Luke 19:22), the ones who fail to multiply that which God has given them, rather found burying the talent because they felt that God's requirements are too difficult, it is these that will suffer loss. Some will be saved: *"but only as one escaping through flames,* (1 Corinthians 3:15)."* What a greater world this would be if the *called out ones* would take the time to reach out and let their Christianity shine (not boastfully) with acts of love, patience, long-suffering and forgiveness of the family, friends, local community members and business associates and fellow employees. When Jesus said it was our mission to spread the Gospel to the entire world, we sincerely believe He didn't mean we had to leave our neighborhood and preach the Gospel a thousand miles away. While certain people (and or churches) are called for these far off missions, we believe the wisdom and knowledge of Jesus Christ should first be extolled to our immediate environs.

The third Passover requirement is seen in verse 4, and it states: *"You are to determine the amount of the Lamb needed in accordance with what each person will eat."* Here we see an example of not only preventing waste, but also of the tremendous onslaught that many people (believers and nonbelievers, alike) face at the hands of pious

Christians. In today's world, we see accounts daily where Christians have been pontifically forcing Jesus Christ on people through obnoxious zeal that literally turns them off, rather than gently leading them to the Lord.

The author was accused of being too pushy with his Christianity when he first came to the Lord in 1975, understandably so; *called out ones* do see truths the natural man cannot. But in recent years, the Lord has sensitized his heart to realize that God doesn't want people to come to Him by force; but, rather, they need to experience (through our gentleness and patience) the love and compassionate nature that is personified in Jesus Christ. In Matthew 7:1-5, we see that great story about the judgmental individual who is always pointing out the speck of sawdust in his brother's eye, and not paying attention to his own weaknesses (the plank in his own eye). How many broken spirits, how many injured souls have been lost because the overzealous and pious Christian has lorded over others their pseudo-holiness. By the same token, Christians are also instructed to handle the word of God in a discriminate manner, *Do not give dogs what is sacred; do not throw your pearls before pigs. If you do, they may trample them under their feet and then turn and tear you to pieces,* (Matthew 7: 6, NIV.) Here we are faced with the need for balance. On the one hand, Jesus entrusted us with the Great Commission to preach the Gospel; but yet, the overzealous manner with which much of modern-day Christianity exemplifies, has been responsible for turning off many who would otherwise come to Christ. We believe that God is not so much concerned with how many souls we claim to have brought into the Kingdom; but, rather, in what manner we brought them in. Did their conversion come about because they saw in us the grace and compassion exhibited by Christ, or did we merely scare or piously badger them to join the flock, fearing retribution at the hand of God?

The author once sent a letter to an elected official who had been severely castigated by many Christians for initiating anti-discrimination legislation to protect victims of AIDS (Acquired Immune Deficiency Syndrome), a disease found mostly among members of the homosexual community. The author asked this individual not to condemn all Christians for this overzealous behavior; but, rather, to forgive them as God would like to forgive the homosexual. The author told the elected official that we are all sinners and come short of the Glory of God. Who can say if this elected official was not later moved to repentance, as the author prayed for him?

The Good News is that once we reach out to Jesus, we can be healed of our past indiscretions, and become fellow partakers of the Kingdom of God. We see this principle coming directly from Jesus as He exhorts us in Matthew 5:43 to *"Love your enemies, and pray for those who persecute you."* We believe that this third requirement in the Passover Feast (determine how much of the Lamb can be eaten) can appropriately apply to this message. Unfortunately, too many people have adopted the saving grace of Jesus and have used it as license to condemn unbelievers, when the fruits of the spirit would have had greater effect. We believe that more people will come to know the real Jesus Christ, the one who personifies in us true love, joy, peace, patience, kindness, goodness, faithfulness, gentleness and self control (Galatians 5:22), if we lovingly share the reality of the Lamb, rather than pontifically forcing the gospel through religious zeal and piety.

The fourth principle we see in the Passover Feast requirements is the condition of the Lamb. In verse 5, it states: *"The animal you choose must be year-old males without defect."* Here we see a beautiful picture of Jesus Christ, the only human ever born without blemish or defect. In Hebrew 9:14, the author speaks about Christ and His sinless condition:

> How much more, then, will the blood of Christ, who
> through the eternal spirit offered Himself unblemished
> to God, cleanse our conscience from acts that lead to
> death, so that we may serve the living God, (Hebrews
> 9:14, NIV).

Many other scriptures attest to Jesus' sinlessness, being born of
a virgin, etc. Here we see a perfect example of how God, in His
omnipotent nature, provided a symbol for Israel that would become
a perfect example of Himself in human form, coming down from
His lofty heights, God in the flesh, without blemish – the only way
that the atoning process could be realized. This unblemished Lamb
was identified for us in John 1:29, where John the Baptist uttered the
greatest words ever: *Behold, the Lamb of God, who taketh away the
sins of the world*, (John 1:29, KJV). Herein lay the reality of what the
Passover truly represents: the fact that God transported Himself (in
the flesh) to earth to be a sacrifice for all humanity, especially for
those who believe and accept this reality! The Israelites (through their
forefathers) were aware of this concept of sacrifices. [For an in-depth
study on the words *blood, redeemed, propitiation* and *sacrifice*, see the
author's book, *Saved? What Do You Mean Saved?* GBM Books]

The first example to Israel's forefathers concerning this sacrifice
principle is seen in the instance where God had to kill an animal
(Genesis 3:21) to appropriate skin to cover Adam and Eve's nakedness
after they sinned. This precept was carried forward, as exemplified
in the sacrifice that God accepted from Abel. But what is developing
here in the Passover requirements is that the Israelites, unfortunately,
saw only a ritual rather than God's prophetic symbolism of things to
come. God was also showing the Israelites (and all mankind, for that
matter) that humanity couldn't be reunited to Him through works.
A people cannot earn their way back to fellowshipping with God
through any efforts of their own. God is omnipotent, omniscient,
never changing. But, more importantly, God is Holy and He can't

compromise that Holiness. The only way that God could reunite Himself with His creation is for a price to be paid. Why God has chosen to accomplish His purpose in this fashion may not be clear to all of us, we can only speculate. But this is the method he has used, a method that requires that something must die before it can live again. This process is seen in the study of nature and its reproductive metamorphism. God has chosen to do things His way and millions try to scientifically unravel that part of His being. It's not necessary for us to know how He does things, but rather, that we believe and obey in faith those things He reveals. It becomes obviously clear that Israel did not understand God's purpose for this ritualistic bloodletting process, but this is the manner in which He chose to reveal His plan of redemption.

The fifth requirement for the Passover Feast was the taking of an unblemished Lamb from either sheep or goats. According to the BDB Lexicon, the words used in verse 5 describe three different types from the sheep family. First, the unblemished lamb is described as *seh*, the Hebrew word denoting *one of the flock*. The word describing the sheep is *kebes*, a male lamb and the word to describe goats is *ez*, the female of the species. In each case where *kebes* and *ez* are used (87 times, especially in Exodus, Leviticus and Numbers) it refers to a special group of sheep that have been destined solely for sacrificial purposes. It is interesting to note (according to T. A. Bryant's Dictionary) that the word *ez* (female goat) literally means *strength*, while the word *kebes* (lamb, the masculine noun) means *meekness* and *innocence*. Here we have, then, a *seh*, which is picture of Jesus, who as the Son of Man was a flesh member of the human flock, possessing both the strength of the *ez* and the meekness and innocence of the *kebes*, which both speak to the embodiment of Jesus Christ. Here we have a beautiful picture of God, Himself (in the person of Jesus), coming into the world, possessing great strength and power, yet allowed Himself in meekness and total innocence to be crucified on the cross as a sacrifice for the sins of the world.

Throughout the New Testament, it speaks about the Christian's walk and attitude being one like Christ. An attitude not depending on conventional strength for protection, but that strength which comes from the Father in the form of the Holy Spirit, thereby manifesting Christ-like innocence and meekness. When the world thinks of meekness, it interprets it as weakness, rather than its true meaning. The Greek word for *meekness* is *praus* or *praos* (in its adjectival form), *prautes* or *praotes* in the noun. Those who demonstrate true meekness are not to be considered weak; but, rather (according to Vine), they possess "an inwrought grace of the soul, and the exercises of it are first and chiefly towards God." Vine goes on to say that meekness "is that temper of spirit in which we accept His dealings with us as good, and therefore without disputing or resisting; it is closely linked with the word *tapeinophrosune* (humility), and follows directly upon it, Eph. 4:2; Col. 3:12, cp. the adjective in the Sept. of Zeph. 3:12, "meek and lowly;" …it is only the humble heart which is also the meek, and which, as such, does not fight against God and more less struggle and contend with Him.

This meekness, however, being first of all meekness before God, is also such in the face of men, even evil men, out of a sense that these, with insults and injuries which they may inflict, are permitted and employed by Him for the chastening and purifying of His elect. In Galatians 5:23, it is associated with *enkkrateia*, self-control." (W. E. Vine, *An Expository Dictionary of Biblical Words*, Pages 727-728, Thomas Nelson Publishers). The verse of Exodus 12:5, which beautifully describes the very nature of Christ, then, presents us with a tremendous symbol for Christians to model themselves after; one of meekness and innocence, yet one of great spiritual strength, which can come only from the power of Holy Spirit gifts.

The sixth requirement (verse 6) addresses the fulfilled prophecy concerning the exact time when Jesus went to the cross. It states: "*take care of them* (the sacrificial lambs) *until the fourteenth day of the*

month, when all the people of Israel must slaughter them at twilight."
For those who have had the opportunity to study the significance
of numerical relationships in the Bible (especially E. W. Bullinger's
Number In Scripture), the number fourteen is very significant in that
it is double the number seven, which stands for spiritual perfection.
The number fourteen therefore signifies a double portion of Jesus
Christ Himself. Those who have studied the numerical implications
in the Bible know that Jesus' name is comprised of six letters (in
the Greek alphabet); the number six representing man and man's
weakness, indicating the humanness of Jesus. The word Christ (His
divine title as the Anointed of God) has seven letters, representing
the spiritual perfection that is provided in the manifestation of the
Messiah (Jesus Christ) in the fullest sense.

The significance of the time of the evening, twilight is consistent with
the Hebrew laws of purification. In Leviticus 11:24, we see where
any person who picks up carcasses of animals with a split hoof, or
that does not chew its cud, was considered unclean until after the
evening time. What exactly is represented here is not known from a
scientific point of view; however, scientists do agree that a cleansing
and purifying process occurs in the human body after evening time,
due to the fasting that ensues while it sleeps. The true significance of
twilight, however, is that it is the exact time when Jesus was crucified,
on the fourteenth day of the seventh month, at twilight time. The
time for cleansing and purification, the time when Jesus' death was
responsible for the eternal cleansing and purification of mankind's
sins (especially for those who believe and accept the gift of salvation)
was on the twilight, another perfect example (and prophetic symbol)
found in the Passover ritual.

The seventh requirement of the Passover Feast was the taking of some
of the blood and placing it on the doorposts and lintel of the houses in
which they eat the Passover Lamb. Here we ask: "Why the doorpost
and the lintels? Why not the windows, the side or top of the house?

Once again, we see in this example how God was revealing to the spiritual man a symbolic example of who was to fulfill the messianic promise: Jesus Christ!

In John 10:7-9, we see where Jesus Christ (God's Passover Lamb) refers to Himself as the "gate" for the sheep (believers, His chosen ones):

> Therefore Jesus said again, I am the gate; whoever enters through me will be saved. He will come in and go out, and find pasture. The Thief (Satan) comes only to steal and kill and destroy; I have come that they might have life and have it to the full, (John 10:7-9, NIV).

Here we read where Jesus Christ Himself is the "gate" to the Kingdom of God, and no one can enter unless they go through Him. In the Passover Feast, the Israelites were given a symbol of this prophecy. But, once again, they didn't see this fact, accepting this feast requirement solely as one of the ritual aspects of the Passover ceremony. As they were instructed, the blood of the Passover Lamb was to be placed on the doorpost and lintel (*masqoph* or *sheqoph*, which literally means the framework or casing of the house). In order for the Israelites to escape the plague of death, they had to be inside the house, the doorpost being the only way in to safety. It is the blood with which people are saved. His shed blood provides the payment for sin (the wages of which is death). It's also a covering, a protection from the eternal perishing that is to come upon those who do not accept or receive the Lord's saving grace. Most people normally do not enter their house through the window or through the roof; they obviously go through the doorway. Jesus is the "gate," His redeeming blood on the doorpost therefore representing the price that was paid. As the believer enters into the Kingdom of God, the entrance way is through the "gate," or the doorpost, which is Jesus

190

Christ Himself. The authority to enter is granted by the payment in blood that the Passover Lamb of God shed on Calvary, the same atoning impact that was realized before the great exodus of Israel, God's chosen people.

In the eighth requirement, we see where the Israelites were to "roast" the Passover Lamb and eat it that same night with bitter herbs and unleavened bread. The Hebrew word for "roast" is *tsali*, which comes from the word *tsaleach*, which literally means, "to succeed, prosper," or is sometimes used in such a way as to indicate "victory!" How beautifully God has provided the believer who searches for His truth, the words that give greater meaning to His messages. Here in this Passover feast requirement, we see where the "roasting" of the Lamb, in and of itself, provides prosperity, success and victory.

In the bitter herbs, we see a perfect example of the "gall" that was mixed in the wine that was dipped on a sponge and put on the mouth of Jesus as He was hanging on the cross (Matthew 27:48; Mark 15:36; Luke 23:36; John 19:29). The word for "bitter herbs" in the Hebrew is *marar* or *maror*, from where we get the Greek word *chole* (a word probably connected with *chloe*, yellow, denotes gall). The word *chole* metaphorically stands for extreme wickedness, productive of evil fruit. In Acts 8:23, we see where the apostle Peter rebuked Simon, the Sorcerer, because Simon wanted to purchase the power and ability to lay hands on people to receive the Holy Spirit. Peter rebuked Simon and told him that the gift of God and the power of the Holy Spirit cannot be purchased with money. Seeing his heart wasn't right with God, Peter rebuked Simon and told him that he had no part in Christian ministry:

> Repent of this wickedness and pray to the Lord. Perhaps he will forgive you for having such a thought in your heart. For I see that you are filled with bitterness (chloe) and captive to sin, (Acts 8:22, 23, NIV). [Parenthesis by the author]

As the Israelites were instructed to eat the roasted Passover Lamb with bitter herbs, they in essence were involved in the beginning of a ritual that symbolized the very act that was fulfilled when Jesus was given the bitter wine. Even more important (if not astounding), at that precise moment, Jesus not only shed His blood as payment for our individual sins, He literally drank all the sins of the world (throughout history), and actually became sin for mankind to set us free of our despicability. The Israelites, when they were partaking of the Passover Feast, didn't realize at that time that what they were doing was literally establishing a prophetic symbolic ritual of what God accomplished at Calvary, the eternal atonement for the sins of the world.

The "unleavened" bread represents meal that did not contain any yeast, a form of bacteria, which causes fermentation, rotting and death. The purpose of using unleavened bread (according to BDB Lexicon) served two primary purposes: "Hastily made bread omitted the fermented (unleavened) dough. Lot *"made them a feast, and did not bake unleavened bread, and they did eat"* (Genesis. 19:3). In this case, the word represents bread hastily prepared for unexpected guests. The Feasts of Israel often involved the use of unleavened bread, perhaps because of the relationship between fermentation, rotting and death (Leviticus 2:4), or because unleavened bread reminded the Israelites of the hasty departure from Egypt and the rigors of the wilderness march." The word for "unleavened bread," is *matstsah*, which is derived from the Hebrew word *matsats*, a primary root meaning to "suck, or to drain out." Here we see a perfect example of sin being drawn out from the individual as they partake of the unleavened bread, a perfect type of Jesus, the bread of life, the bread without the leaven (yeast, a form of bacteria), He the perfect food for mankind! In John 6:35, Jesus declared, *"I am the bread of life. He who comes to me will never go hungry, and he who believes in me will never be thirsty."* Here Jesus is not solely talking about bread for food's sake; He was talking about the negative ingredient (yeast, bacteria, rottenness, death) in bread, Himself being the only true sinless bread, that which gives eternal life!

Regarding the leaven, in 1 Corinthians 5:6-8, we see the apostle Paul exhorting the Christian about sexual immorality existing in the assemblies. He chides the church for this behavior and exhorts the brethren to *"hand this man over to Satan, so that the sinful nature may be destroyed and his spirit saved on the day of the Lord* (vs. 5). Paul is warning the church that a little sin (leaven), or what might appear to be morally insignificant, can grow into a greater infection, as all bacteria will if it goes unchecked. Many Christian assemblies fail to address the issue of leaven in their midst for fear that offending some members of the congregation will result in their fleeing and thereby losing out on tithes and offerings. So be it; the size of the church is not what matters, it's the effectiveness of its parishioners regardless of its numbers. Paul, speaking to the many who gloat that large membership alone constitutes successful churches, states:

> Your boasting is not good. Don't you know that a little yeast works through the whole batch of dough? Get rid of the old yeast that you may be a new batch without yeast – as you really are. For Christ, our Passover Lamb has been sacrificed. Therefore, let us keep the Festival, not with the old yeast, the yeast of malice and wickedness, but with bread without yeast, the bread of sincerity and truth, (1 Corinthians 5:6-8, NIV).

In the remainder of this exhortation, Paul commences to tell the *called out ones* exactly what they must do to solve the problems of the *ecclesia*, especially those dealing with sexual immorality:

> I have written you in my letter not to associate with sexually immoral people – 10 not at all meaning the people of this world who are immoral, or the greedy and swindlers, or idolaters. In that case you would have to leave this world. 11 But now I am writing you that

> you must not associate with anyone who calls himself
> a brother but is sexually immoral or greedy, an idolater
> or a slanderer, a drunkard or a swindler. With such a
> man do not even eat. 12 What business is it of mine to
> judge those outside the church? Are you not to judge
> those inside? 13 God will judge those outside. "Expel
> the wicked man from among you, (1 Corinthians 5:9-
> 13, NIV).

True, we are saved by grace and should not be found plucking out the sawdust in other people's eye when there is a big log in ours. However, too often the church leadership turns away from such problems rather than praying for a healing of the individuals involved. Whether it is sexual immorality, jealousy, anger, strife, etc., the church leadership must address these problems rather than solely praying for a healing of the individuals involved. Whatever the leaven of sin it may represent, the elders must address these problems with compassion, yet with firmness in correcting the problem before its spiritual bacteria grows to greater proportion.

As we continue the roasted lamb aspect of the Passover, we see that the eating of the "roasted" lamb provides us with "success, prosperity and victory;" the "bitter herbs" represent the wickedness and sins of the world, which Jesus took upon Himself for our sake. We also see the partaking of the "unleavened bread," which represents the bread without the yeast, representing Jesus Christ in His sinless nature, the perfect food for life. The Israelites knew not of the symbolic aspects of these ritualistic requirements, but the faithful Christian should be clearly aware of their symbolic significance as they pertain to the Christian walk.

The ninth requirement of the Passover Feast is that the Passover Lamb is not to be eaten raw. The word for "raw" in the Hebrew is *na*, and it is used only once in the entire Bible. According to the

BDB Lexicon, the word literally means *flesh*. It is, however, obvious that this requirement represents the curse that fell upon mankind in the Garden of Eden. When Adam and Eve were cast out from the Garden, they lost access to the Tree of Life, which would have provided them with immortality (Genesis 3:22) and, subsequently, death of the *flesh* entered the world. The body, without direct access to the Tree of Life, was destined to decay. When Jesus Christ paid the price on Calvary, all those who believe and accept Him as Lord and Savior have been redeemed and will qualify to receive immortal bodies (1 Corinthians 15:53) when He returns. From a practical point of view, it is known scientifically and medically that ingesting raw meat can be hazardous to one's health. The myriads of living parasites that are found in raw meat bring with them diseases and affliction. But more important, the symbolic meaning of not eating the lamb raw is in direct opposition to the benefits provided once it has been roasted. Obviously cooking meat kills bacteria contained therein, the roasting thereby symbolizing the killing of sin which prevents us from being successful, prosperous and victorious in these mortal bodies of ours. Also, throughout the entire Bible, we see where the eternal battle being faced today (and from the time of the great fall) is the battle between spirit and *flesh*. But as it states in Romans 8:11, those who have believed in Messiah, and have accepted Jesus Christ as their personal Lord and Savior now have the new spiritual nature from the Holy Spirit, guaranteeing them resurrection from death to eternal life:

> But if the Spirit of him that raised up Jesus from the dead dwell in you, he that raised up Christ from the dead shall also quicken your mortal bodies by his Spirit that dwelleth in you, (Romans 8:11, KJV).

The tenth requirement of the Passover Feast was for the Israelites to "eat all of the Passover Lamb." "Do not leave any of it till morning, if some is left till morning, you must burn it." Here, again, we see a perfect example of "eating all" or of the total and complete acceptance of Jesus Christ as Lord and Savior. Too often we see people coming to Jesus, verbally accepting Him as Lord and Savior, then forsaking the Christian walk, using His grace as license to pursue the demands of the flesh: *These people honor me with their lips, but their hearts are far from me. They worship me in vain; their teachings are but rules taught by men...* (Mark 7:6-7, NIV). How sad it will be when the Lord returns, when many will be filled great anguish, wailing,

> Lord, Lord, did we not prophesy in your name, and in your name drive out demons and perform many miracles? Then I will tell them plainly, 'I never knew you. Away form me, you evildoers, (Matthew 7:22, NIV).

Partaking of the Lamb cannot be merely the appropriation of those benefits that solely appease our wants and desires; but, rather, it needs be the acceptance of the totality of Jesus Christ, which includes trials and tribulations (and possibly death) as He Himself experienced.

That which is not eaten, that which is left over must be "burned" outside, is the other portion of this tenth requirement. Here we see, in the burning of the remaining portion of the Passover Lamb, an example of how the burnt remains of a sacrificed animal act as an ash of purification. The word "burn," in the Hebrew, is *saraph*, the verb denoting the destruction of objects of all kinds. It is interesting to note that *saraph* is never used for the "burning" of the sacrifice on the altar, although a few times it designates the disposal of the refuse, the unused sacrificial parts of the lamb. In Numbers 19:9-17; we see a part of a ritual that calls for the gathering of ashes for purification from sin. However, while the Israelites used this ritual for cleansing and purification (tossing the ashes in their water of cleansing for purification of sins), in Hebrews 9:11-14, we see where Jesus (our high priest) did not enter the tabernacle by means of the blood of goats and calves, but entered the Most Holy Place once and for all by His own blood, having obtained eternal redemption. The blood of goats and bulls and the ashes of a heifer sprinkled on those who are ceremonially unclean sanctify them so that they are outwardly clean; but in reality, their sins still remained on them. But, in partaking of the entire roasted Lamb (in the person of Jesus Christ), the *called out ones* benefit from being totally cleansed, totally freed, and coinheritors of the promises of God!

> How much more, then, will the blood of Christ, who through the eternal Spirit offered himself unblemished to God, cleanse our consciences from acts that led to death, so that we may serve the living God! 15 For this reason Christ is the mediator of a new covenant, that those who are called may receive the promised eternal inheritance – now that he has died as a ransom to set them free from the sins committed under the first covenant, (Hebrews 9:14-15, NIV).

Once again, we see where God used ritual symbolism as examples of what He would eventually fulfill in the person of Jesus Christ.

The eleventh requirement of the Passover Feast, included the Israelites eating the Passover Lamb *"with your cloak tucked into your belt, your sandals on your feet and your staff in your hand, (vs. 11)."* Here we see three symbols of how the Christian must receive Jesus Christ. First of all, the cloak tucked in your belt is symbolic of the Christian who stands firm with the belt of truth buckled around his waist. The sandals on their feet represent the Christian who, with the staff (sword of the Spirit), is prepared to preach the word of God (Ephesians 6:14-17). Once again, we see where God has used ritual symbolism as examples for Christians to use today, as members of the Passover Lamb's army.

The Last Passover Feast requirement involves the manner in which the Israelites were to partake of the Passover Lamb: "Eat it in haste;

it is the Lord's Passover, (vs. 11)." The only example that the author was able to discern from this edict is the accepting of Jesus Christ, as Lord and Savior, as quickly as possible, before it's too late. In 2 Corinthians 6:1, 2, it states:

> As God's fellow workers we urge you not to receive God's grace in vain. For He says, 'In the time of my favor I heard you, and in the day of salvation I helped you.' I tell you, now is the time of God's favor, now is the day of salvation, (2 Corinthians 6:1-2, NIV).

How sad it is to see so many people pondering whether to respond to the nudging of the Holy Spirit, whose power gifts were poured out in these latter days to give His children power they never had before Pentecost. How sad it is to see people scoffing at the gospel that is being preached for their benefit. How great it is to see those who in the past lived contrary to God's will, but who today hold onto the promise of eternal life with our Creator, Almighty God. How blessed to see the millions of people who are turning their lives over in forgiveness of past sins and to follow and serve Jesus Christ, now!

If the reader has gotten this far, and is not completely sure of his or her status with Jesus Christ, God's Passover Lamb, and may doubt whether he or she has yet to surrender completely their lives to Jesus, *now* is the time! *Now* is the day for salvation, the partaking of God's Passover Lamb. Do it *now* and do it quickly!

How does one turn their life over to Jesus? In Romans 10:9, 10, it states:

> That if you confess with your mouth, 'Jesus is Lord,' and believe in your heart that God raised Him from the dead, you will be saved. For it is with your heart that you believe and are justified, and it is with your mouth that you confess and are saved, Romans 10:9-10, NIV).

What greater confidence could a born-again believer have than knowing they are truly a chosen child of God, being prepared for possibly the greatest time of evangelization, ministering and witnessing to a dying world? What greater confidence could the Christian have at this very moment, than knowing they are truly saved and will be able to stand firm to the very end when Jesus Christ returns to rule and reign as King of Kings and Lord of Lords?

Stop for a moment, place this book to the side, and go into you prayer closet by yourself. Reach out with all your heart and soul and ask Jesus to create in you a new heart, to heal past wounds, to forgive you for past sins, to forgive you for your slackness and half-hearted commitment to your prayer and fellowship with Him, to renew your spirit, to restore in you a joy unspeakable, to place in your heart the complete and total confidence that you are His son or daughter. Ask Him for an extra portion of power from the Holy Spirit. Ask Him for greater power to help you to better understand His word, for sound instruction that will help you to become more obedient to His will for you and in your life. Ask Him for the strength to be willing to pick up your cross and follow Him wherever He leads you, even if it means dying for His will, as He died for your eternal salvation. Go ahead, reach out and let Him come into your life, your heart, your total being – and then, begin to praise Him for what He has done. Begin to praise Him for providing you with the Passover Lamb. Begin to praise Him for His grace, His mercy, and His loving kindness, but most of all, begin to praise Him for providing us with Jesus, His glorious Passover Lamb, who took away the sins of the world!

Chapter 11
THE DUAL PURPOSE OF GOD'S MIRACLES

In the last chapter, we examined the Passover Feast requirements and their spiritual significance to the believer. We were able to see how God, in His omniscient nature, not only provided the ceremonial requirements for *The Passover*; He also provided spiritual types and symbols that can (and should) be applied to our present Christian walk. We saw how God not only established the methods with which the Israelites were to partake the Passover Feast, we also saw that God ordained these rituals be observed as a permanent reminder for Israel (and her faith-believing descendants) as to how God was able to free them from their captors in Egypt.

What the Israelites failed to grasp, however, was that these very same rituals were (and are today) perfect symbols and types of how God would fulfill His overall redemption plan for mankind. What the Israelites then and today's Jewish community failed to comprehend, was that the Passover Lamb they sacrificed was (and is) a prophetic symbol of the coming Messiah. As a matter of fact, if the Christian community will take the time to carefully read and study the Old Testament, it will be found that most of what God performed through

His chosen *called out* people was prophecy through types and symbols that hold the keys to history and the events we see unfolding before our very eyes. God not only provided a systematic program of rules and regulations by which Israel was to follow, but this system of governance also included types or symbols that provide clues (and patterns) that reveal God's unchanging nature, especially as it applies to these "latter days." If examined carefully, we can see how God operated during Old Testament times, and those methods are still applicable today. One major difference is the obvious outpouring of His Holy Spirit gifts on the Day of Pentecost. While the Holy Spirit did indeed work through specific individuals throughout the Old Testament, the outpouring of the Holy Spirit on the Day of Pentecost was a fulfillment of prophecy (Joel 2:28,29) that God's *ecclesia* would receive power from on high to broadcast the gospel to all mankind. This blessed act did not negate the fact that God is still dealing with His chosen people in accordance with His original plan. There is no new dispensation or differing application in the way God has been dealing with His *called out ones* throughout history. True, national Israel experienced a falling away (Romans 11:25), but that was only to allow the Gentiles (all non-Israel nations) the opportunity to accept Jesus Christ as Lord and Savior and thereby become grafted into His Olive Tree (faith-believing Israel) and co-inherit all the promises God made to Abraham, (Galatians 3:29).

If examined very carefully, we can see the things that happened to Israel occurred as examples to keep us from setting our hearts on evil things as they did (1 Corinthians 10:6); but they also reveal, through types and symbols, the very unchanging character and nature of God. As *The Passover* has become an obvious prophetic type of God's revelation (that Jesus would be sacrificed for our sins), the Bible also has many other incidents in the Old Testament that not only record other significant and historical events, but also show us how they serve as prophetic symbols of God's original plans for His people; and, more importantly, the unchanging and consistent nature with which He accomplishes

His goals. These prophetic symbols not only provide insights to God's unchanging nature, they also provide clues concerning the process God will use to accomplish the last phase of His redemptive plan.

As has been recorded in Genesis, the main purpose for the great flood was to punish mankind for its totally deteriorated condition. Unfortunately for that generation, their self-seeking, self-indulgent lifestyle had become so repugnant to God, He had no alternative but to destroy the creation:

> The Lord saw how great man's wickedness on earth had become, and that every inclination of the thoughts of his heart was only on evil all the time, (Genesis 6:5, NIV).

The Lord was grieved that He had made man on the earth, and His heart was filled with pain. So He did the only thing He could:

> So the Lord said, 'I will wipe mankind, whom I have created, from the face of the earth – men and animals, and creatures that move along the ground, and the birds of the air – for I am grieved that I made them.' **But Noah found favor in the eyes of the Lord**, (Genesis 6:6, 7, 8, NIV). [Bold and underline is by the author, solely for emphasis]

The actual account of the Noahaic Flood is found in Genesis 6:9 through 9:17. After careful examination of that historical event, spiritual concepts can be seen that not only provide great examples for a dedicated Christian walk, but they also provide prophetic types and symbols of God's magnificent and unchanging nature.

First of all, the great floodwaters are a type of baptism that provides both salvation and judgment. In 1 Peter 3:21-22, we clearly can understand this message where it states,

> ... and this (flood) water symbolizes baptism that now
> saves you also -- not the removal of dirt from the body
> but the pledge of a good conscience toward God. It
> saves you by the resurrection of Jesus Christ, 22 who
> has gone into heaven and is at God's right hand--with
> angels, authorities and powers in submission to him,
> (1 Peter 3:21, 22, NIV). [Parenthesis by the author]

In the judgment sense, it is clearly evident that God used the great flood to purify His green earth from all that was sinful. In the flood, we see where God flushed the world of sin, and by the very same act, saved righteous Noah and his family.

Here we see a perfect example of how God, through one act, is able to accomplish a dual purpose: the purification from sin (by destroying the world's sinful mass) and the salvation of the righteous. As we will see later on, God's dual purpose principle will be in effect during the end times period, where we will see God pouring out His wrath upon an unbelieving world and still safely carry the righteous ones through the great onslaught without having to remove them from planet earth. Just as God was able to *pass over* the Israelites during the plague He poured out on Egypt, God will also be able to safely carry His *ecclesia* through great tribulation without having to remove it from its evangelizing position here on earth. We say "evangelizing position" because we believe scripture prove that the *ecclesia* will be kept on earth for the purpose of witnessing to the unsaved and bringing more people into the Kingdom of God before Christ returns.

According to Genesis 6:3, God told Noah that His Spirit would not contend with man forever, "*for he is mortal; his days will be a hundred and twenty years*, (Genesis 6:3, NIV)." It obviously took Noah and his sons this much time to not only build the Ark, but also to gather the different species of existing animals and foul that would accompany Noah during the forty days and nights of torrential flood. One can very well imagine the scornful epithets cast toward Noah by an unbelieving world. According to Hebrew 11:7, it appears that Noah not only warned the scoffers about their impending doom, 2 Peter 2:5 specifically states that Noah was "*a preacher of righteousness.*"

We also see this principle in play during the period preceding the plague that God brought on Egypt. Right before the plague hit, Moses and Aaron were seen exhorting Pharaoh to loose Israel to worship God. Pharaoh relented not and was therefore victim to the plague which subsequently passed over the Israelites who responded to God's Passover Feast requirements. The point being made here is that prior to those times where God is seen pouring out His wrath on unrepentant societies, we always see the righteous proclaiming the Word of God! More importantly, you will note that in each of these circumstances, the righteous are never removed from that particular arena; but, rather, we see them being divinely protected by God. Noah was not "raptured" to heaven, nor was Israel. In each case, we see where God safely carries the righteous through his wrath outpouring without having to remove them from impending doom. God's people are always seen escaping from, but not necessarily out of, the arena of terror that befalls the unrighteous. Once again, these two examples clearly show the nature of God's duality of purpose. In these examples, we see where God was able to not only punish the wicked, but also provide a rescue (Passover) scenario for his righteous ones. Let's look at other examples of God's dual purpose, where we can clearly see this principle in effect.

In the Book of Daniel, we see two more examples of this dual principle where God is able to protect (but does not remove) His righteous ones from peril. In Daniel, Chapter 3, we read about three Godly men who stood fast in their faith to God, to the extent that they were prepared to die rather than bow to another god. As the story goes, King Nebuchadnezzar was furious with Shadrach, Meshach and Abednego because they wouldn't bow down to his ninety-foot image of gold. In his edict, Nebuchadnezzar ordered those who wouldn't bow to be tossed into a blazing furnace. Let's read part of this account:

> But there are some Jews whom you have set over the affairs of the providence of Babylon – Shadrach, Meshach and Abednego – who pay no attention to you, O king. They neither serve your gods nor worship the image of gold you have set up. 13 Furious with rage, Nebuchadnezzar summoned Shadrach, Meshach and Abednego. So these men were brought before the king, 14 and Nebuchadnezzar said to them, "Is it true, Shadrach, Meshach and Abednego that you do not serve my gods or worship the image of gold I have set up? 15 Now when you hear the sound of the horn, flute, zither, lyre, harp, pipes and all kinds of music, if you are ready to fall down and worship the image I made, very good. But if you do not worship it, you will be thrown immediately into a blazing furnace. Then what god will be able to rescue from my hand?" 16 Shadrach, Meshach and Abednego replied to the king, "O Nebuchadnezzar, we do not need to defend ourselves before you in this matter. 17 **If we are thrown into the Blazing furnace, the God we serve is able to save us from it, and he will rescue us from your hand, O king.** 18 **But even if he does not, we want you to know, O king, that we will not serve your gods or worship the image of gold you have set up**, (Daniel 3:12-18, NIV)." [Underline and bold is by the author, solely for emphasis]

As the story goes, Nebuchadnezzar ordered the three Godly men tossed into the furnace; however, the three were not affected whatsoever by the blazing fire. The strong men that the king ordered to toss them into the furnace were burned instantly, but the three righteous ones experienced not even a single singed hair on their heads. Their robes weren't scorched and, for that matter, they didn't even smell like they had even come close to the flames. The most interesting part of this incident is the amazed look on the King's face as he watched the entire incident:

> 'He said, "Look! I see four men walking around in the
> fire, unbound and unharmed, and the fourth looks like
> a son of the Gods, (Daniel 3:25, NIV).'

Much conjecture has been made about the identity of the fourth individual in the fire; but whomever you choose to name, the author's spirit tells him that Jesus Christ Himself was in the blazing furnace providing the protection. But even more important is what these three men stated, in regards to their faithfulness and loyalty to God. These committed *called out ones* not only believed that God was able to rescue them, their commitment to God was so great that they said: "*But even if he does not* (rescue us), *we want you to know, O king, that we will not serve your gods or worship the image of gold you have set up*, (Daniel 3:18, NIV)." [Parenthesis is by the author, solely for emphasis]

What modern-day Christian can make such a courageous claim or commitment to God in the face of death? What member of God's *ecclesia*, when under such extreme financial burden may buckle under and give in to the 666 system, or when being tortured by the man of lawlessness to renounce Jesus Christ as Lord and Savior, is prepared to look into the face of death and make such a bold proclamation as did these three? What *called out ones* can say, at this present moment, that he or she is prepared to die for Christ, knowing that He may not even rescue them from that imminent peril? Who truly knows if our destiny calls for death or rescue? In this particular case, Shadrach, Meshach and Abednego *were* rescued, proving that God *is* able to protect *called out ones* regardless of how hopeless the imminent peril

207

appears. More important than God's ability to rescue the *called out ones*, these three valiant believers were willing to give up their lives rather than serve or worship any god except their own! Is today's *Christian Church* prepared to make such a commitment?

Nevertheless, what we see here is a beautiful example of God's ability to protect (without removing) His *called out ones* during times of peril. The prophetically profound part of this story is that, once again, the righteous are seen proclaiming allegiance and faith toward God while facing death squarely in the face! The net result of their faith is seen not only in them being protected from the burning flames, but more importantly gaining glory and praise to God from the lips of unbelievers. King Nebuchadnezzar said:

> **Praise be to the God of Shadrach, Meshach and Abednego, who has sent his angel and rescued his servants**! They trusted in him and defied the king's command and were willing to give up their lives rather than serve or worship any god except their own God, (Daniel 3:28, NIV). [Bold and underline is by the author, solely for emphasis]

Once again we see where God is glorified by the demonstrated faith of His children, even when facing death. The author sincerely believes that had Shadrach, Meshach and Abednego been lifted out of the furnace through a "secret rapture" process, the king would not have responded in such a praiseful manner. He would have merely discounted their disappearance as one would when a piece of paper hits a blazing inferno. Poof! Up in smoke they went! But instead, he witnessed the power of Almighty God at work in and through those *called out ones* of faith.

In Daniel, Chapter 6, we see this same dual principal applied once again. In the famed story of Daniel and the lion's den, we again see

208

where one of God's righteous ones chose death rather than serve or pray to another god. Nebuchadnezzar's cronies were jealous of Daniel and his prophetic gifts from God. They were forever trying to paint him with disfavor in the eyes of the king. They cajoled the king to declare an edict that no one should pray to any god or man for thirty days except for the king. Rather than obey that order, Daniel went to his upstairs room, as he always did three times a day, and got on his knees and prayed, giving thanks to his God. The king's cronies sneaked up to his room in hopes of catching Daniel violating the King's orders and caught him praying. They immediately rushed to the king and relayed that Daniel had, in fact, been caught praying to his God. The king was furious and gave the command for Daniel to be tossed into the lion's den:

> A stone was brought and placed over the mouth of the den, and the king sealed it with his own signet ring and with the rings of his nobles, so that Daniel's situation might not be changed. 18 Then the king returned to his palace and spent the night without eating and without any entertainment being brought to him. And he could not sleep. 19 At the first light of dawn, the king got up and hurried to the lions' den. 20 When he came near the den, he called to Daniel in an anguished voice, "Daniel, servant of the living God, has your God, whom you serve continually, been able to rescue you from the lions?" 21 Daniel answered, "O king, live forever. 22 **My God sent his angel, and he shut the mouths of the lions. They have not hurt me, because I was found innocent in his sight**. Nor have I ever done any wrong before you, O king." 23 **The king was overjoyed** and gave orders to lift Daniel out of the den. **And when Daniel was lifted from the den, no wound was found on him, because he had trusted in his God**, (Daniel 6:17-23). [Bold and underline is by the author, solely for emphasis]

Once again, as was the case with Shadrach, Meshach and Abednego, one of God's righteous ones was not only delivered by God's protective hand, it also resulted in God being glorified again. As we review that scenario, the key points to be made are that God's righteous ones, when looking at death squarely in the face, are always seen proclaiming their faith in God, not only to be delivered, but also resulting in God being glorified by virtue of their faith and testimony.

The same principle will apply during the increased times of tribulation, which will be experienced by the *called out ones* before Jesus returns to rule and reign. We see a perfect example of this principle in Jesus' exhortation to the disciples in Luke 21:10-19. In this group of scriptures, Luke expands with more detail on the Lord's Sermon on the Mount:

> Then He said to them: "Nation will rise against nation, and kingdom against Kingdom. There will be great earthquakes, famines and pestilences in various places, and fearful events and great signs from Heaven. But before all this, they will lay hands on you and persecute you. They will deliver you to synagogues and prisons, and you will be brought before kings and governors, and all on account of my name. This will result in your being witnesses to them. **But make up your mind not to worry beforehand how you will defend yourselves. For I will give you words and wisdom that none of your adversaries will be able to resist or contradict.** You will be betrayed by parents, brothers, relatives and friends, and they will put some of you to death. **All men will hate you because of me.** But not a hair of your head will perish. By standing firm you will save yourselves, (Luke 21:10-19). [Underline and bold is by the author, solely for emphasis]

In this group of scriptures, we see a perfect example of what many Christians will experience immediately before Jesus returns, at which time they *"will see the Son of Man coming in a cloud with power and great glory,* (Luke 21:27, NIV)." Jesus goes on to say, in the following verse, *"When these things begin to take place, stand up and lift up your heads, because your redemption is drawing near,* (Luke 21:28, NIV)."

Many theorists interpret the persecutions found in Luke, Chapter 21, solely from an historical perspective, believing these things have already taken place, citing the destruction of Jerusalem by the Romans in 70 A.D., as proof. There is scripture and historical data to validate much truth to this interpretation. However, I'm certain that most theologians will agree that the Son of Man has yet to make His final arrival on earth with power and great glory. What we do see in Luke 21:10-19 is the exact same principle we saw when Shadrach, Meshach and Abednego were tossed into the furnace for holding fast to the testimony of God. This same principle was witnessed when the apostle Paul was brought before King Agrippa in Acts 26. Paul was being tried for upholding the testimony of Jesus Christ, and although facing a death sentence, he commenced to utter words to the king, words and wisdom that none of his adversaries were able to resist or contradict; Holy Spirit-filled words that eventually caused Agrippa to soften his heart. Although it isn't recorded that King Agrippa accepted Jesus Christ as his Lord and Savior (it is recorded that he was almost persuaded to become a Christian), he did repent his position to a degree.

The important point being made here is that Christians will be brought before various authorities, kings, magistrates and governors, whatever ruling groups will be on earth during the persecution immediately preceding *The Second Advent*; and God's purpose for this will be two-fold. One, to persuade as many people as possible to accept the Lord before He pours out His wrath; and two, to cause situations that will bring glory to God! These verses (Luke 21:10-19 and all of Acts 26) are not only proof that God's *ecclesia* will be used for a greater purpose during times of great tribulation, they are also proof that it is not necessary for God to have to remove His *called out ones* from earth through a secret escape to heaven scenario to fulfill His redemption plan.

The author realizes that many new (and even long-time believers) are still concerned about the fact that Luke 21 states that many Christians will be put to death. This is still a very horrible thought for many to imagine. In our final chapter, we will be sharing scriptures that should help to allay those fears. However, the message we are attempting to bring forth in this chapter is that God's word, especially in the verses covered so far, reveals that He can accomplish the dual task of punishing unbelievers and at the same time *pass over* the faithful without removing them from the situation.

Throughout the Old Testament, the Bible is replete with similar stories and incidents where Almighty God is not only able to rescue His righteous ones from impending doom, but the manner in which He accomplishes these acts can never be questioned as to who is responsible for the deliverance. Man cannot steal the glory away from God. King David's strength was not responsible for Goliath's downfall. The walls of Jericho did not crumble due to Joshua's effort, but rather, due to the Lord's deliverance, (Joshua 6:1-27). The Midianites were not defeated by Gideon, they were given to him by God, (Judges 7:15). Poor Gideon didn't even have the faith (he tested God's sincerity with the fleece); but, yet, God handed the Midianites over to him. It wasn't Samson's individual strength that was responsible for the slaying of over a thousand Philistines, nor did he possess a magical donkey's jawbone; it was the power of God's Holy Spirit, (Judges 15:14).

On and on we see where God's Almighty power has rescued the righteous from the beginning of time. Yet, not once do we see God secretly "catching up" His righteous ones up to heaven to escape peril. We always see God bringing His righteous ones *through the peril*, not out of it, especially those who are found faithfully proclaiming the word of God for His everlasting glory! God's character is unchanging! God has been dealing with His *called out ones* the same way He has dealt with His original *ecclesia*, His chosen people, from the beginning. God has not been dispensing nor administering the affairs of His people in various manners and various levels of grace and mercy, as dispensationalists hope He has, solely to fit their eschatological mythologies. The Lord is the same today, yesterday and forever, (Hebrews 13:8)! God's duality of purpose and His ways of accomplishing His will are not determined by mere men who interpret scripture to infer erroneous epochs, places and people. They erroneously interpret scripture solely to suit their soothing agenda, always compartmentalizing God's set times and purpose, and denying Him His due glory. The God, who is, who will be and always has been the same from eternity, will rescue those who trust in Him. They will be delivered, even if they should die!

As God was able to bring Shadrach, Meshach and Abednego through the blazing furnace, God will also be able to protect the remaining faithful through the end times. Just as God was able to deliver Israel from Egypt, passing the plague over them, God will be able to *pass over* His righteous ones when He pours out His wrath on the unrepentant. Just as God was able to deliver Noah and his flock from the flood, God also will be able to carry His righteous ones through great tribulation before *The Second Advent*! It would appear to many comfortable Christians that it would be easier for God to "snatch" us out of earth and have us wait patiently for an undisclosed period of time in heaven. However, the author believes that scripture supports the fact that God will use His *called out ones*, His *ecclesia*, you and me, all of us who believe that He is able to protect us during this horrendous period, for the sole purpose of bringing as many more people as possible to His kingdom, and this for His everlasting glory!

But, beware! Many theorists will continue to espouse soothing and titillating theories, as they puff up themselves as being holier and more knowledgeable of God's words, when in reality their greed for money, power and fame will result in Christians being lulled into a false sense of physical security. Great distress *is* in store for the *called out ones* during the imminent period of increasing tribulation, such as has never been seen before. But God can and is able to rescue the Christian from these horrendous persecutions through *The End Times Passover*, even while in the process of pouring out His punishment on the ungodly:

> **But there were also false prophets among the people, just as there will be false teachers among you. They will secretly introduce destructive heresies,** even denying the sovereign Lord who bought them-- bringing swift destruction on themselves. 2 **Many will follow their shameful ways and will bring the way of truth into disrepute.** 3 **In their greed these teachers will exploit you with stories they have made up.** Their condemnation has long been hanging over them, and their destruction has not been sleeping. 4 For if God did not spare angels when they sinned, but sent them to hell, putting them into gloomy dungeons to be held for judgment; 5 if he did not spare the ancient world when he brought the flood on its ungodly people, **but protected Noah, a preacher of righteousness, and seven others**; 6 if he condemned the cities of Sodom and Gomorrah by burning them to ashes, and made them an example of what is going to happen to the ungodly; 7 **and if he rescued Lot, a righteous man, who was distressed by the filthy lives of lawless men** 8 (for that righteous man, living among them day after day, was tormented in his righteous soul by the lawless deeds he saw and heard)-- 9 if this is

so, **then the Lord knows how to rescue godly men from trials and to hold the unrighteous for the day of judgment, while continuing their punishment**, (2 Peter 2:1-9, NIV). [Bold or underlined is by the author, solely for emphasis]

Chapter 12
GOD'S END TIMES PASSOVER!

In a previous chapter we pretty much explained the original Passover, demonstrating how God was able to symbolically and prophetically show the nation of Israel what the significance of the Passover rituals represented. Unfortunately, the Israelites (the Ten Northern tribes of Ephraim) and the Jews (the Southern tribes of Judah) of those times, as well as those of today, failed to see that the sacrificing of the lamb actually represented the propitiatory act that God (through the incarnate Jesus) performed on the cross at Calvary. This miraculous sacrifice to end all sacrifices provided humanity with the greatest gift it could ever receive, payment for the sins of all mankind, by where those who accept that gift now share in the protective grace of God. This salvation was prophesied to the Israelites through The Passover. That Passover applies as well to all of the Gentiles who have been engrafted into His original *ecclesia* body after the crucifixion and resurrections of Jesus Christ, and the subsequent power gifts poured out by the Holy Spirit on Day of Pentecost.

The author also feels that throughout this book (and our first book) he has exhaustively covered a myriad of topics, and presented specific scriptures, to show that a secret pre-tribulation escape to heaven is not part of God's redemption program; but, rather, the *called out ones*, the *ecclesia* of Christ, will remain on earth throughout the most horrendous times of persecution ever seen in the history of mankind. Yes, the living *called out ones* will be *caught together* with the resurrected ones who currently sleep in Christ, and there will be a *meeting* in the air for the purpose of greeting and escorting the Lord as He makes His final descent back to earth, accompanied by a mighty army of His holy angels.

Many of those who will be *caught together* will be martyred immediately before *The Second Advent*, victims of Satan's and the man of lawlessness' diabolical efforts during the increased times of tribulation prior to the Lord's return. Those who are executed during the times of tribulation imminent to the return of Christ will have been in the forefront extolling the gospel, awaiting their resurrection at the Lord's return. And those who are martyred during that increased time of tribulation will (and should) not be classified as a different group of people (supposedly unrepentant Jews or descendants of Jacob) who supposedly will convert to Christ merely and solely because they experienced God's wrath outpouring. The author believes scripture clearly states that God does not want us to come to Him by force. At least not the God the author knows and loves. The author can't imagine a group of nonbelievers being beaten down to point of accepting salvation after the *Christian Church* has supposedly been 'Raptured' to heaven anywhere from three and a half to seven years before Christ returns. No, my friends, God doesn't beat people into submission. He knocks on the door of our hearts and beckons us to come to Him like little children, crying "Abba Father." Yes, my friends, those faith-believing remnant remaining to the very end will all be followers of Christ, God's *called out ones*, the *ecclesia* of Jesus Christ, preaching the gospel to the very end, as witnesses (martyrs) for our Lord and Savior, Jesus Christ. Many will be killed, martyred for Christ, just as have so many others who experienced persecution and great sufferings throughout history for their hope in Messiah!

It is interesting to note here, that the word for *witness* in the Greek is defined as *martyr*. So many times Christians have boasted about *witnessing* for the Lord, as if *witnessing* means solely preaching or extolling the Gospel, never realizing that the true *witnesses* are those who have carried their cross, or will be picking up their crosses, as Christ did, and laying down their lives so that others may also have eternal life.

There will be two classifications of *called out ones* that will be participating in that great *meeting* (Gr. *apentesis,* face-to-face meeting) in the air with the Lord during His descent to earth. One, those who throughout history have fallen asleep in the Messiah, either by martyrdom or natural death; which will include the many who will be victims of the antichristian forces prevalent during the last days. The other classification will be *called out ones* who will be alive at the time of increased tribulation, moments before the Lord returns. Both groups will be changed into immortal and spiritual bodies and *caught* together to meet and greet and escort back the returning Lord. Those who are asleep now have no need to worry anymore about experiencing the antichristian oppression and torture at the hands of the man of lawlessness and his military forces. So we won't dwell as much on them as we will on those "who are alive" at *The Second Advent.* However, we will point to Matthew 24:1-29, which very clearly describes what those martyred Christians have faced in the past, and what will be facing those *called out ones* who are alive during the final hour:

> Jesus left the temple and was walking away when his disciples came up to him to call his attention to its buildings. 2 "Do you see all these things?" he asked.

"I tell you the truth, not one stone here will be left on another; every one will be thrown down." 3 As Jesus was sitting on the Mount of Olives, the disciples came to him privately. "Tell us," they said, "when will this happen, and what will be the sign of your coming and of the end of the age?" 4 Jesus answered: " Watch out that no one deceives you. 5 For many will come in my name, claiming, 'I am the Christ," and will deceive many. 6 You will hear of wars and rumors of wars, but see to it that you are not alarmed. Such things must happen, but the end is still to come. 7 Nation will rise against nation, and kingdom against kingdom. There will be famines and earthquakes in various places. 8 All these are the beginning of birth pains. 9 **'Then you will be handed over to be persecuted and put to death, and you will be hated by all nations because of me**. 10 **At that time many will turn away from the faith and will betray and hate each other**, 11 **and many false prophets will appear and deceive many people.** 12 Because of the increase of wickedness, the love of most will grow cold, 13 **but he who stands firm to the end will be saved.** 14 And this gospel of the kingdom will be preached in the whole world as a testimony to all nations, and then the end will come. 15 "So when you see standing in the holy place 'the abomination that causes desolation,' spoken of through the prophet Daniel – let the reader understand – 16 then let those who are in Judea flee to the mountains. 17 Let no one on the roof of his house go down to take anything out of the house. 18 let no one in the field go back to get his cloak. 19 **How dreadful it will be in those days** for pregnant women and nursing mothers! 20 Pray that your flight will not take place in winter or on the

Sabbath. 21 **For then there will be great distress, unequaled from the beginning of the world until now – and never to be equaled again**. 22 **if those days had not been cut short, no one would survive, but for the sake of the elect those days will be shortened**. 23 **At that time if anyone says to you, 'Look, here is the Christ!' or, 'There he is!' do not believe it**. 24 For false Christs and false prophets will appear and perform great signs and miracles to deceive even the elect – if that were possible. 25 See I have told you ahead of time. 26 "So if anyone tells you, 'There he is out in the desert,' do not go out; or 'Here he is, in the inner rooms,' do not believe it. 27 For as the lightning comes from the east and flashes to the west, so will be the coming of the Son of Man. 28 Wherever there is a carcass, there the vultures will gather. 29 "immediately after the distress of those days, "'the sun will be darkened, and the moon will not give its light; the stars will fall from the sky, and the heavenly bodies will be shaken, (Matthew 24:1-29, NIV). [Bold and underline is by the author, solely for emphasis]

For those who remain alive immediately before the Lord returns, God, through His word, has foretold of the protection He will be providing them, and no more boldly and clearly does He describe this 'End Times Passover' than He does in Psalms 91. Let's read this chapter in its entirety.

He who dwells in the shelter of the Most High will rest in the shadow of the Almighty. 2 I will say of the Lord, "He is my refuge and my fortress, my God, in whom I trust." 3 **Surely he will save you from the fowler's snare and from the deadly pestilence.** 4 He will cover you with his feathers, and under his wings you will find refuge; his faithfulness will be your shield and rampart. 5 You will not fear the terror of night, nor the arrow that flies by day, 6 nor the pestilence that stalks in the darkness, nor the plague that destroys at midday. 7 A thousand may fall at your side, ten thousand at your right hand, but it will not come near you. 8 **You will only observe with your eyes and see the punishment of the wicked.** 9 If you make the Most High your dwelling – even the Lord, who is my refuge – 10 **then no harm will befall you, no disaster will come near your tent.** 11 **For he will command his angels concerning you to guard you in all your ways;** 12 they will lift you up in their hands, so that you will not strike your foot against a stone. 13 You will tread upon the lion and the cobra; you will trample the great lion and the serpent. 14 **"Because he loves me," says the Lord, "I will rescue him; I will protect him, for he acknowledges my name.** 15 **He will call upon me, and I will answer him; I will be with him in trouble, I will deliver him and honor him**. 16 With long life will I satisfy him and show him my salvation, (Psalm 91:1-16, NIV). [Bold and underline is by the author, solely for emphasis]

The reader will note in verse 8 that those *called out ones* who remain *alive* during the period the Lord begins to punish the wicked, will be observing with their eyes (not participating) in the meting out of this punishment of *the wicked*. The 10th and 11th verse clearly states that the Lord's angels will be guarding the *called out ones* while He pours out His wrath on the unjust. This is the Lord's End Times Passover!

Another group of scriptures that speaks about His End Times Passover protective power, while at the same time He will be pouring out His wrath on unbelievers, is found in Isaiah 43: 1-7. Let's read:

But now, this is what the Lord says – he who created you, O Jacob, he who formed you, O Israel; "**Fear not, for I have redeemed you**; I have called you by name; you are mine. 2 **When you pass through the waters, I will be with you; and when you pass through the rivers, they will not sweep over you. When you walk through the fire, you will not be burned; the flames will not set you ablaze.** 3 For I am the Lord, your God, the Holy One of Israel, your Savior; I give Egypt for your ransom, Cush and Seba in your stead. 4 **Since you are precious and honored in my sight, and because I love you, I will give men in exchange for you, and people in exchange for your life**. 5 **Do not be afraid, for I am with you; I will bring your children from the east and gather you from the west. 6 I will say to the north, 'Give them up!' and to the south, 'Do not hold them back.'** Bring my sons from afar and my daughters from the ends of the earth – 7 everyone who is called by my name, whom I created for my glory, whom I formed and made, (Isaiah 43:1-7, NIV). [Bold and underline is by the author, solely for emphasis]

The reader will notice that this End Times Passover protection applies to His *redeemed people,* Jacob, Israel: "*O Jacob, he who formed you, O Israel; "Fear not, for I have redeemed you; I have called you by name; you are mine* (vs1)." Therefore, the only conclusion that can be made is that this reference applies to those He purchased with the blood of Christ, God's church, His *ecclesia*, and cannot apply to national Israel or the legalistic Jews, as so many theorists profess.

Both the group of scriptures above and the following one attest to the fact that as *The Resurrection* ensues, the Lord pours out His wrath on the unrepentant. For example here is another group of scriptures that allude to God's End Times Passover program:

> As a woman with child and about to give birth
> writhes and cries out in her pain, so were we in your
> presence, O Lord. 18 We were with child, we writhed
> in pain, but we gave birth to wind. We have not
> brought salvation to the earth; we have not given
> birth to people of the world. 19 **But your dead will
> live; their bodies will rise. You, who dwell in the
> dust, wake up and shout for joy.** Your dew is like
> the dew of the morning; the earth will give birth to
> her dead. 20 Go, my people, **enter your rooms** and
> shut the doors behind you; hide yourselves for a little
> while **until his wrath has passed by**. 21 **See, the
> Lord is coming out of his dwelling to punish the
> people of the earth for their Sins**. The earth will
> disclose the blood shed upon her; she will conceal her
> Slain no longer, (Isaiah 26:17-21, NIV). [Bold, italics
> and underline by the author, solely for emphasis]

It is interesting to note that in this particular group of scriptures *The Resurrection* is mentioned before the Lord asks us to enter our chambers for protection as He commences to pour out His wrath on those who refused to repent and turn to Him. The author's experience has taught him that many scriptural chapters have breaking points between them, and do not necessarily mean that one comes before the other in chronological order. Nevertheless, the verse above (20) that states, *enter your rooms ...until His wrath has passed by,* could not be referring to a Rapture three-and-a-half to seven years earlier. This command from God is stated simultaneously along with *The Resurrection* and His pouring out of wrath. Therefore, one must conclude that *The Resurrection* and being *caught* together to meet the Lord in the air happen at the same time, which is at *The Second Advent*! Ergo, Post-Tribulationists are more on target as to the timing of the return of Christ than Pre or Mid-Tribulationists. The only thing Post-Tribulationists fail to see is that *called out ones* never get *caught up* to heaven; but, rather, they are *caught* together with those that sleep solely to have a meeting in the air with the returning Lord!

What these rooms represent is not made succinctly clear. However it appears that they represent a place where the Lord secretly hides (Psalm 27:5) His *called out ones* while He pours out His wrath. This is a perfect example of the tribulation protection that God has provided a myriad of *called out ones* throughout history (without having to remove them to heaven), including the protection he provided to Daniel in the lion's den; Meshach, Shadrach and Abednego in the fiery furnace; and, of course, the same protection God provided Noah in the Ark, (Luke 17: 27).

The author might add that in Isaiah 26, verse 20, the Hebrew word for *rooms* is *cheder* (chambers), which corresponds to the Greek word *tameion* (chambers), which should not to be confused with the words *rooms* or *mansions* mentioned in John 14:2, which uses the Greek word *mone* (an abiding, an abode). [Refer back to Chapter 10 (*Heavenly Minded*) of our first book, for extensive explanation regarding the differences between *room* (Gr. *topos*, condition, opportunity, occasion, and license,) and *chambers* (Gr. *tameion*, private rooms, and secret chambers).

Could these *rooms* Isaiah speaks of be situated inside God's Holy City, which is seen descending at *The Second Advent*? Could these *chambers* be where the *ecclesia* will be caught up to have that meeting in the air with our Lord, rather than being taken to up to a stationary heaven for three and a half to seven years? Could these *chambers* possibly be where the Lord, through His End Times Passover, will house those who are *caught up* while He pours out His wrath on the unrepentant? Whereas the Bible doesn't clearly or specifically state (in 1 Thessalonians 4:17) that the *meeting* will take place in the descending New Jerusalem, neither does that verse state that the snatched *ecclesia* is taken up to a stationary heaven. No Bible expositor has ever provided scripture that specifically states the *called out ones* are taken to *up* to heaven, whether they are advocates of a secret Pre-Tribulation escape to heaven scenario, or not.

The author is not proffering a new theory here. However, if the scriptures he provided in an earlier chapter (in our first book) concerning the Holy City of God, New Jerusalem, the Bride of the Lamb, can be viewed as descending at *The Second Advent* of Jesus Christ. And, if the scriptures he provided in Chapter 10 (*Heavenly Minded*) of our first book prove no one goes up to heaven immediately after death, nor at the so-called Rapture, scripture does provide for the possibility that the *meeting in the air* with the *called out ones* and Jesus Christ could very well happen inside of God's descending Holy City. Those whose names are written in the Lamb's Book of Life will be the only ones that will be allowed entrance into New Jerusalem, which will descend to earth, which will be the headquarters of Jesus Christ, to rule and reign on earth forever. Therefore, even though scripture doesn't clearly state that these chambers are inside of the descending Holy City of God, there is scripture that clearly states that God does provide these chambers for His *called out ones* while He pours out His wrath on the unrepentant. Following is Matthew Henry's observation on this aspect in his commentary of Isaiah 26:20:

> He invites them into their chambers (v. 20): "Come, my people, come to me, come with me" (he calls them nowhere but where he himself will accompany them); "let the storm that disperses others bring you nearer together. Come, and enter into thy chambers; stay not abroad, lest you be caught in the storm, as the Egyptians in the hail," Ex. 9:21. 1. "Come into chambers of distinction; come into your own apartments, and continue not any longer mixed with the children of Babylon. Come out

from among them, and be you separate," 2 Co. 6:17; Rev. 18:4. If God has set apart those that are godly for himself, they ought to set themselves apart. 2. "Into chambers of defence, in which by the secresy or the strength of them you may be safe in the worst of times." The attributes of God are the secret of his tabernacle, Ps. 27:5. His name is a strong tower, into which we may run for shelter, Prov. 18:10. We must by faith find a way into these chambers, and there hide ourselves; that is, with a holy security and serenity of mind, we must put ourselves under the divine protection. Come, as Noah into the ark, for he shut the doors about him. When dangers are threatening it is good to retire, and lie hid, as Elijah did by the brook Cherith. 3. Into chambers of devotion. "Enter into thy closet, and shut thy door, Mt. 6:6. Be private with God: Enter into thy chamber, to examine thyself, and commune with thy own heart, to pray, and humble thyself before God." This work is to be done in times of distress and danger; and thus we hide ourselves, that is, we recommend ourselves to God to hide us, **and he will hide us either under heaven or in heaven**. Israel must keep within doors when the destroying angel is slaying the first-born of Egypt, else the blood on the door-posts will not secure them. So must Rahab and her family when Jericho is being destroyed. Those are most safe that are least seen. Qui bene latuit, benevixit—He has lived well who has sought a proper degree of concealment. (Matthew Henry's Commentary, Isaiah 26:20) [Bold and underlines is by the author, solely for emphasis]

Matthew Henry could make no definite pronouncement as to whether these chambers mentioned in Isaiah 26:17-21 are *under heaven* or *in heaven*. Theorists would choose these chambers be located up and inside heaven. The author chooses to believe these chambers are inside God's Holy City, which is seen descending to earth when He begins to pour out His wrath on the unrepentant. If theorists choose these chambers to be up in heaven, and the call to enter these chambers is being made to the *ecclesia*, as it speaks about the time that God's wrath is being poured out, then this cannot paint a picture of a secret Pre-Tribulation escape to heaven. As theorists claim, the so-called Rapture is supposed to happen three and a half to seven years before God pours out His wrath on the unjust! If anything, God's *called out ones* have been on earth giving testimony to God's saving grace. They have been experiencing great tribulation at the hands of the man of lawlessness, bringing others to Christ. Now, as Jesus Christ leads His vast army of angels to rescue His *ecclesia* from this tribulation, He *snatches* His *ecclesia* (both those who are asleep in Christ, along with those alive and waiting for His return) through His End Times Passover, and commences to pour out His wrath on the unjust!

Tribulation or Wrath?

The biggest confusion the author has seen coming from the secret escape from tribulation camps has been their inability to recognize the difference between tribulation and wrath. The man of lawlessness and his cohorts will *afflict* (Gr. *thlipsis*, tribulations) and even kill many Christians, but God's wrath is designed solely for the unbelieving and unrepentant. The wrath by the man of lawlessness is the *called out ones*' tribulation, but God's wrath is His vengeful punishment on the unrepentant, that wrath which He will pour out on those who did not accept His gift of salvation:

> **For God did not appoint us to suffer wrath but to receive salvation through our Lord Jesus Christ.**10 He died for us so that, whether we are awake or asleep, we may live together with him, (1 Thessalonians 5:9, 10 NIV).[Bold and underline is by the author, solely for emphasis]

All of the scriptures mentioned so far in this chapter prove that God is able to deliver His people from any calamity. He did so throughout the Bible as previously mentioned with Daniel, Meshach, Shadrach and Abednego, Noah and so many others. Why would anyone think that God is not able to protect His chosen people while at the same time He is pouring out His wrath on the unrepentant?

Unfortunately, what many Christians are not prepared for, nor even want to imagine, is what was spoken about in Matthew 24, where it states that Christians will be persecuted, and even at the hands of relatives and other loved ones. That's the true horror, that many of our so-called friends and loved ones (and maybe even fellow church members) will abandon the faith and acquiesce to the pressures of the world and literally sell out their souls to antichristian forces. Many in exchange even for mere scraps of food and water, and to avoid any pain being inflicted on them. The treachery by those who we once befriended, loved, trusted and supported in all things, will, in a self preservation mode, betray their former friends and relatives. "*The horror, the horror,*" is the appropriate and descriptive phrase for this time, words which actor Marlon Brando uttered so agonizingly in the movie, *Apocalypse Now*.

So, the truth remains that many, hundreds of thousands, maybe even millions of Christians will be brought before the magistrates, kings, or government officials that will comprise the authorities of the Beast state, to face charges of treason and sedition for preaching the Gospel of Jesus Christ. Many *called out ones* will be tortured and even killed for what will be perceived as blasphemy against the world's new ruling order, which will (by then) have abolished the freedom of religion. However, God said not to worry, He will provide His *called out ones* with words to speak that cannot be dissuaded, words that will pierce the hardest of hearts in order to bring great glory to God and to His Kingdom. These select Christians will become witnesses (martyrs) as a result of being accused, judged and executed as enemies of the state, at those diabolically controlled tribunals. Many in attendance at (or who view through media) these trials, who do not believe in Christ, will be moved by the power of the Holy Spirit. They will stirred by the testimonies of these *called out ones* to also pick up their cross for Jesus, as they themselves will witness those innocent soldiers of the cross being convicted of no crime save their belief in Jesus Christ. Many will be moved by the power of the Holy Spirit as they witness the diabolically induced injustice against the *called out ones*, and will repent and hitherto will instantly convert to the Lord, also placing them in harm's way. Unfortunately, the Pre-Tribulation theory, that bespeaks Christians will be secretly caught away to safety in heaven before God pours out His wrath, has literally lulled millions into a false sense of security. When in fact, millions *will* suffer for Christ's sake and *will* be put to death at the hands of antichristian forces.

No one wants to think about death or dying, primarily because no one really knows what death truly entails. Ecclesiastes states that when a person dies, they remember or know nothing henceforth, until *The Resurrection*. There have been numerous recorded accounts of out-of-body experiences by those who came close to death. And in each of those cases, those who came back have reported experiencing either a hellish encounter or seeing a wonderful white light (or even seeing Jesus) or departed family members. It is interesting that after being resuscitated back to life; claimants have never reported or could remember the pain of death or dying. Who really knows what death is like until it is experienced? There must be something about death that God knows needs not to be feared.

Humans fear death for many reasons. Fear of leaving loved ones behind uncared for, fear of leaving their earthly possessions to others, fear of not being able to finish a work. However, as the Bible clearly states, the biggest fear is in not knowing what death holds in store. The biblical reality is that we have this fear because we don't know true love, the love that one can only know and experience from God.

Those who don't know the love of God have fear of punishment, because there is punishment for sin, our daily sinful actions. Those who know true love have experienced the forgiveness God provided them when Christ died on the cross to pay for our sins. If we have not accepted this grace and forgiveness, we will always fear death because the only judgment for those who do not accept this forgiveness is eternal punishment. In the book of 1 John 4:10-21, the author clearly explains this profound truth:

> This is love: not that we loved God, but that he loved us and sent his Son as an atoning sacrifice for our sins. 11 Dear friends, since God so loved us, we also ought to love one another. 12 No one has ever seen God; but if we love one another, God lives in us and his love is made complete in us. 13 We know that we live in him and he in us, because he has given us of his Spirit. 14 And we have seen and testify that the Father has sent his Son to be the Savior of the world. 15 If anyone acknowledges that Jesus is the Son of God, God lives in him and he in God. 16 And so we know and rely on the love God has for us. God is love. Whoever lives in love lives in God, and God in Him. 17 In this way, **love is made complete among us so that we will have confidence on the Day of Judgment**, because in this world we are like him. 18 **There is no fear in love. But perfect love drives out fear, *because fear has to do with punishment*.** The one who fears is not made perfect in love. 19 We love because he first loved us. 20 If anyone says, "I love God," yet hates his brother, he is a liar. For anyone who does not love his brother, whom he has seen, cannot love God, whom he has not seen. 21 And he has given us this command: Whoever loves God must also love his brother, (1 John 4:10-21, NIV). [Bold, italics and underline is by the author, solely for emphasis]

Based on our understanding of this group of scriptures, an important question begs to be asked. If Christians have already been caught up to heaven for safety reasons, seven or three and a half years before Christ returns to pour out His wrath on the unrepentant, why would John be giving Christians a warning about love being complete among them so that they should have confidence on the Day of Judgment? If the *Christian Church* has already been Raptured (before this great onslaught of tribulation), obviously it has already made it to heaven and needs not fear death or judgment. The answer is that we fear death because fear has to do with punishment. If the *Christian Church* is already in heaven, God's love for it is made complete and, at this point in time, there is no punishment due to the church because living in God is love and whoever lives in love lives in God and, if we live in God, we need not have the want for confidence on the Day of Judgment. Therefore this exhortation would not be necessary. However John does warn the *called out ones* about this aspect, because the *ecclesia* will be here on earth when Christ returns to pour out His wrath on the unrepentant. While many fear this aspect, they fail to understand that experiencing martyrdom so others can obtain salvation is the zenith of the human experience. Jesus Christ showed mankind this great love, and conquered sin and Satan by giving His life so others may live, and *called out ones*, during this most horrific period in history, will also have an opportunity to be conquerors themselves:

> Greater love hath no man than this, that a man lay down his life for his friends, (John 15:13, KJV).

Next to God's (in the person of Jesus Christ) willingness to lay down His life so others can live, there exists no greater example than the love resident in martyr Stephen's heart. One of the author's all-time favorite Bible chapters is Acts 7, because it paints a perfect picture and example of what he believes Christians will be experiencing at the End Times. This chapter ends with how Stephen's soon-to-be assassins reacted to the words of his piercing truth; and, his last dying wish as he succumbed to the stoning by those very same people, was a prayer that God had to answer:

> **When they heard this, they were furious and gnashed their teeth at him**. 55 But Stephen, full of the Holy Spirit, looked up to heaven and saw the glory of God, and Jesus standing at the right hand of God. 56 "Look," he said, "I see heaven open and the Son of Man standing at the right hand of God." 57 At this they covered their ears and, yelling at the top of their voices, they all rushed at him, 58 dragged him out of the city and began to stone him. Meanwhile, the witnesses laid their clothes at the feet of a young man named Saul. 59 **While they were stoning him, Stephen prayed, "Lord Jesus, receive my spirit"**. 60 **Then he fell on his knees and cried out, "Lord, do not hold this sin against them." When he had said this, he fell asleep**, (Acts 7:1-60, NIV). [Bold and underline is by the author, solely for emphasis]

As mentioned in an earlier chapter in our first book, the author is convinced that God answered Stephen's last prayer, and thereby called out Paul (and possibly many others) amongst this band of legalistic Jews, a man He converted and used like no other man has been used by God to bring others to His Kingdom. The entire Chapter of Acts 7 shows us how Stephen was not only one of the greatest martyrs in Bible history, but it shows us a profound role model and a perfect example of what Christians can truly expect to experience immediately before the Lord's return. Like Stephen, God will use many *called out ones* during the End Times to bring others to Christ. And the author believes that many of those *called out ones* will be mere humble and faith-believing servants of God, unknown by many, and not necessarily will include renowned evangelists, pastors,

Bible teachers, prophecy writers and others who take so much pride in their knowledge of theology and seek worldly acceptance as great religious leaders:

> But before all these, they shall lay their hands on you, and persecute you, delivering you up to the synagogues, and into prisons, being brought before kings and rulers for my name's sake.13 and it shall turn to you for a testimony. 14 **Settle it therefore in your hearts, not to meditate before what ye shall answer**: 15 **For I will give you a mouth and wisdom, which all your adversaries shall not be able to gainsay nor resist.** 16 And ye shall be betrayed both by parents, and brethren, and kinsfolks, and friends; and some of you shall they cause to be put to death. 17 And ye shall be hated of all men for my name's sake. 18 **But there shall not an hair of your head perish**. 19 In your patience possess ye your souls, (Luke 21:12-19, KJV). [Bold and underline by the author, solely for emphasis]

Of course, none of us wants to think about death and dying, but that's what many Christians will truly experience in the End Times, especially those who choose not to shrink back, those who hate their lives and will find it, as opposed to those who love their lives and will lose them. [To grasp a greater understanding of the phenomenon of dying for Christ, please read *Fox's Book of Martyrs* after finishing this book]

It is interesting to note that the true beauty of Acts, Chapter 7, is that the word Stephen (*stephanos*, in the Greek) is the very word used for the 'crown of life' reward Jesus brings with Him upon His return, as mentioned in Revelation 22:12. Nevertheless, as profound an example of what true Christians can and should be prepared to experience during the End Times, most humans (Christians, too) still have this inbuilt fear of death. The author is not claiming that all Christians will experience martyrdom during this period immediately before *The Second Advent*. However, the possibility of persecution unto death is highly probable for many Christians. No one truly knows if God has chosen us for this fate; but, individually, each and every true believing Christian alive today is a strong candidate for martyrdom. Some (or many) will have to face this possibility. Others may escape death before *The Second Advent*.

To Know and Feel the Love of God

Scriptures abound that speak of the love of God for His creation. Those who have experienced the regenerative power of forgiveness can attest to the knowledge and feeling of God's love. Many a Christian who was once bogged down in the swamp of sin, who openly welcomed the forgiveness of God, can attest to the wondrous feeling of His love.

The author believes Christ loves each and every one of us and does not want us to suffer pain. This is so clear especially in the Book of John, Chapter 17. While true faith is not based on feeling, as we read this following chapter, one can feel the special and personal closeness and love Jesus has for each and every one of us, as He prays to the Father for our protection during the End Times. Read this in its entirety, and feel His tremendous love:

> After Jesus said this, he looked toward heaven and prayed: "Father, the time has come. Glorify your Son, that your Son may glorify you. 2 For you granted him authority over all people that he might give eternal life to all those you have given him. 3 Now this is eternal life: that they may know you, the only true God, and Jesus Christ, whom you have sent. 4 I have brought you glory on earth by completing the work

you gave me to do. 5 And now, Father, glorify me in your presence with the glory I had with you before the world began. 6 **I have revealed you to those whom you gave me out of the world.** They were yours; you gave them to me and they have obeyed your word. 7 Now they know that everything you have given me comes from you. 8 **For I gave them the words you gave me and they accepted them. They knew with certainty that I came from you, and they believed that you sent me.** 9 I pray for them. I am not praying for the world, but for those you have given me, for they are yours. 10 All I have is yours, and all you have is mine. And glory has come to me through them. 11 I will remain in the world no longer, **but they are still in the world**, and I am coming to you. Holy Father, **protect them by the power of your name**--the name you gave me-- so that they may be one as we are one. 12 While I was with them, I protected them and kept them safe by that name you gave me. None has been lost except the one doomed to destruction so that Scripture would be fulfilled. 13 "I am coming to you now, but I say these things while I am still in the world, so that they may have the full measure of my joy within them. 14 **I have given them your word and the world has hated them**, for they are not of the world any more than I am of the world. 15 **My prayer is not that you take them out of the world but that you protect them from the evil one**. 16 They are not of the world, even as I am not of it. 17 Sanctify them by the truth; your word is truth. 18 As you sent me into the world, I have sent them into the world. 19 For them I sanctify myself, that they too may be truly sanctified. 20 My prayer is not for them alone. **I pray also for those who will believe in me through their message**, 21 that all of them may be one, Father, just as you are in me and I am in you. May they also be in us so that the world may believe that you have sent me. 22 I have given them the glory that you gave me, that they may be one as we are one: 23 I in them and you in me. **May they be brought to complete unity to let the world know that you sent me and have loved them even as you have loved me**. 24 "Father, I want those you have given me to be with me where I am, and to see my glory, the glory you have given me because you loved me before the creation of the world. 25 "Righteous Father, though the world does not know you, I know you, and they know that you have sent me. 26 I have made you known to them, and will continue to make you known in order that the love you have for me may be in them and that I myself may be in them, (John 17:1-26, NIV). [Bold and underlines is by the author, solely for emphasis]

The most important verse in this chapter, which is crucial to the major premise of this book, is verse 15, which bears repeating. *"My prayer is not that you take them out of the world but that you protect them from the evil one."* If there is any one scripture that confirms that there will be no secret Pre-Tribulation escape to heaven before *The Second Advent*, it is this one verse. Here, Jesus Christ Himself is praying to God for Him *not* to take us out of this world, but to protect us from the evil one. God is perfectly able to do this without removing us anywhere. God is able to pour out His wrath on the unrepentant, and still provide protection for all of His saints, as Peter so boldly states:

For if God did not spare angels, when they sinned, but sent them to hell, putting them into gloomy dungeons to be held for judgment; 5 if he did not spare the ancient world when he brought the flood on its ungodly people, but protected Noah, a preacher of righteousness, and seven others; 6 if he condemned the cities of Sodom and Gomorrah by burning them to ashes, and made them an example of what is going to happen to the ungodly; 7 and if he rescued Lot, a righteous man, who was distressed by the filthy lives of lawless men 8 (for that righteous man, living among them day after day, was tormented in his righteous soul by the lawless deeds he saw and heard) – 9 **if this is so, then the Lord knows how to rescue godly men from trials and to Hold the unrighteous for the day of judgment, while continuing their punishment**, (2 Peter 2:4-9, NIV). [Bold and underline is by the author, solely for emphasis]

Yes, my friends, God truly has an End Times Passover program. Many of the *called out ones* will be persecuted and killed by the man of lawlessness and his demonic minions, and maybe even by friends, neighbors and relatives; and, sadly, even by former church members. Many will be alive when the Lord *snatches* His *ecclesia* to meet and greet Him in the air, to escort Him back to earth, where each *called out one* will actually see Him pouring out His wrath upon the unrepentant. Some of members of the *ecclesia* might still feel a little squeamish about the possibility that they will be tortured or killed for standing up for Him, while others will escape unscathed through His End Times Passover. Regardless, when He does return, whether we die a martyr's death or remain alive upon His return, we will finally be united forever with Jesus Christ, our Lord and our God; we will be able to look Him in the face and hear Him say *"Well-done, good and faithful servant, you were faithful in a few things; I will put you in charge of many,* (Mathew 25:23, NIV).

Therefore, the author herewith boldly encourages his fellow *called out ones*. As we begin to faintly hear in the distance, the imminent hoof beats of that great white horse, carrying our soon-to-return Messiah, to stand firm and, as Ephesians 6:10-18 so boldly exhorts, let us:

> ...be strong in the Lord and in his mighty power. 11 put on the full armor of God so that you can take your stand against the devil's schemes. 12 For our struggle is not against flesh and blood, but against the rulers, against the authorities, against the powers of this dark world and against the spiritual forces of evil in the heavenly realms.13 Therefore put on the full armor of God, so that when the day of evil comes, you may be able to stand your ground, and after you have done everything, to stand. 14 Stand firm then, with the belt of truth buckled around your waist, with the breastplate of righteousness in place, 15 and with your feet fitted with the readiness that comes from the gospel of peace. 16 In addition to all this, take up the shield of faith, with which you can extinguish all the flaming arrows of the evil one. 17 Take the helmet of salvation and the sword of the Spirit, which is the word of God.18 and pray in the Spirit on all occasions with all kinds of prayers and requests. With this in mind, be alert and always keep on praying for all the saints, (Ephesians 6:10-18, NIV).

In conclusion, the author believes he has provided in these two books sufficient scriptures that literally refute both the secret Pre-Tribulation escape to heaven theory, and the establishment of a 1000-year geopolitical kingdom reign for Nationalistic Jews. God's Kingdom reign will be established on earth, its headquarters will be inside of the soon-to-descend New Jerusalem, and it will be an eternal kingdom. Until this day arrives, the world and its people will continue to slide further down the diabolical trash heap of history. One only has to see on television, hear on radio, read in newspapers and the Internet, to realize that mankind is drifting farther and farther away from God. The world is being dragged asunder by demonic forces, appearing as angels of light, twisting God's message set forth in His Holy word. Heathen religions (and even many Protestant denominations) are fomenting a different Gospel than the one Paul was given by Jesus Christ, the very God of creation Himself!

In the United States (especially), many churches and their leaders are propagating a soothing, titillating Gospel and lulling many uninformed Christians into a false sense of religious security. Many American citizens (especially), believing they are true God-fearing people, are being duped by religious charlatans, whose sole mission is to glorify themselves and fill their coffers by writing and promoting false doctrines at the expense of people who genuinely seek the truth, who genuinely seek forgiveness for their sinful lives, and the proper direction to serve God in truth. Many of them have fallen victim to "quick fix" religious formulae used by the thousands of false teachers and prophets, who use the media as their pulpit of expediency, charming and seducing many of God's children away from their local congregations, and the faithful service required in their immediate households and in their respective neighborhoods. These demonically inspired (and so-called) men of God are *snatching* our loved ones from the flock right before our very eyes.

Yet, while many who boldly speak forth the gospel truth, which calls for the genuine sacrifice of prayer and faithful service to the poor, hungry and homeless, they are being told that they will be *Left Behind* to suffer God's wrath, while their adherents are being craftily seduced to believe they will not experience tribulation through secret escape to heaven mythologies.

The choice is yours. Keep waiting for a secret escape to heaven, or pick up your cross and follow Jesus, wherever that path may lead.

Are you ready to pick up your cross, and follow Him? Are you ready to lay down your life so others can also share eternal life with Jesus Christ, our God?

Until next time, maybe sooner, when we will be joined together in that great meeting in the air at His Coming, the author leaves you with this profound message:

> **We must pay more careful attention, therefore, to what we have heard, so that we do not drift away.** 2 For if the message spoken by angels was binding, and every violation and disobedience received its just punishment, 3 how shall we escape if we ignore such a great salvation? This salvation, which was first announced by the Lord, was confirmed to us by those who heard him. 4 God also testified to it by signs, wonders and various miracles, and gifts of the Holy Spirit distributed according to his will. 5 It is not to angels that he has subjected the world to come, about which we are speaking. 6 But there is a place where someone has testified: "What is man that you are mindful of him, the son of man that you care for him? 7 You made him a little lower than the angels; you crowned him with glory and honor 8 and put everything under his feet." In putting everything under him, God left nothing that is not subject to him. Yet at present we do not see everything subject to him. 9 **But we see Jesus, who was made a little lower than the angels, now crowned with glory and honor because he suffered death, so that by the grace of God he might taste death for everyone.** 10 In bringing many sons to glory, it was fitting that God, for whom and through whom everything exists, **should make the author of their salvation perfect through suffering.** 11 Both the one who makes men holy and those who are made holy are of the same family. So Jesus

is not ashamed to call them brothers. 12 He says, "I will declare your name to my brothers; in the presence of the congregation I will sing your praises." 13 And again, "I will put my trust in him. And again he says, "Here am I, and the children God has given me." 14 Since the children have flesh and blood, he too shared in their humanity so that by his death he might destroy him who holds the power of death--that is, the devil-- 15 **and free those who all their lives were held in slavery by their fear of death**, (Hebrews 2:1-15, NIV). [Bold and underline is by the author, solely for emphasis]

Joe Ortiz

Printed in the United States
76057LV00004B/307-348